FRAMING BORDERS

MW01070293

Principle and Practicality in the Akwesasne Mohawk Territory

Framing Borders addresses a fundamental disjuncture between scholastic portrayals of settler colonialism and what actually takes place in Akwesasne Territory, the largest cross-border Indigenous community in North America. Whereas most existing portrayals of Indigenous nationalism emphasize border crossing as a site of conflict between officers and Indigenous nationalists, in this book Ian Kalman observes a much more diverse range of interactions, from conflict to banality to joking and camaraderie.

Framing Borders explores how border crossing represents a conversation in which different actors "frame" themselves, the law, and the space that they occupy in diverse ways. Kalman addresses what goes on when border officers and Akwesasne residents meet, and what these exchanges tell us about the relationship between Indigenous actors and public servants in Canada. Written in accessible, lively prose, this book provides an ethnographic examination of the experiences of the border by Mohawk community members, the history of local border enforcement, and the paradoxes, self-contradictions, and confusions that underlie the border and its enforcement.

IAN KALMAN is a founding faculty member at Fulbright University Vietnam.

Framing Borders

Principle and Practicality in the Akwesasne Mohawk Territory

IAN KALMAN

UNIVERSITY OF TORONTO PRESS
Toronto Buffalo London

ISBN 978-1-4875-0921-7 (cloth)   ISBN 978-1-4875-3992-4 (EPUB)
ISBN 978-1-4875-2653-5 (paper)   ISBN 978-1-4875-3991-7 (PDF)

Library and Archives Canada Cataloguing in Publication

Title: Framing borders : principle and practicality in the Akwesasne
    Mohawk Territory / Ian Kalman.
Names: Kalman, Ian, author.
Description: Includes bibliographical references and index.
Identifiers: Canadiana (print) 20210090154 | Canadiana (ebook)
    20210092149 | ISBN 9781487526535 (softcover) | ISBN 9781487509217
    (hardcover) | ISBN 9781487539924 (EPUB) | ISBN 9781487539917 (PDF)
Subjects: LCSH: Mohawk Nation at Akwesasne. | LCSH: Mohawk Nation
    at Akwesasne – Social conditions. | LCSH: Canadian-American Border
    Region. | LCSH: Borderlands – Social aspects – Mohawk Nation at
    Akwesasne. | LCSH: Borderlands – Political aspects – Mohawk Nation
    at Akwesasne. | LCSH: Border crossing – Social aspects – Mohawk
    Nation at Akwesasne. | LCSH: Border crossing – Political aspects –
    Mohawk Nation at Akwesasne. | LCSH: Border crossing – Social
    aspects – Canadian-American Border Region. | LCSH: Border crossing –
    Political aspects – Canadian-American Border Region.
Classification: LCC E99.M8 K35 2021 | DDC 971.3/7004975542 – dc23

University of Toronto Press acknowledges the financial assistance to its
publishing program of the Canada Council for the Arts and the Ontario
Arts Council, an agency of the Government of Ontario.

Canada Council   Conseil des Arts
for the Arts   du Canada

ONTARIO ARTS COUNCIL
CONSEIL DES ARTS DE L'ONTARIO
an Ontario government agency
un organisme du gouvernement de l'Ontario

Funded by the   Financé par le
Government   gouvernement
of Canada   du Canada

Contents

Figures

Acknowledgments

This book was a lot of hard work – not for me so much as for the many people who have put up with me over the past decade. The number of people and organizations without whom this text would have been far poorer (or not existed at all) is immense. The project spanned several continents and four nations (Akwesasne, Canada, the United States, and Germany); consequently, there is a lot of acknowledging to do. Readers have my apologies for the length of this section. Digital readers may save time by pressing "Control-F" to search for their own names.

My family has supported me through every stage of this process, offering advice, encouragement, and a substantial number of bagels. First and foremost, I wish to thank my mother, Andrea Kalman, and my father, Kenneth Kalman, who never wavered in their support and love. My sister, Rachel Kalman, offered clever bits of advice and was never afraid to challenge me. My grandparents, Eli and Zelda Kalman and Robert and Rita Kessler, always provided unconditional affection.

The reason this book has been published is thanks to the persistent, never-ending encouragement of Christopher Alcantara. Chris never gave up on me, and in so doing, made it impossible for me to give up on this project.

It may be overdoing it to thank the entire populations of New York, China, Ukraine, and Turkey, but I'd like to point out a few people whose friendship has remained a constant beacon throughout my travels. Drew Gulley, Bedra Girgin, Lisa Brunner, Laura Frantz, Lilya Askarova, George Rowe, Anna Matviyenko, Sean Speciale, Shanti Marthaller, Tyson Pierce, Gillian Groenen, Jacqueline Haslam, and Olga Andrusych have all conspired to make me a more fun and caring person. Jena Barchas-Liechtenstein gets a sentence but deserves a chapter for her seamless balancing of hugs and brilliance. Lee Solomon and my brothers in all but genetics, Jeremy and Adam Scholem, were always there for sharing cheap Scotch and priceless advice. In Montreal, my ideas were developed over video games with Steven Sych; beers with Brodie Noga, Sean Desjardins, Nicholas Barber, and Jennie Glassco; whisky with Takeshi Uesugi, Fern Thompsett, Sarah Sandham, and Joshua Friesen; magic soup with Doerte Bemme and Stephanie Alexander; Marxism with Marco Poppalardo; walks with Hannah Kiezenler and Cees Van Dyke; pho with Karen McAllister; tea with Julia Bailey; raclette with Marie-Pierre Gadoua; tavla with Giulia El-Dardiry; papusas with Alonso Gamara; kale and anarchy with Erica Lagalisse; salt with Saman Tabasi-Najad; carnitas with Camilo Gomez; barbecue with Amber Silva; hot chocolate with Monica Cuellar Gempeler; board games with Katie Sinclair; *Game of Thrones* with Adam Fleischmann, Kristin Flemons, and Raad Fadaak; football with Loes Knappen and Andrew McCaan; cake with Stephanie Olson and Rob Boddice; dim sum(day) with Claudia Masferrer and Renato Calleja; lobster rolls with Ivet Reyes Maturano and Richard Feldman; karaoke with Victor "Corey" Wright; and Chinese food with everyone else.

Jessica Dolan and Daniel Rueck helped me learn about Haudenosaunee studies from new perspectives, and Phillip Messier taught me to always justify myself. Sebastien Bluteau and Gregory Brass were exceptional roommates and helped me ask questions I had not even thought of. Rine Vieth taught me that just because anthropologists ruin everything, that does not mean we cannot be fun. A special thanks to my dear Belgians, Melanie Chaplier and Lionel Neyts, whose gastronomic, emotional, and intellectual contributions are too numerous for this page.

At McGill, Kristin Norget, Eduardo Kohn, and Setrag Manoukian gave me insights I never would have had otherwise. John Hall, Katherine Muller, Diana Allan, Allan Young, Katherine Lemons, and Nicole Couture also met with me to develop the project. At the University of Montreal, Karine Côté-Boucher and John Leavitt dedicated their time to discuss border officers and myths and helped me see the ways in which the two are more similar than one may first imagine. Toby Morantz welcomed me into her home and made me feel that I had a Jewish family north of the border. I am also grateful to my colleagues Mike Loft, Nicole Ives, Kirsten Anker, Jill Hanley, and Courtney Montour for organizing the Interdisciplinary Field Course in Indigenous Studies and enabling me to spend my summers in Kahnawake with exceptional students. Rose-Marie Stano, Diane Mann, Anne Farray, and Connie Di Giuseppe always had time for "just one more question" from me. Olga Harmazy gets special mention, both for providing assistance and for a brief respite any time we spoke.

Most graduate students are fortunate if they have a good supervisor. I was blessed with two. Colin Scott and Ronald Niezen provided encouragement when I needed it, work when I needed it, advice when I needed it, and positive models of scholarship and integrity always.

Richard C. Jeffrey, on the other hand, did not help.

In Germany, I am indebted to Jonathan Bernearts and Faduma Abukar for the advice and laughs over superhero stories. Thanks as well to Agathe Mora, Jon Schubert, Mareike Reidel, Andrea Klein, Hendrik Tieke, Miriam Francina, Lucia and Jens Frobel, Esther Horat, Sajjad Safaei, the Advokaten Piraten, Kiran Morjaria, Kalindi Kokal, Harika Dauth, and vegan soup. Special gratitude to Timm Sureau, Christina Turzer, Markus Klank, and Susanne Vollert, for giving me a true sense of home in Halle and Leipzig respectively.

At the Max Planck Institute, Bertram and Jutta Turner provided advice, maps, wine, and a cat, with the first two transforming this book into a more complete and rigorous piece of scholarship. Maria Sapignoli, Julie Billaud, Brian Donahoe, and Katrin Seidel taught me not simply how to develop my project but how to develop as a scholar. Marie-Claire Foblets has my dearest gratitude; she supported my time at the institute, and her advice made it possible for me to develop ideas I never would have had the confidence to explore otherwise.

Here in Vietnam, my life is made sane through collaborations with my amazing students and my friends and colleagues: Jill Sirikantraporn, Kevin Hart, Nguyễn Cẩm Vân, Lương Ngọc Trâm, Aaron Anderson, Andrew Bellisari, Tram Luong, Phan Vũ Xuân Hùng, Trương Thị Thạch Thảo, Antoine Touch, Sebastian Dziallas, and Samhitha Raj. Extra *cảm ơn* for Lê Nguyễn Thiên Hương, for helping make every day worthwhile.

None of this would have been possible without the support of my friends in Akwesasne. Ashley Tarbell introduced me to the community and remains a friend to this day – I have been blessed to know her and her amazing family. Curtis Lazore shared his love of the land and some of my favorite conversations over our lunch breaks. I am especially glad I met Phillip White-Cree on a bus ride to Ottawa, as I continue to take pleasure in our conversations on traditional knowledge and Doctor Who. Debbie Rourke, Jacey Rourke, and Jeffrey Rodriguez were my family when I was far away from my own.

I was fortunate to have tremendous institutional support in Akwesasne. I am grateful to Mike Mitchell for meeting with me and supporting my project in the territory along with the Mohawk Council of Akwesasne (MCA), the Saint Regis Mohawk Tribe, and the Mohawk Nation Council of Chiefs. At the MCA, I am especially indebted to the Aboriginal rights research office where I spent most of my year of fieldwork. I also wish to thank Joyce King and the Justice Department, and Cactus Cook-Sunday, the director of ARRO. In the Mohawk Nation, I want to extend a *nia:wen* to Bula Hill and Richard Mitchell. Although Rasennes Pembleton may not know it, he always asked me the hardest questions and had the deepest insights of anyone I spoke with. While most of my interviews with border officers are kept anonymous, I wish to thank those who took the time and accepted the risk of speaking to me, and J.D. Marchand for going above and beyond in his patience and willingness to meet with me.

Raymond Fogelson is not the reason I am an anthropologist, but if I am ever to be considered a good anthropologist, it will be because of him. Professor Fogelson showed an eager, confused, curious under-graduate that a well-told story teaches a whole lot more than a well-written textbook. He was the educator and scholar I aspire to be some day. He is also possibly to blame if there are too many jokes in this text.

Everything good in the next several hundred pages is thanks to the above individuals, and many whom I was unable to name. Everything bad, or false, is because I did not listen to them when I should have.

I wish to end these acknowledgments with my thanks to both the Mohawk Community of Akwesasne and the lands and waters occupied by their ancestors since time immemorial.

FRAMING BORDERS

Principle and Practicality in the Akwesasne
Mohawk Territory

Prologue

20 June 2013

Today I've been given the opportunity to ride along with the Akwesasne Mohawk Ambulance Service unit. A mutual colleague introduced me to the ambulance unit's director during one of the cross-border protests. He told me, "If you want to see what the border's like, you need to see what we have to deal with."

I leave my apartment in the city of Cornwall around 8:00 a.m. and start driving to the Kanonkwat'sheri:io Health Facility in St. Regis Village. Even though the facility is technically in Canada, I'll have to drive through the United States to get there. I've been doing this commute from Cornwall to St. Regis Village for nearly a year now, but this will be my first time at the health facility. I set out with enthusiasm – and a light jacket – on the cool summer morning.

It takes only a few minutes of driving past Cornwall's innumerable strip malls and fast-food eateries before I make my way to the foot of the Three Nations Bridge connecting Akwesasne, the United States, and Canada. After paying the $3.00 bridge toll, I head across the long and rickety northern span of the bridge, driving south onto Cornwall Island. The thumping of my car against the bridge's many potholes has become the soundtrack to my morning commute. After a few more minutes of rattling, I'm on the island. I am now in the Akwesasne Mohawk Territory (see figure P.1).

I'm only on the island for the blink of an eye, passing the old Canadian port facilities, abandoned nearly half a decade ago. Their heavily fortified structure stands in contrast to the otherwise bucolic landscape of the island. Even the Peace Tree Mall, standing across from the port, seems designed with a lot of browns and greens. It looks as though the mall has seen better days; many of its shops are closed or closing now that it is illegal for cross-border traffic to stop on the island before heading into mainland Canada (I discuss this in greater detail in chapter 5).

Before I know it, I've traversed the island and am taking the much smoother southern bridge into mainland New York State. By reflex, my foot leaves the gas pedal when I see the sign notifying me I've reached the US port of entry. I get ready for my daily shell game – trying to determine which lane will get me across the fastest. I look for trucks with a purple Six Nations flag, or lacrosse or clan bumper stickers. Those travellers will likely be old pros from Akwesasne, and tend to get processed a lot faster. Plus, the trucks take up a bit more space, making the lines seem longer when really they're not. I go for my old standard – the last lane in service. If they open a new one next to it, I can move over and be the first in line. Fortunately, I choose a good one, and it moves quickly.

When I pull up to the booth, I notice Kathy, an officer I've met several times previously in my daily commute. "What are you up to today, Ian?" she asks jovially as I hand over my passport. "I'm doing a ride along with the ambulance unit," I tell her with a smile. She asks me to let her know how it goes, and hands the passport back to me. "Have a nice day," she says, as the arm of the gate lifts and I drive forward into New York State.

I hang a left turn at the port facility and am now back in the Akwesasne Mohawk Territory (south of the borderline). I continue along route 37, Akwesasne's main thoroughfare, past recently renovated gas stations, now expanded into restaurants and convenience stores. "Twin Leaf" and "The Bear's Den," the two largest, sell discount petrol, cigarettes, and all-you-can-eat spaghetti or turkey dinners to residents or people passing through. A few of these places have started selling handmade baskets and novelty lacrosse sticks. There are a few cows grazing behind the Tim Horton's where I usually get my breakfast. I continue past closed-down casinos with torn-up parking lots, chip stands, the offices of the Saint Regis Mohawk Tribe, and the Akwesasne Public Library. There are a few houses along the way; some are ramshackle, a few palatial, but most are indistinguishable from the wooden homes I grew up seeing every summer in upstate New York.

I reach "the four corners," the intersection of St. Regis Road and route 37, and turn left again, heading back up north. This is the part of Akwesasne few outsiders see. It's not as commercial as route 37, with a convenience store here and there selling soda and whatever soup is in the slow cooker for the day (probably hamburger or corn soup), but it's mostly large houses with larger yards. I keep my eyes open for "rez dogs," border-patrol officers, or the occasional deer. I'm also making sure I don't go over the speed limit (local traffic police have a reputation for preferring to stop non-residents), or too slowly, to avoid annoying the car behind me.

At some point, I cross the border back into Canada. There are no ports of entry, no check points, no signs. A border post was torn up a few years ago by a resident with some heavy machinery.

I notice "the border" (when I notice it at all) when the roadwork changes from concrete to asphalt, sidewalks appear on the side of the road, and my mobile phone buzzes "Welcome to Canada." I know I'm north of the line when a sign gives me the speed limit in kilometres rather than miles per hour.

This will be my first time in the health facility, but I know where it is, just a few blocks away from my office at the Mohawk Council administrative building.

It's a slow morning for the ambulance unit. I'm introduced to the four EMTs (emergency medical technicians) on shift. John tells me he grew up between the reserve and Syracuse, New York, but he came back to raise a family. His wife is also an EMT, working part time. As he heats up a cup of tea (he quit drinking coffee), his friendly demeanour exudes quiet confidence and measured responsibility. Paul is the newest member of the unit, transitioning out of a lucrative career in the cigarette trade. He seems, like me, eager to learn anything new that's put in front of him. George grew up in Kahnawake but decided to stay in Akwesasne after doing a stint as a medic in the armed forces. We spend a couple of minutes trying to figure out if we know some of the same people in Kahnawake (we do). Linda is also from Kahnawake and commutes from there every morning. She says she can make it from her home to the office in around half an hour, and I try not to think about how fast she must drive to accomplish that. I'm relieved to hear that I'll be riding with John and Paul for the day and not Linda. The crew, on the whole, reminds me of Anthony Bourdain's description of the cooking underground – tattooed, foul-tongued, crude-humoured, and eminently competent.

We head back down to 37 to grab lunch and return to the office for equipment checks. I start to think we won't receive any calls, when the phone suddenly rings. A man in Snye (another part of the reserve that, like St. Regis Village, is ostensibly in Quebec) fell and dislocated his shoulder while doing housework. Concerned, his wife called for an ambulance. I feel fortunate we've received the call, and then immediately guilty for doing so.

John, Paul, and I get into the ambulance and are gone in a matter of minutes. Riding in the ambulance is one of the few times in Akwesasne I don't feel like I'm in the smallest vehicle on the road. The ambulance is a big white metal box with state-of-the-art lifesaving technologies, checked and rechecked at the end of each shift. There's a spot on the dash where a GPS would go, but John tells me that they aren't reliable in the territory – people don't like giving information that would make it easier for unwelcome outsiders, especially US or Canadian law-enforcement officers, to get around. I get to sit in the front, while Paul sits in the back with the stretcher.

In order to drive from our headquarters in St. Regis, Quebec, to Snye, Quebec, we must first drive back through New York State. We head back down St. Regis Road, back into New York State, but only for a couple of minutes.

We return to 37 and turn left yet again a few kilometres down the road. This time, we're going to Snye. Snye is a lot more rural than the other parts of the community – a land of large farmsteads, much of it swampy, and right along the water. Mosquitos like helicopters are especially aggressive at this time of year. It's an easy place to get lost in, and I rarely drive to Snye on my own. John points out the border's location for my benefit as we drive along borderline road. Fortunately, he spent time here growing up and has an idea where the man's house is. We briefly stop to ask for directions at a house doubling as a convenience store, but get there quickly.

What looks like three generations of women are sitting in the living room attending the injured man, as he sits on a white sofa covered in blankets. Some crime-scene-investigation show I've never seen plays muted on the back wall in faux HD. It's a spacious house, but cramped with the addition of me, John, Paul, and mementos from what seems to be a large extended family.

Randy, the injured man, is of wiry build, wearing work clothes, a Toronto Blue Jays cap, and what could be described as a "NASCAR" moustache. He's visibly in pain, but grimacing quietly. He tells us he doesn't want to go to the hospital because he hasn't picked up his health card. "We have to call this in," John tells me, stepping outside, while Paul remains in the house bandaging Randy's arm.

John explains that even though they are based in Quebec and funded by the Canadian government, the Akwesasne Mohawk Ambulance is licensed out of New York State. Most EMTs don't speak French, and New York's licensing gives them a greater liberty for cross-border service. However, as a consequence, they must follow New York State protocols, which require getting a doctor to sign off on any patient's decision not to be admitted to the hospital. Even though Randy is a Canadian citizen, and we are ostensibly in Quebec, we have to call the nearest New York State hospital in order to get approval for releasing him. This is standard procedure, I'm told, though John looks chagrined when the doctor tells him we have to send the patient to the hospital for treatment. "This hasn't happened before," John tells me.

He explains that had we been in New York State, the police would have had the authority to escort an unwilling Randy to the hospital. But we can't do that in Canada, and we certainly can't do that in Snye. Legally, we're in a bind. If we don't bring Randy to the hospital, the ambulance unit would be violating its licensing, but we have no way to force him to go to the hospital if he chooses not to. John calls his boss for advice, while Paul, now finished bandaging the injury, heads back inside to convince Randy to change his mind. He suggests that the hospital might be flexible in waiting for him to get his health card before they charge him. Fortunately, Randy decides to take the chance. Though he had been sitting and walking around, we load him onto the stretcher and radio to Dispatch.

Dispatch first lets the hospital know that we're on our way, and then calls the Canada Border Services Agency (CBSA) to tell them the same. At some point we cross back into New York State, but this time John doesn't bother pointing it out.

We drive back down route 37, past US customs, over the southern bridge, across Cornwall Island, over the northern bridge, banging up and down against potholes, while Randy sweats in the back of the ambulance. Now that we're driving into the city of Cornwall, we must go through Canadian customs at the end of the bridge. I've waited up to an hour in line to get to the foot of the bridge in the past. Today, however, since we're answering an emergency call, the bridge corporation closes one lane of the bridge, transforming it into an ambulance-only express lane. We breeze along the road. The toll booth opens and we slow down just enough for a uniformed CBSA officer to wave us to an empty lane, give us a thumbs-up, and let us pass. I'm back in Canada.

We drop Randy off at the hospital, while making small talk with the police officers and other emergency medical technicians. Randy's family is on the way, but they had to take the slow route, waiting in line to go through customs along with all the other cars. Once Randy is admitted, John and Paul look at their watches – it's a bit after 5:00 p.m., and their shifts have ended. It's time to head back to the office and head home.

They tell me I have to report to the Canadian port of entry now that we've dealt with the emergency. A non-Indigenous colleague had failed to do so once after joining them on a similar call and got harangued the next time he went through customs. We park the ambulance by the port facility, and as I walk to the Canadian port of entry, Paul heads across the street to pick up a St. Hubert rotisserie chicken dinner for his wife and children. They're looking forward to the treat, as the dining options are much more limited south of the border, and no one wants to wait in line to get to Cornwall for dinner at this time of day.

Walking into the port of entry office, I'm surprised to see Louis, an officer who usually works commercial customs in the back office. I'd gotten to know him after conducting a few interviews in the building he usually works in. He tells me he's filling in for someone today, and I tell him I just came from the hospital. He asks me the same standard questions – whether I stopped anywhere in Canada besides the hospital (no), what I've been up to (research), whether I bought anything (no), and then says thanks for checking in.

I get back into the ambulance and it smells like warm chicken. We start heading back to the station. As we drive along the bridge toward Cornwall Island, I notice that the line of cars heading into the city of Cornwall has grown. I dread having to wait in that line for a half-hour or so when I return from headquarters at the end of the day. I contemplate grabbing dinner in Massena or visiting some friends until later to avoid the wait.

We drive once again over the rickety bridge, once again across Cornwall Island, and again across the smoother bridge, and then stop in line at US customs. We're not answering any emergency calls, and we wait in line with everyone else. It's not a long line, and when we arrive at the booth, I notice Kathy is still working. She looks into the ambulance and sees me in the passenger's seat. She's laughing when I hand her my passport. "I guess you got to go on your ride-along." I agree, also laughing, and she returns the passport. She says, "Have a nice day," and we're back along route 37, back along St. Regis Road, and back at the health centre.

John and Paul park the ambulance and sign off for the day. I get back into my own car for one last stop before heading home. As a non-Indigenous person, I'm obligated to drive without stopping (for gas, cigarettes, food, the library, to visit a friend, etc.) to the US port of entry as soon as I've left the northern, "Canadian" portion of Akwesasne. After driving back down St. Regis Road and across the border, wherever it is, I get back on route 37 and park my car when I reach the US port of entry facility. Shutting off my car and phone, I grab my passport and walk inside. A border officer is sitting and eating out of a Tupperware container – her dinner, I suppose. I wait for her to look up. "Just checking in?" she asks me between bites. "Yup," I tell her. "Did you stop anywhere along the way." "Nope." "You're good to go," she says, not even bothering to look at my passport.

I could spend a bit more time in New York, but decide against it – wanting to start writing up my notes at home. I head back into my car and back toward Cornwall Island. I cross the island for the fourth time that day, hoping the line at the bridge won't be so bad. It's not. I pay another $3.00 at the toll booth and get funnelled into the Cornwall port of entry. Choosing the lane that seems shortest, when I get to the booth, I see Louis. Apparently, he's been moved to yet another position today. "You're everywhere," I tell him with a smile as I hand over my passport. He replies, "Some days I get to do everything." I know how he feels, as he returns my passport and says "Have a nice day." Tired and hungry, I pick up some chicken just across the street before heading home.

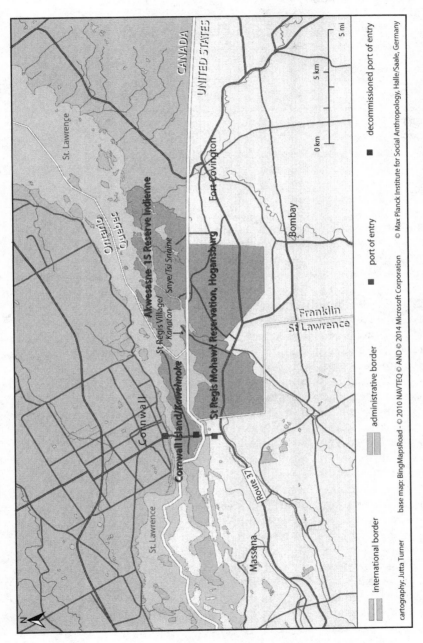

Figure P.1. Map of the Akwesasne Mohawk Territory and surrounding political geography. I reproduce this map again and discuss it critically in chapter 2. Map courtesy of the Max Planck Institute.

cartography: Jutta Turner   base map: BingMapsRoad - © 2010 NAVTEQ © AND © 2014 Microsoft Corporation   © Max Planck Institute for Social Anthropology, Halle/Saale, Germany

Chapter One

Introduction

Throughout most of my travels with the Akwesasne Mohawk Ambulance Service, the border was invisible. It appeared, if at all, in a change in pavement, street signs, or mobile phone service as we drove. At other times, the border constrained our work and mobility – forcing us to convince an injured man to come with us to a hospital, and requiring us to cross the border twice to bring him there. The border accounted for the long line-ups at the bridge and made it necessary for border officers to expedite our travel by shutting down one lane. We were frustrated at various junctures, but there were no fights or shouting matches. As with the border, Indigenous narratives of resistance and refusal simultaneously saturated our experience while remaining largely invisible.

This book sets out to reconcile a fundamental disjuncture between current portrayals of Indigeneity at the Canada-US border and what takes place in Akwesasne, North America's largest cross-border Indigenous community. Most depictions of Indigenous people crossing the border emphasize crossing as a site of conflict between largely ignorant officers and Indigenous nationalists for whom the border is a site of resistance, refusal, or contestation. The border is frequently understood as a concrete manifestation of settler colonialism, and border crossing as a fundamental rights issue. Alternatively, some media outlets have depicted borderland communities like Akwesasne as zones of lawlessness, clandestine trade, and vice industries. Summarizing the literature, Circe Sturm writes that "border crossings that demand settler-state passports are met with tribally generated documents that insist on Mohawk nationhood. Refusal is affective, material, historical, ideal, and even pleasurable – an act possibly more ontological than anything else of indigenous people insisting on their own way of being" (2017, 345).

Yet juxtaposed with these narratives of the border, my day with the Akwesasne Mohawk Ambulance Service does not quite fit the mould. There were more instances in which the border was accepted or nego-tiated than refused. The day was largely peaceful; conflicts that did occur were over law and policy. The injured man initially refused to go to the hospital not because he insisted on Mohawk nationhood and contested the legitimacy of the Canadian state but because he did not have his Canadian health card. Rather than being freed by lawlessness at the border, we were stymied by our efforts to abide by incommen-surable federal, state, provincial, and local laws. Border officers forced us to move in certain ways but also created policies to ameliorate a situation they seemed equally displeased with. They did not demand any passports as we drove past the entry port in an ambulance. As a non-Indigenous visitor, I, a white settler, was subjected to more rather than less scrutiny than the Mohawk national medical technicians. Undoubtedly, settler colonialism, Mohawk nationalism, rights, refusal, racism, resistance, clandestine trade, and concerns over law and order formed the border we had to cross and recross. Yet at the same time, these themes are insufficient to make sense of how border officers and Akwesasne residents acted and interacted.

Akwesasne, a single Indigenous community straddling the border between Canada and the United States, is often cited as a "jurisdictional nightmare" (Bonaparte 2017)). It is one of the most complicated border-lands in North America. This book explores the meaning of "the bor-der" and "border crossing" in a place where even the most fundamental terms of borders can be called into question. In doing so, I offer both the first book-length depiction of North America's largest Indigenous cross-border community and an examination of how borders work in a place where they often fail to.

Origins of This Project

My interest in studying the Canada-US border in Indigenous commu-nities, and subsequently in Akwesasne, was first piqued in the early 2000s when I read a quotation by Tuscarora artist Jolene Rickard. Rick-ard described her experience of an annual border-crossing demonstra-tion in which participants march across the border from Canada into the United States without stopping for border officers. She wrote:

> I crossed with my newborn and husband in 1991. I felt part of a long line of honor as we quietly marched from the Canadian side to the US side. I've lobbied at the UN, followed the longest run, protested on the Capitol steps

in Washington, wrote poems and made art about our rights, but nothing made me feel so strong as passing the customs guards at the bridge without uttering a word.[1]

I was fascinated by the experience Rickard described – crossing the border not simply as an act of protest but as one of conscious non-recognition. There was something compelling in gathering with hundreds of people to march across a border and proclaim that, for you, that border does not, or should not, exist. Reading Rickard's words as a New Yorker whose family rarely crossed state lines, let alone international ones, I found it difficult to fathom how someone could deny something like a border. For me, borders were immutable, so real that I could not imagine denying them. I wanted to know what is at stake when a population rejects those immutable borders, especially an Indigenous population for whom historically they did not exist.[2]

I was subsequently directed to the work of Audra Simpson, who coined the term "refusal" to describe how Haudenosaunee people, and specifically the Mohawks[3] of Akwesasne's sister community of Kahnawake, refuse the various impositions of settler states (2007, 2014). Refusal makes more sense than resistance as a theoretical paradigm to understand Mohawk nationalism and Mohawk peoples' continued denial of the "embrace" (Scott 1998) of American or Canadian colonialism.

Haudenosaunee political philosophies, and especially Mohawk voices, have played prominent roles in the North American scholarship of Indigenous-state relations. Akwesasne was at the forefront of both the pan-Indigenous North American "red power" movement in the 1960s and 1970s and the locally centred warrior societies' movements that gained notoriety from the 1980s onward (T. Alfred and Lowe 2005).

---

1 I recorded the quotation in my notes (and mentioned it to Rickard when I met her some years later) but have since been unable to find the source. Both the internet and my citational rigour have changed in the past decade.
2 Jolene Rickard is a globally celebrated Tuscarora artist and educator. She is also the granddaughter of storied Tuscarora chief Clinton Rickard, who organized both the Indian Defense League of America to fund the defence of the seminal *Diabo v. McCandless* (US) border-crossing-rights test case and the first annual border-crossing demonstrations at Niagara. His autobiography, *Fighting Tuscarora* (1994), provides an exceptional account of his life and numerous efforts to support and protect border-crossing rights for Indigenous North Americans.
3 Akwesasne is the capital of the Mohawk Nation, one of the Six Nations of the Haudenosaunee (Iroquois) confederacy along with the Cayuga, Seneca, Onondaga, Tuscarora, and Oneida nations.

Indeed, Haudenosaunee political principles (especially as interpreted and employed by Mohawk peoples) have been offered as a productive model for pan-continental Indigenous praxis (putting theory into practice) (see, e.g., Johnston 1986; Mohawk 2005; T. Alfred 2005, 2009; Simpson 2014).

Haudenosaunee political beliefs and practices stand out among those of North America as especially prominent. And the Canada-US border stands out as a site in which these beliefs are brought to bear most regularly and starkly. Simpson points to the border as "a site not of transgression, but rather a site for the activation and articulation of their *rights*" (2014, 116). After all, it is when crossing a border that someone is most likely to be asked their citizenship and nationality, and required to provide state-produced documents to support their claim. It is when crossing the border that the stakes for refusal are highest – as travellers may risk detainment or even imprisonment for failing to comply with state-employed officers. At that moment, rights, identity, and the state intersect with potentially volatile significance. Simpson fleshes out her observation with several anecdotes of her own crossing experiences, including a powerful account of a dispute with a border officer in which she shouts, "I am a Mohawk," at the officer's insistence on calling her American (ibid., 119).

"Doing What's Right" versus "Doing What's Easy"

When I asked a Mohawk Council chief how people in their community interacted with border officers, they told me that at the end of the day, it came down to a question of principle versus practicality. They expressed the opinion that practicality tends to win out in the end – people have to go to work, go to school, take care of their families, and so forth. In their mind, the practicality of answering the officers' questions and providing the most easily accepted documentation typically outweighed the cost of refusing. Indeed, many Akwesasronon (people of Akwesasne) I met told me that this was how they crossed the border. Any study of Akwesasne must study the ways in which the practicalities of everyday life influence how people engage with a contentious border.

I asked a former Mohawk Council chief the same question. They told me that, at the end of the day, it came down to a question of doing what's right versus doing what's easy. They expressed the opinion that doing what's right tends to win out in the end – people who stand up for their beliefs will be rewarded in the long term and do not have to compromise their sense of what is right. In their mind, doing what's right – refusing to be anything other than Akwesasronon and not kowtowing to the demands of border officers – outweighed the simplicity of submitting. Indeed, many Akwesasronon I met told me that this was how they crossed the border. Any study of Akwesasne must study the ways in which their history, rights, and beliefs influence how people engage with a contentious border.

In the face of such a diversity of border interactions, how do we account for what goes on there and what these exchanges tell us about the relationship between Indigenous peoples and state officers? How do these interactions make the border real? How do they deny that reality?

This book addresses these questions through an examination of (1) the experiences of the border by Akwesasronon and border officers; (2) the history of the border and its enforcement; and (3) the paradoxes, self-contradictions, and confusions that underlie the border. Akwesasne is certainly unique among territories along the border, both as an Indigenous community and as a contiguous community straddling the border. Yet the frequency and diversity of encounters with the border and border officers in Akwesasne also reflect the border more broadly. Many of Akwesasne's issues magnify the border to such an extent that otherwise taken-for-granted aspects of it are rendered visible.

Border Crossing as Interaction

You may find that, for an introduction to a book on "the border," I have spent much of my writing concerned with interactions between border officers and cross-border travellers. One facet of the border that appears starkly in Akwesasne is the role of face-to-face interaction in defining the experience of border crossing. As much as borders may be imagined as lines on a political map, most people experience crossing a border in terms of an interaction with a border officer rather than in terms of traversing a line. Later in this text, I consider how different conceptions of "what is a border" manifest in Akwesasne. For now, I offer a brief thought experiment to exemplify the role of interaction in border crossing.

Imagine yourself driving from New York to Montreal (I choose this example as a native New Yorker who drove back and forth between cities dozens of times – but you can choose two different locations if you prefer). Your car follows a highway north until you see a large sign, "Welcome to Canada," and several lanes of cars leading to a PIL (primary inspection lane) booth staffed by a border officer. You choose to queue up at one lane and immediately regret your decision, as the other lanes seem to be moving much faster. After waiting on line (New Yorkers wait "on" line rather than "in" line), you reach a booth housing a border officer. The officer takes your travel document and asks you a few questions: "Where are you from?" "Where are you going?" "What is your status?" "What are you doing?" "Do you have over five thousand dollars in currency?," and so forth. You answer. Assuming there are no problems, the officer returns your document and says, "Have a nice day." You drive forward along a Canadian highway.

Imagine that a friend has asked you to call them when you have crossed the border. When would you have called? After crossing the invisible line separating the countries? After you saw a sign that said "Welcome to Canada"? As you were waiting on/in line? Or would you have called after the border officer returned your document and said, "Have a nice day"?

People generally do not see themselves as crossing a border when they traverse an invisible line. Even if they have passed that borderline, they likely do not know where it is. The experience of border crossing is often incomplete until an officer has let you go. Crossing a border is often more a matter of which side of a conversation you find yourself on than which side of a line. Face-to-face conversations often "frame" the experience of border crossing. They create the circumstances in which the answer to the often-unasked question "What is going on?" is "You are crossing a border."

These interactions are events in which the questions asked and the answers given demand framings of a great many things. As Audra Simpson has shown, Mohawk people crossing the border are put in a situation where they must frame themselves as "American," "Canadian," "Mohawk" – some, all, or none of the above. Non-Mohawk travellers are also required to frame themselves when answering questions, even if those answers are less frequently contentious. Viewed from a wider angle, the conversations that take place at a PIL booth demand a framing of "who is in charge," what rights are at play, and who can claim them.

Jolene Rickard's account of walking past the customs booth without uttering a word represents her framing of the border as something that did not exist for her, at least not in the same way as it would for a non-Indigenous person walking past that booth. Her refusal to have the conversation was a refusal of the border. The officer in the booth chose to accept that framing, allowing her to pass without detaining her. But that officer could also have stopped her, thereby offering an alternative framing, that this border must exist for her.

Because these conversations are so central to the experience of border crossing, studying a border requires studying an interaction produced by and productive of that border. It is as much a study of interaction as a study of geography. In this text, I integrate some theoretical approaches to the study of border with some theoretical approaches to the study of interaction. Specifically, I draw upon Harold Garfinkel's "praxeological" approach to the relationship between ideology and action and Erving Goffman's "frame analysis."

Towards a Praxeological Approach to Border Crossing

Conventional thinking suggests that action follows ideas – in other words, that first we think about how we should act, and then we act accordingly. However, contributions from sociology to neuropsychology have contested the ubiquity of that fact, suggesting that we often begin acting before we think to do so.

Perhaps the earliest modern example of this perspective was that of mid-twentieth-century social theorist Harold Garfinkel, whose studies of juries (1967) demonstrated that people act unreflexively and then justify their actions after the fact, using whatever facts are available. This approach has proven especially fruitful in the study of law – for example, Pratt's (2010) study of Canadian border officers, which, though not citing Garfinkel, parallels his contributions in showing how border officers often investigate travellers on a "hunch," only justifying that hunch through specific observations or legal statutes after the fact if they are obligated to do so in court. In other words, we often act first and then create a narrative in order to justify, or make sense of, that action after the fact.

This "praxeological" approach has recently seen a resurgence among scholars looking at the ways in which legal and political principles associated with Islam manifest, or fail to manifest, in the activities of adherents to the faith (Dupret, Berger, and Al-Zwaini 1999; Dupret 2011; Dupret, Lynch, and Berard 2015; Schielke 2010). These scholars have suggested that it is problematic for one to simply assume that someone acts blindly in accordance with their religion. Rather, they demonstrate that people act in accordance with a wide variety of factors, and contingent upon each particular situation, but often look to their faith to say, and feel, "This is why I did that."

A comparable approach is useful, I find, in looking to the ways in which political principles associated with an Indigenous population manifest, or fail to manifest, among members of that population. In both instances, a praxeological approach examines how complex ideologies not only inform action but are the lenses by which actions are interpreted after the fact; in other words, how dogma works as post-facto explanation as much as pre-facto cause.

What does this have to do with border crossing in Akwesasne? Garfinkel warned against what he called "cultural dopes" – the assumption that individuals are "slavishly beholden" (1967, 68) to the shared ideology of their culture. This understanding helps make sense of how people act at the border. Border officers are not legal dopes, slavishly beholden to the law (indeed the law is often self-contradictory). Indigenous peoples are not cultural dopes, and nor is anyone else who is crossing a border. Culture and law, broadly conceived, are potential explanations and justifications for how people act, but there are many other ones.

Indigenous peoples are not unique in refusing the imposition of state authority. Most people, regardless of their status or historical situation, do not like being told what to do and how to live their lives. Akwesasronon are unique in having more reasons to refuse and more ways to understand their refusal than others. Yet even if someone in Akwesasne argues with an officer, that does not mean that they are doing so because they are Mohawk. Non-Mohawks often argue with officers, and often for the same reasons. There are many reasons to argue with an officer.

Similarly, border officers are not unique in trying to tell other people what to do and how to live their lives. Many people, regardless of their job title, try to exert their authority over others. Indeed, several of my interviewees suggested that the sort of people who try to become border officers are likely predisposed to such behaviour before they apply. Border officers are unique in having more reasons to tell people what to do and more means to force them to do so. Yet even if a border officer is pushy or aggressive, that does not mean they are doing so because that is what the job demands. Non-border officers often argue with people, and often for the same reasons. There are many reasons to be pushy.

Both border officers and Akwesasronon are historically and culturally situated beings with distinct histories, roles, and beliefs that have been shaped by the ongoing colonial projects of settler states. They are legally situated beings with distinct rights and responsibilities. They are at the same time human beings living in North America in the twenty-first century, with many shared motivations, influences, and ideas about what constitutes the right way to live. Akwesasronon are not cultural dopes but nor are they a-cultural. Border officers are not "legal" dopes, but the law matters quite a bit in what they do and how they do it.

The challenge for this project, then, is providing a depiction of the border that considers these unique and general motivations proportionally. In this book, I attempt a balance between an ideology-first and a practice-first approach to what takes place at the border. While the former is well-mapped in the study of Indigenous experiences of the border, the latter is less so. A practice-first approach looks at the minutiae of what occurs in instances of border crossing. Ultimately, it is the context of a given interaction – who is involved, what is at stake, personal and collective histories, and a wide range of other on-the-ground factors – that determines what occurs when officers and travellers meet.

This orientation results in a less uniform treatment of "power relations" at the border than the unilateral one conventionally found in popular accounts of Indigenous peoples at borders. As recent anthropological work on settler colonialism and bordering have pointed out, "the state power generated by colonialism, in any of its forms, remains highly insecure and not a privileged site of sovereign authority" (Sturm 2017, 344). On the one hand, border officers consistently claim power over cross-border travellers from Akwesasne in the form of legal authority and the threat of state-sanctioned violence. On the other hand, officers were often concerned about causing trouble with Akwesasne – expressing resentment at the limits on the power they could effectively exercise. Power, as an analytic descriptor of a constellation of factors, is always in the background but fades in and out of the foreground in terms of what goes on at the border.

An Akwesasne resident reluctant to accede to an officer's demands may nevertheless comply because of fear of arrest, or out of an exasperated desire to move things along, or because an officer convinces them that they want to comply. Similarly, an officer may give up on scrutinizing an Akwesasne resident out of fear of getting in trouble with their supervisors, out of an exasperated desire to move things along, or because the resident convinces them that they do not need high scrutiny. One could attribute any one of these factors to power, in the abstract, but doing so would not contribute much, productively, to understanding what happened.

Both the officers and the travellers I interviewed expressed both a feeling of power and a lack of it when interacting with one another. Ultimately, "power" can account for everything that happens at the border, but it offers little to help us anticipate what will happen in a given interaction. I do not want to present the reader with the false impression that my work is unique in its efforts to transcend binary notions of ideology and practice by replacing them with a more subtle depiction of what is going on locally. That is the project of most, if not all, anthropological research. With a moment's thoughtful consideration, most people would not consider somebody a cultural or legal "dope." At the same time, we often do not take that moment. Indeed, the need for, and role of, "hunches" in law enforcement (discussed in greater detail in chapter 6) can involve a tactical lack of thoughtful consideration on the part of officers. Similarly, the need for, and role of, essentialized notions of culture in order to make legal rights claims can involve intentionally painting Indigenous practices with broad brush strokes.

The observation that people do not simply match onto binaries is an important one that informs this text, but it is a means to an end rather than an end in itself. I go further to demonstrate (1) how locally understood binaries (ideology/practice; doing what's right/doing what's easy; pragmatism/discretion, etc.) are understood and employed by border officers and Akwesasne residents; (2) how the relationships between ideology and action are locally enacted; and (3) the usefulness of "frame analysis" in navigating these binaries.

Framing Borders

Frame analysis is a form of analysis developed by Canadian-born sociologist Erving Goffman in his magnum opus, *Frame Analysis* (1974). Although Goffman never wrote about borders, I find much of his work useful in thinking about them. Frame analysis looks to the ways in which people answer the questions "What is going on here?" and "Under what circumstances do we think things are real?" These are important questions to consider when thinking about a border – often invisible, often contested, often real while always imaginary. They are also important questions to consider when considering "border stories" – what makes these stories real?

Earlier in this introduction I put forward the argument that face-to-face interactions frequently frame the experience of border crossing. It is through an interaction with a border officer that the answer to the unasked question "What is going on here?" would be "I am crossing a border."

To frame a situation is to give it context (Scheff 2006, 374). To frame a person or a place is to give them or it context. We frame ourselves when we communicate with other people. We may frame ourselves as friendly, aggressive, indifferent, American, Canadian, Mohawk, in charge, and so forth. As much as interactions frame border crossing, what takes place in those interactions often determines how that interaction will play out. As a Mohawk Council chief was quick to tell me,

> The American CBSA, or whatever they're called, customs and immigration. They went out of their way to learn more about the community. And it reflected on your day-to-day encounter. When you came through, American customs officers would routinely refer to you by name, say "How's the family?" "Where're you going?" etcetera. And you didn't mind telling them where your point of destination was because of the way it was framed.

This observation points to the fact that the same question asked by two different officers may yield two different responses. A friendlier American officer asking "Where're you going?" will receive a different response from a less friendly Canadian one. It is the context of the question – what is said and asked beforehand, any personal familiarity with the officer, the way they comport themselves – that matters in this situation.

We can compare this chief's observation with a brief anecdote an Akwesasne resident shared with me of a recent experience he had at the border:

> He [the border officer] asks me where I came from. I tell him, "Akwesasne." He says, "Which part?" I say, "Akwesasne." He says, "I know there's an American part and a Canadian part. We can do this the easy way, or I can take you in."

In this instance, it was not simply a matter of the officer's asking "Where do you come from?" that resulted in a conflict. The Akwesasne resident's response, "Akwesasne," offered a framing of the territory consistent with his view of its political geography: Akwesasne is Akwesasne. It is neither American nor Canadian. The officer, in turn, refused to accept that framing – contesting it with his own: Akwesasne has an American part and a Canadian part. The officer then reframed the conversation in a threatening manner: If the resident does not answer "America" or "Canada," they will be taken in. This is a "frame dispute," and one that is resolved through the officer's threats to "take you in."

Arguments such as the one described above make for a much more interesting discussion than a quick, quiet, and easy crossing, yet they are more the exception than the rule. While the border is a site of suffering at the hands of the state –of argument, contestation, and noble assertions of autonomy against overwhelming odds – it is also a site of tedious boredom.

Grand theories of the border as a site of settler colonialism and its refusal are necessary. To borrow from Erving Goffman's dramaturgical metaphor (thinking of culture as a performance), we can think of border crossing as a one-act play with innumerable repeat performances. Settler colonialism has set the stage in which border officers and Akwesasronon meet. It has determined the roles ascribed to the participants, and the fact that they must perform in the first place. It accounts for many of the tropes one finds. But while there may be guidelines, there is not a script. Participants improvise. They act off each other, rather. People are free to be silent, talkative, bellicose, pacific, humble, bombastic, pragmatic, dogmatic, antagonistic, friendly, and so forth. On one level, the play is a tragedy, merely by the fact that it has been forced into being by states exerting contestable authority over the original peoples of the land. Yet each performance can be a comedy or a drama, though most frequently they are dull and uneventful.

In my survey-analysis work for the Mohawk Council of Akwesasne, I found that the travellers with the highest rate of dissatisfaction with border enforcement were not the "frequent flyers" who cross the border many times a day but those who cross less frequently. Frequent travellers are more likely to develop rapport with officers, provide requested identification without complaint, and answer questions clearly and concisely. Elected officials in Akwesasne are highly aware that many in the community simply want their experiences to be brief and uneventful. Studying how this "ideal boredom" operates provides data in support of the Mohawk government's efforts to improve everyday life amid the challenges of the border. This has direct implications for policy and peace building as well as in the broader intellectual discourse on how Indigenous peoples and states can interact. At a bare minimum, improving the everyday experience of crossing can diminish, though certainly not eliminate, the likelihood of big blow-ups, shouting matches, and flagrant human-rights violations. At another scale, my emphasis on negotiation, context, and banality offers a counterpart (or counterweight) to anthropology's discursive focus on power, identity, and resistance.

A One-Minded Approach to the Border

This book is shaped largely by my understanding of the Haudenosaunee principle of one-mindedness. This understanding is shaped both by conversations with elders and Longhouse adherents over the past eight years and by the way the principle has been presented by scholars in published literature. (For a more substantial discussion, see Alcantara and Kalman 2019.) The concept of one-mindedness, most prominently represented in the *Ohenten Kariwatekwen*, or "Thanksgiving Address," suggests that coercion (like the border officer's comment, "We can do this the easy way, or I can take you in") is not the only way to resolve a frame dispute. Shared gratitude, including a recognition of what is shared, also has the power to align understandings and is an important step toward peace building.

The Thanksgiving Address is relevant as an Indigenous theory of frame dispute resolution, and one specifically useful in the training of border officers. Indeed, it is used to open presentations to officers and other governments, although often in the Mohawk language. The Thanksgiving Address is among the most well-known and oft-quoted Haudenosaunee addresses, and a selection can (ironically) be found in US passports. The passage reads as follows:

> We send thanks to all the Animal life in the world. They have many things to teach people. We are glad that they are still here and hope it will always be so.

The "we" in the address assumes a shared belief, one that transcends any cultural divides. There are many different structures to the address (Foster 1974; Venables 2010, 39), but it inevitably includes a series of refrains that reflect a shared recognition of and appreciation for the natural world so that the minds of different participants in the address can be "as one." Variations of "now we are of one mind" or "now our minds are as one" are common. Below, I offer a Tuscarora version of the address recorded by Anthony Wallace. This address was chosen for its concision.

> We are thankful for the people. Now we are of one mind.
> We are thankful for mother Earth. Now we are of one mind.
> We are thankful for the Strawberries and Grasses. Now we are of one mind.
> We are thankful for the Trees. Now we are of one mind.
> We are thankful for the Animals. Now we are of one mind.
> We are thankful for the Birds. Now we are of one mind.
> We are thankful for the Corn, Beans, and Squash. Now we are of one mind.
> We are thankful for the Four winds. Now we are of one mind.
> We are thankful for the Thunders. Now we are of one mind.
> We are thankful for the Sun. Now we are of one mind.
> We are thankful for Grandmother Moon. Now we are of one mind.
> We are thankful for the Stars. Now we are of one mind.
> We are thankful for the Creator. Now we are of one mind.
> (F.C. Wallace 2012, 218)

These, or similar words, when delivered before a political (or academic) meeting have the power to orient interlocutors on the same "footing" (Goffman 1981) at the start of a discussion. Taiaiake Alfred's *Wasáse: Indigenous Pathways of Action and Freedom* (2005) begins with a version of the address for, presumably, similar reasons. It is a way of saying, in effect, "Before we start disagreeing about things, let's all agree about the things that we share, care about, and are responsible for." Whereas people may disagree as to what constitutes a border, or nationality, and so on, the stars, the sun, the thunder, and the seas are understood and valued across divides. In the address there is a sense that giving thanks and recognizing shared responsibility toward the natural world will carry over into familiar discussions.

This is not to say that one-mindedness is always attainable or maintainable. Regardless, one-mindedness serves as a potent and practical objective for people who would like to see border officers and Akwesasne residents have a more pacific relationship or no relationship at all.

By this point in the text, a reader may have noticed that, in several sections, I structure my words to place descriptions of border officers and Akwesasronon in parallel. One sentence or paragraph will talk about officers, and the next will follow a similar structure while talking about Akwesasronon (or vice versa). This mirrored structuring is intentional. While it may result in a few clunky sentences or paragraphs, it shows what is shared between the two, especially when it comes to motivations, anxieties, responsibilities, and uncertainties.[4]

One-mindedness is a long-standing objective of the Mohawk government with regard to their own practices and interactions with settlers. This objective was implicit in my discussions with officials, and they agreed with my framing when I discussed it with them in person (see also Alcantara and Kalman 2019). Nevertheless, it is undeniable that local border officers operate with a limited degree of autonomy, given their directives from Washington and Ottawa. At the same time, as I demonstrate in this text, localized relationships, discretion, and simply "being on the same page" have a tremendous impact on the success, or failure, of border officers' operations and interactions in Akwesasne.

Departures from Current Literature

Audra Simpson's work is, to date, the most serious, substantial, and successful interrogation of Mohawk nationalism, and Indigenous-settler relations in North America more broadly. In this book, many of my

---

4 My efforts to produce a parallel between the structure of my argument and the argument itself are inspired by Gregory Bateson's and Mary Bateson's (Bateson 1972; Bateson and Bateson 2005) metalogue, which they define as "a conversation about some problematic subject. This conversation should be such that not only do the participants discuss the problem but the structure of the conversation as a whole is also relevant to the same subject" (1972, 1). This structures the book on the whole but is most pronounced in (1) my treatment of one-mindedness; (2) my discussion of "border stories" in chapter 6 (which is indebted to Bateson's theorization of stories); and (3) my framing of the text itself in the introduction and conclusion, much as one would the start and conclusion of a border-crossing interaction.

observations respond to her oeuvre, and especially her book *Mohawk Interruptus* (2014), which includes a chapter on border crossing. Her observations of Kahnawake:ronon experiences of the border mesh with what I have heard and seen at first hand in Akwesasne. The border is a site through which identity is activated and the settler state manifests. Refusal is a very real and fundamental facet of everyday life and being in Akwesasne, and especially at the border.

It is unfortunate that some scholars and readers have understood Simpson's depictions of Mohawk refusal and nationalism as essential and inevitable. As one reviewer put it, "readers are left with the impression that each border crossing for the 'average' Mohawk is an overt political act" (Holcombe 2018; but I make a similar observation in my own 2014 review).

My students, reading articles and books and watching films about Mohawk nationalism, are consistently surprised when they find out that Akwesasne residents often have a more sanguine and complicated relationship with the Canadian (and American) state than they had been led to believe. Students were gobsmacked when I mentioned a "blue lives matter, all lives matter" poster hanging from the "Warrior Society" Longhouse, that most commonly associated with refusal. The poster, not uncontentious in its own right, was placed by a community member who developed a strong affection for the NYPD after working alongside them at the World Trade Center clean-up efforts after 9/11. Yet while Simpson may emphasize the distinctions between Mohawk nationalism and moments of conflict, her work is more subtle than a cursory impression might suggest. *Mohawk Interruptus* contains several sections describing humorous interactions with officers, positive ones, and the ways in which Mohawk identities are multifaceted and layered. Simpson's final chapter's discussion of "feeling citizenship" directly engages with the ways in which pragmatism plays into Mohawk border crossing.

Simpson suggests that the history of anthropology is a history of "desire," showing the ways in which a fetishized desire for "tradition" led to the creation of an "Iroquois studies" canon that ignored the dynamism of Haudenosaunee peoples and privileged the voices of some individuals and communities over others (2014, 69–71). Rather than going away, I find that the objects of disciplinary desire have merely shifted. Today, many scholars, journalists, and activists who work with Indigenous communities may desire refusal, transgression, and righteousness instead of tradition. Over the course of my work in Akwesasne, the Mohawk Council often put me in contact with visiting scholars and journalists. I found that nearly all of them tended to seek out and speak primarily with members of the community who voiced their opposition to the state most loudly. My students in Kahnawake preferred to speak with and write about the more politically engaged people they met, and found themselves more challenged when interacting with apolitical interlocutors. Granted, current studies of resistance and refusal may serve the interest of communities better than past ones of "tradition." Nevertheless, in our desires, we still risk attending to some voices over others.

There are substantive differences between Akwesasne and Kahnawake that complicate and expand current Kahnawake-oriented research on Mohawk political engagement with settler states. Whereas Kahnawake was historically ignored by anthropologists and historians for not being "traditional enough," it has, in recent years, become a major player in intellectual and popular considerations of Indigeneity in North America. Several Kahnawake:ronon scholars such as Taiaiake Alfred and Audra Simpson represent leading voices in First Nations and Indigenous scholarship in North America. Scholars and leaders in Kahnawake are often interviewed and cited both in university settings and in mass media. Akwesasne, on the other hand, remains more isolated – speaking with the voice of the Mohawk Nation at the confederacy's central fire, but not nearly as often in conferences. (However, one may want to look at Griest 2018 for a more literary and very engaging discussion of Akwesasne.)

Though neither Kahnawake nor Akwesasne was studied for generations because they were the wrong kind of "traditional," Kahnawake has shown just the right kind of "resistance" or "refusal" to attract attention today. It is the media darling of the Mohawk Nation, the topic of several documentaries (e.g., Deer et al. 2008; Tarbell et al. 2009; Obomsawin et al. 1997), a popular television show entitled *Mohawk Girls* (described as "a native take on *Sex and the City*" [Hays 2013]), and numerous research papers. It is also the only singular community to be accorded a dedicated section of the National Museum of the American Indian, as other sections of the museum focus on whole nations or geographic regions. The section on Kahnawake prominently features a Haudenosaunee passport and a discussion of border crossing.

Without a media presence or proximity to a major urban centre, Akwesasne seems a less attractive site for media or scholastic attention than its sister community of Kahnawake. The depictions and studies of Akwesasne that do exist often reify the community's stigmatizing association with smuggling and illegality, and are typically the product of short-term research (see, e.g., Jamieson 1998; Dickson-Gilmore and Whitehead 2002).

A few of my friends in Akwesasne were frustrated that Kahnawake has become the voice of Mohawk border crossing. One said that Kahnawake was like the older sister that always demanded attention; another simply said, "They don't speak for us."

As much as border crossing is an issue of importance in Kahnawake, which is located wholly north of the Canada-US border, it is a fundamental facet of everyday life in Akwesasne, which literally straddles that line. While some residents, especially those whose homes are south of the border, may find themselves entering the Canadian mainland infrequently, others must traverse borders and ports of entry to simply go about their daily lives. In some parts of the territory, crossing the border is as simple as crossing the street or moving from one side of a building to another. In other parts, people must go through customs even if they have not crossed an international borderline. In my year of commuting from my apartment in Cornwall, Ontario, to my desk in the Mohawk Council of Akwesasne's government office, I traversed the borderline well over a thousand times.

In planning this research project, I initially reasoned that if people who crossed the border several times a month described it as a frequent site of conflict and the activation of their rights, then among people who crossed the border several times a day, this would be magnified. I expected to find, in Akwesasne, a story of conflict, refusal, and settler colonialism (see Sturm 2017, 345). Ultimately, this was only partially true.

For every crossing in Akwesasne with a tribally generated document that insists on Mohawk nationhood there are far more crossings using documents that either are produced by settler states (like a US or Canadian passport) or, though tribally manufactured (such as status cards), do not insist on any sort of Mohawk nationhood. And nationalism is not the only reason for one's document preference. Many respondents told me they prefer status cards because those cards are easier to acquire than a passport and fit in their wallet. Crossings on tribally generated documents that affirm sovereignty such as Haudenosaunee passports certainly exist. And many more such crossings would undoubtedly exist if state regimes did not punish or challenge travellers for using them. Yet any empirically grounded treatment of border crossing in Akwesasne demands attention to the many instances in which people prefer to use a US passport, a Canadian passport, or no document at all.

If someone expects an argument every time an Akwesasronon crosses the border, they will be disappointed by what they find on the ground, as they will if they expect to find a clueless border officer mechanically applying the letter of the law. For every shouting match between a Mohawk traveller and a border officer in Akwesasne there are thousands of banal interactions in which nothing memorable takes place. Sometimes officers and residents fight, sometimes they joke, and on some rare occasions, they get married.

This is not to say that arguments do not matter. A single tense relationship can inform a lifetime of interactions and attitudes toward the border regime, whereas a thousand uneventful interactions may have little observable influence. At the same time, this does not mean that those "uneventful" interactions are not influential. While I am interested in the arguments that occur at borders, I also look at the spaces between those arguments. This book is as much an examination of how rights and power manifest at the border as an exploration of how they fail to manifest. I am interested in the border as a site in which people refuse, refuse to refuse, choose not to refuse, or simply don't think of refusal as an option.

Akwesasne is a community that, like Kahnawake, refuses to be anything other than itself. But as with selves more broadly, what constitutes Akwesasne "itself" is contextually variable. It is something as much felt as presented. Sometimes Akwesasne is a site of refusal, and sometimes it is a site of negotiation, collaboration, or complacency. Sometimes it is American and Canadian, sometimes it is anything but. Sometimes it is a no man's land, and sometimes it is a vibrant community.

Settler colonialism is an assumption rather than a conclusion in this study. This book is not a depiction of the border as an epitomizing event in the broader history of colonialism that includes residential schools, racist legislation, Indian agents, and violence – symbolic, structural, and physical. Books of that sort have been written and have been written well (see, e.g., Hele 2008; Fine-dare and Rubenstein 2009). My goal is to make sense of the relationship between these histories of power and what takes place when two people are talking to each other at a border crossing – what goes into these conversations, and what comes out of them. We can take the already strong theorization of settler colonialism and bolster it with an examination of how it intersects with the minutiae of everyday life. I do so by bringing a micro-analytic approach to a field that has largely been dominated by macro-analytic perspectives.

Research Methods and Data Collection

I conducted primary fieldwork from 2012 to 2013 and continue to spend a month or so in Akwesasne each year, usually over half a dozen or more visits to catch up with friends and discuss past and future research projects. Before commencing interviews in Akwesasne, I received the permission of the Mohawk Council of Akwesasne (MCA; a Canada-recognized government), the Saint Regis Mohawk Tribe (a US-recognized government), and the Mohawk Nation Council of Chiefs (hereafter "the Nation"; the territory's predominant traditional government). The Nation gave me the opportunity to speak with elders about contemporary border issues, tradition, history, and cosmology. This supplemented both my background in literature concerning traditional knowledge and my years of involvement co-teaching a field course in Akwesasne's sister community of Kahnawake. I employ this background at several junctures, such as in the above section on one-mindedness. I gave two presentations to the Nation (one to the whole Longhouse, and one to the chiefs), and several community presentations organized by the Mohawk Council.

During my year of primary fieldwork, I resided in the city of Cornwall, Ontario, located directly north of Akwesasne, and commuted to an office space in Akwesasne that was kindly provided by the Mohawk Council. This office space was in Akwesasne's Aboriginal Rights Research Office (ARRO). While there, in addition to my own work, I helped design and analyse community-wide surveys and policy reports, and index ARRO's archives.

My daily commute from my apartment in Cornwall to the office in Akwesasne involved crossing the borderline a total of four times at a minimum. I had to first drive down to the United States and through US customs before continuing along the road and driving up into Canada (this time not crossing customs). When I left the office, I repeated this trip in reverse – first parking my car at the US port of entry in order to "report in" to officers there, and then continuing across Canadian customs. If I wanted to get lunch at a local restaurant, I often had to leave the part of Akwesasne I was in and cross the borderline two more times (once to get food, and once to get back). This will be clearer in chapter 2, which provides an overview of Akwesasne's geography along with a map.

Over the course of a year's fieldwork, I went through border controls more than 400 times and crossed the borderline roughly 2,000 times. I crossed by myself primarily, keeping an audio recorder in my dash to repeat my interactions with border officers from memory out loud as soon as I finished going through a port of entry. These recordings were not done in situ, but the next best thing. I crossed with friends and neighbours whenever possible, both as a driver and as a passenger. By the end of the year I got to know some officers, and a few remarked, "Oh, I've heard about you," when I explained my research project.

This experience was not "participant observation." As a non-Indigenous, non-resident researcher in Akwesasne, I was subject to different types of scrutiny than members of the community. I traversed the border on a US passport with a Canadian student visa, never crossing "as" anything other than an American living in Canada. I was not put in a situation in which an officer would deny my national identity nor a situation in which I found myself fighting over whether I was "really" American. Yet at the same time, I could travel with people who can and do claim Mohawk identity and speak, daily, with friends and colleagues who had crossed the border earlier that day.

I arrived at a fortunate time for border research but a less fortunate time for life along the border. The period of my primary fieldwork was one in which tensions between Akwesasne and the Canada Border Services Agency (CBSA) had heightened following vehicle seizures that I discuss in greater detail later in this book. Both the MCA and the CBSA had hired liaison officers in order to improve their relationship. The Mohawk government was receptive to supporting me as an independent researcher documenting both the challenges Akwesasronon faced at the border and learning more about local border enforcement. In their efforts to demonstrate conciliation with Akwesasne, the CBSA gave me permission to talk with currently employed officers, tour the facilities, and circulate a questionnaire. I also met many retired officers who wished to share their stories. Of course, with great access comes great responsibility – to both the communities and the individuals I worked with. Within this book, I prioritize protecting the people who took the risk of speaking with me. My emphasis on peace building is, further, rooted both in the wishes of my primary interlocutors and in my genuine belief that the relationship between border officers and Akwesasne can improve.

In addition to spending my days in Akwesasne, I was fortunate to be able to interview retired and current border officers at the Canadian port of entry, administrators at the US port of entry, and US border-patrol officers working in the region, and to conduct a questionnaire of currently employed officers. I also had typically brief, though sometimes more substantial, exchanges with officers while crossing at ports of entry and reporting into the US port of entry. My study draws upon nearly a hundred hours of conversations with Canadian border officers that were not recorded but transcribed by hand, and several dozen hours of recorded and transcribed interviews with four officers, some of them retired and some currently employed. My most substantial conversations with US-based officers comprised a tour and interview with the acting director of the port of entry in Massena and a meeting, presentation, and Q&A with the administration for local border-patrol operations.

I also spent more than one hundred hours observing court cases, in particular the testimonies of border officers, and working with transcriptions of court cases pertaining to the border. As one officer told me, "Court is the only place you have to tell the truth." I consider this observation in greater detail in chapters 3 and 4. Given the fact that the Canada Border Services Agency is "one of the most secretive of the publicly funded bodies in Canada" (Côté-Boucher 2013, 116), such insights have proven invaluable.

In contradistinction to the work of Shahram Khosravi's "The 'Illegal Traveller': An Autoethnography of Borders" (2007), my approach constitutes a "legal" traveller's auto-ethnography of a legally nebulous border. Despite the vast differences between illegal and legal (or perhaps quasi-legal) border crossing, an auto-ethnographic approach like Khosravi's remains as valuable along the Canada-US border as it does in the Middle East and Europe, perhaps even more so because the everydayness of the border risks rendering so much invisible. The sheer banality of daily crossing in Akwesasne is neither glorious nor status-enhancing (contra Khosravi 2007, 331), yet it is rife with rituals, assumptions, affective weight, and consequences for human and minority rights.

In crossing, I occupied a position of intersectional privilege – a cisgender white male with a high level of education and legal status in both countries (though, as I elaborate below, my status as an outsider sometimes made cross-border movement harder rather than easier). In terms of my physical appearance, I have been diplomatically referred to as "unimposing." When a border officer called me into the office for "looking nervous," I was able to jokingly defuse the situation by attributing my demeanour to my Jewish upbringing. Within this text, I clearly delineate those experiences that were specific to me, and those I recorded through observation of others or from second-hand accounts. Some readers may wish to discount my narrative as another instantiation of a white man speaking "for" Indigenous peoples. Nevertheless, it is my hope that the empirical, reflexive, and collaborative focus of this research is received with the same openness it has been granted by my friends and colleagues in Akwesasne and interlocutors in border enforcement.

A reader may notice that my attention toward the border disproportionately emphasizes Canadian operations. The reasons for this are twofold. Firstly, while I had initially planned to emphasize US-based operations when I commenced fieldwork, my initial contacts in Akwesasne asked me to focus on CBSA-community relations because of recent challenges involving the relocation of the port of entry and vehicle seizures. There was more "going on" in the Canadian context, including a human-rights tribunal, policy changes, infrastructure changes, and complaints about officer behaviour. Canadian operations were seen as more important in Akwesasne, and therefore I made studying them the priority. Secondly, my work within the Mohawk Council of Akwesasne, which represents sections of the community north of the border, afforded me greater access to and awareness of Canadian enforcement. This emphasis on Canada has had the added advantage of enabling me to respond more closely to the Canada-centric literature on Indigenous, and especially Mohawk, nationalism and sovereignty.

Organization of This Text

Taking into account the importance of "context" in determining what is going on at the border, this text is organized to best examine the many contexts that overlie one another at that site. We can distil these emphases into several questions: "What/where is Akwesasne?" "How did the border come to Akwesasne in the first place?" "How did contemporary border enforcement practices come to Akwesasne?" "What brings Akwesasronon and border officers into contact with each other?" "What takes place when the two interact?" And, "What do people take away from their interactions?"

This introduction has laid out my justification for the study of the border as a study of interaction and framing. I have also brought forward some of the theoretical approaches that inform my writing and the structure of that writing.

Chapter 2, "Welcome to Akwesasne," takes a step back to introduce Akwesasne and the surrounding area. I depict Akwesasne as a "flexible geography," a space that permits, and often demands, a variety of representations – some of which may even seem contradictory. Akwesasne is rarely "just one thing," even if some officers, courtrooms, and legal statutes can only understand it if it is. Through this introduction, I consider the difficulties of both naming and map making. This chapter is organized around how the seemingly simple question, "Where are you from?" is loaded with social and historical meaning.

Chapter 3, "Doing History in Akwesasne," considers the early history of Akwesasne and the border. I look at how the border came to Akwesasne or, from another perspective, how Akwesasne came to the border. In doing so, I argue that the border did not simply land on Akwesasne. Rather, Akwesasne's residents chose to create a permanent settlement in the area because of its historical location as a traditional territory and its strategic value as a nexus of trade and diplomacy. I also consider what it means to "do" history in Akwesasne and how legal rights claims influence the ways in which the past is viewed today.

Chapter 4, "The Changing Face of the Cornwall-Akwesasne Border," offers a recent history of Akwesasne and the border. In the chapter, I look at how *this* border came to Akwesasne – focusing on changes within Akwesasne, Canadian border enforcement, and transnational agreements from 1969 to 2009. This approach offers a local contextualization to Karine Côté-Boucher's (2013) assertion that Canadian border work underwent a period of "disembedding" in the 1980s. I supplement her thesis by suggesting that Akwesasne-CBSA relations underwent a parallel period of "depersonalization" that began in the 1980s but reached its apex in the withdrawal of the CBSA from the port of entry on Cornwall Island (Kawehnoke) in 2009. My use of the term "face" is intentional here – showing how new enforcement technologies and practices changed the ways in which border officers could present their "face" to cross-border travellers (and vice versa).

Chapter 5, "'Reporting in' to/from Akwesasne," is concerned with what brings people to the border. There are numerous ways to traverse the borderline in the region without ever encountering an officer. Canadian and American "reporting-in" policies seek to force travellers to visit ports of entry even if they otherwise would not have to. I suggest that these policies, which have had a deleterious effect on the community, can be interpreted as a fundamental disjuncture between the "ideal type" of border upon which policy is designed and the practical realities of the Akwesasne Mohawk Territory. This chapter examines the different definitions of "the border" at play and how those definitions manifest when people interact. Unable to bring "the border" to the Mohawks, border officers try to bring the Mohawks to the border. At the end of the chapter, I compare American and Canadian reporting-in policies with the historical "Edge of the Woods" protocols by which Haudenosaunee people have regulated movement within and into their territories.

Chapter 6, "Processing," focuses on what goes on when officers and Akwesasronon meet. I discuss the diverse ways in which officers conceptualize processing and their own discretionary activities in border work. I also look at the strategies, techniques, and logics that make up "border practices" of both officers and cross-border travellers. While they occupy very different roles, both border officers and cross-border travellers orient their actions along axes of dogmatism and pragmatism. In processing, the law is simultaneously negotiable and inflexible, and people may find themselves torn between "doing what's right" and "doing what's easy."

Chapter 7, "Talking Borders," looks at what border officers and travellers take away from their interaction. I focus on "border stories" and, expanding on Yael Navaro-Yashin's (2002) discussion of the state as creating a self-fulfilling prophecy, consider the ways in which the citizenry may also be creating a self-fulfilling prophecy. Regardless of the veracity of their content, these stories of what happened in the past are often true, as they are meaningful in the present and produce the future of the border. In addition to the stories themselves, I reflect upon the media through which these stories circulate, suggesting that, as much as communications technologies make it easier to communicate across borders, the infrastructures of these technologies reproduce borders in new ways.

The Passport

I conclude this chapter with a consideration of the Haudenosaunee passport. It offers a justification for the sort of analysis I provide, an example of Mohawk nationalism, and a microcosm of this study. I briefly discuss it here to highlight the shortcomings of an epistemological approach to the border that places too much emphasis on powerful symbols and too little emphasis on quiet banalities. (I discuss Haudenosaunee refusal to provide a passport, and border officers' historic willingness to accept that refusal, at length in Kalman 2018.)

For nearly a century, Haudenosaunee people have been producing and travelling on their own passports. The first such instance was that of Cayuga Chief Levi General (whose chiefly name/title was Deskaheh), who travelled on one such passport to lobby for Haudenosaunee inclusion in the League of Nations in Geneva (Rickard 1994; Niezen 2009). There were pictures of the passport on the front page of major news outlets in 2010 when members of the Iroquois Nationals lacrosse team were denied the opportunity to compete in the United Kingdom when trying to travel on their Haudenosaunee passports (as the team had done for many years).

While teaching a field course in Kahnawake, I did a quick and unscientific survey of my McGill students, most of whom had some background in Indigenous studies. I asked them what percentage of Mohawk people they believed used the Haudenosaunee passport when crossing the border. Answers averaged at between 50 and 75 per cent, although one student said 5 per cent.

By the numbers, according to a survey conducted by the Mohawk Council of Akwesasne (n = 413), less than 1 per cent of respondents listed the passport among the top three documents they use when crossing the border. A few respondents added the comment that they would like to use the passport, but it is often not accepted by border officers. People in Akwesasne showed me a wide variety of documents they used to cross the border, but none presented a Haudenosaunee passport.

In my roughly seven years as a researcher studying Haudenosaunee border crossing and speaking with thousands of cross-border travellers, I have seen the passport four times in person. Twice was behind glass in museums, once was at a border-crossing demonstration in Akwesasne (held up by a prominent chief from another community), and once was in a presentation by an activist, educator, and scholar from Kahnawake. In these international fora – museums, newspapers, speeches – the passport represents the experience of Haudenosaunee peoples at the border to publics largely unfamiliar with their situation. In presenting my research, I have often mentioned the passport to grab an audience's attention and interest, showing one of several pictures readily available online. Nearly every time I have written about border crossing in Akwesasne, an editor has asked me to say more about the passport.

How, then, to make sense of a document that is so important yet so rarely utilized? The passport matters in Akwesasne. The confederacy has worked alongside the US government to modernize the passport in accordance with biometric and other security features. Successful modernization of the passport is a source of pride and future vision for a better relationship with the United States, which recognizes and respects Haudenosaunee sovereignty in Akwesasne and beyond. Another news story reached beyond the community when the head of Akwesasne's justice department, Joyce King, had her passport confiscated as a "fantasy document" by a Canadian border officer, the official designation for non-recognized passports. The passport was subsequently returned, with apologies, to the Mohawk Nation, the predominant traditional government in the community; yet the fact that an officer stationed in the region had never seen such a passport before suggests the infrequency of its use.

Like most people in Akwesasne, King had not planned on providing any ID. As I mentioned previously, for many years, this was the standard way people in the community crossed the border. The Haudenosaunee passport was provided, as she did not have any other photo ID at the time. As one article written shortly after the confiscation remarked,

She said because of the frequency of her border travels, she rarely is asked to provide any identification [...] when King was asked to provide some

ID, her first thought was that she could not show her driver's license because it had expired. She said she had a new temporary one on her, but it did not include a photo. So instead she took out her Haudenosaunee passport. And her difficulties began as she was taken inside the customs office for a secondary inspection. (Laskaris 2011)

In an interview with the Aboriginal Peoples Television Network (APTN), King remarked,

> I look in my purse and there is my Haudenosaunee passport, so I asked what kind of identification do you want? And he said, and I memorized this, "Any documentation that has your identification on it" [...] They weren't direct, they changed their mind, they took their passport, how I identify myself. Okay, if it's not good, I'll give you something else. They chose to seize it. So they stole my identity. (Blackburn 2011)

It was the particularities of that specific interaction that resulted in the passport's being offered, and the vagaries of the officer's training or understanding of the law at that moment that resulted in its confiscation. At the moment, King's decision to hand over the passport was not understood as refusal of the settler state but rather as the choice of an appropriate document at any appropriate time. King, an active voice in Akwesasne's rights claims, certainly understood the significance of the passport, but interviews suggested that the decision to hand it to an officer at that moment was more pragmatic than ideological.

Yet subsequent articles discussing the confiscation de-emphasized the underlying context of King's decision to provide the passport (Carlson 2011). Instead, they emphasized the absurdity of the CBSA's confiscating an Indigenous nation's passport, contesting the heart of their identity, and labelling it a fantasy document. What was important in these treatments was not what the passport represented at that moment but what it represents in the larger picture of an Indigenous nation whose very identity is denied by a settler state.

The Haudenosaunee passport tells one part of the story of Haudenosaunee peoples and the border. It tells the part that focuses on sovereignty and identity, and the complex refusals of settler colonialism that have arisen in communities such as Akwesasne. Yet it does not say much about how someone will cross a border in their day-to-day life. It says more about what someone *can* say to an officer than what someone *will* say to an officer when asked about who they are and where they are from. Every crossing in which a Haudenosaunee passport was not presented is one in which it *could* have been. Similarly, a complex understanding of the history and qualities of Mohawk nationalism can give someone a sense of how the border is understood and how some interactions will take place, but it is incomplete as a measure of how people will interact with border officers.

The problem of the passport is a problem of the border in general. The symbolic often overshadows the banal in the eyes of scholars and media and the imagination of actors involved with border crossing. History and symbolism, however rich, are not enough, in themselves, to account for how people choose to act on a day-to-day basis. One must also look to the contexts in which the passport may or may not appear at a port of entry. This is the analysis I attempt in the following pages.

PORT CLOSED
PROCEED THRU
DO NOT STOP
Wa'tkwanonhwera:ton / Greetings

You have entered the Akwesasne Mohawk Territory. Be aware and respectful of our Nation and our laws. Respect our Mother Earth. Nia:wen tanon O:nen
    Thank you and travel safely

> *– Signage at the former site of the Cornwall Port of Entry, Cornwall Island (Kawehnoke), Ontario, Canada/Akwesasne Mohawk Territory*

NOTICE
THIS IS AN INDIAN RESERVE

Any person who trespasses on an Indian Reserve is guilty of an offense and is on summary conviction to a fine not exceeding fifty dollars or to imprisonment for a term not exceeding one month, or both fine and imprisonment.

> *– Signage on a small island in Akwesasne Mohawk Territory accessible only by boat*

Chapter Two

Welcome to Akwesasne

Not too long ago, a friend from Akwesasne posted one of those Facebook images with a "Please share." The image was a woman holding a sign that read, "I'm a teacher trying to show my class how quickly a message can be shared on Facebook. Please 'like,' 'share,' and 'comment' on your location."

The friend who posted the message wrote, "Hogansburg, NY," in reply. On her comment thread were several other answers including, "Northern NY, Akwesasne"; "Akwesasne. Ontario/Quebec/Northern New York State"; "Akwesasne. Allow all Iroquois to travel on their Haudenosaunee passports!" Though these respondents all lived in Akwesasne, they each chose a different way to respond to the teacher. At least one response was tied to a broader struggle related to border crossing. Most answers referenced New York, and one also included Quebec and Ontario.

There is something about Akwesasne that makes "Where are you from?" a question that must be asked, and answered, in a wide variety of ways.

The Akwesasne Mohawk Territory is one of the most complicated geopolitical landscapes one can find in North America, if not the world. It is a single community encapsulating the legal and administrative boundaries of two elected Mohawk governments, New York State, Quebec, Ontario, and the federal governments of Canada and the United States. Several Longhouses also claim traditional authority in the area. Akwesasne is Canada, America, Haudenosaunee territory; it is some, all, or none of those things.

I had more false starts in writing this chapter than with any other chapter in the book, even if a "basic geographic overview" may seem less consequential than sections on the history and policing of the border. The reason for this is, simply, that Akwesasne's social and political geography is complicated – and writing about it inevitably privileges some representations over others, either through ordering or through omission. While, with some familiarity, a resident (or researcher) can accommodate multiple possibilities, even seemingly self-contradictory ones, in their head, arriving at that point takes time and is hard to do via words on the page.

This chapter offers an ethnographic geography of Akwesasne. This means that I discuss Akwesasne's geography, but I also consider how people talk about that geography and what is at stake when they do so.

I discuss the "where" of Akwesasne as it appears both on maps and in conversations. To start, I introduce the idea of Akwesasne as a community and unpack what it means to call Akwesasne a "community." Afterwards, I briefly provide some demographic information about Akwesasne – its language, religion, economy, education, and so forth. Showing a map of the community, I discuss its political geography while also considering how hard it is to discuss that political geography.

Akwesasne is what I call a "flexible geography." It can be different things at different times, while nevertheless remaining a single community. Flexibility rather than hybridity or assemblage makes the most sense in thinking about Akwesasne. The space of Akwesasne is defined more by the possibilities and contexts in which it manifests than by any singular or "true" understanding.

Akwesasne – Driving in the Territory

In what follows, I drive the reader through the territory (people rarely walk any great distance, although a few ride a bicycle). I introduce the territory as I've experienced it, highlighting some points of contention long the way.

The first sense one gets of Akwesasne's location is often through the radio. Turning the dial in one's car, the stations transition from English-language pop music; classic rock; liberal or conservative political commentary; country music; local college stations; Québécois stations playing French-language rock, hip-hop, and classics; and finally CKON, Akwesasne's own "pirate" radio station.

CKON's office and tower literally straddle the borderline, rendering the station unregulated by US or Canadian officials. One quickly gets accustomed to the familiar tags of radio host Reen Cook, the *Akwesasne weather* jingle, Mohawk language lessons (I learned how to say, "I slipped on the ice and hurt my butt" in Mohawk), and, of course, weekly radio Bingo.

Indeed, even if one does not decide to stick with CKON, this ability to switch stations is part of what makes a driver feel that they are in Akwesasne. In the car, you can choose background music from English, French, or Mohawk. Switching between stations, you can feel yourself in Quebec, Ontario, New York, and Akwesasne. You can bounce to contemporary pop music, or ramble to something more classic. You can find yourself a little bit of country, or a little bit of rock and roll, without ever leaving your car.

The population of Akwesasne is usually cited as 12,000 to 14,000. There are, however, several obstacles to precise census taking. Many Akwesasronon live off-reserve/reservation land in neighbouring towns. Some people have legal status as a member of Akwesasne but visit rarely (an employee of the Saint Regis Mohawk Tribe once proudly told me that there are Akwesasronon living in each of the fifty American states, although he did not have specific information about who was in North Dakota). Alternatively, some people do not have legal status but are active members of the community. Some residents get counted twice, and may even have two or three names, an "American" name, a "Canadian" name, and a Mohawk name. For every resident who gets counted more than once, there are one or more who refuse to be counted at all and resist any efforts at census taking.

English is the dominant language throughout the territory, with Mohawk (*Kanienkehaka*) spoken most fluently by very old and very young Akwesasronon. The Mohawk spoken among members of my age group (late twenties to early thirties) reminded me of my third-generation Jewish-American family's use of Yiddish. Mohawk is peppered into conversations and used when other words fail. Much as I spoke of my *bubby* (grandmother), so did my friends speak of their *totas*. Today, an increasing number of youths are learning Kanienkehaka. The Akwesasne Freedom School, established with community support in 1979, teaches Mohawk immersion classes from pre-Kindergarten to Grade 8. There are also many free Mohawk classes in schools and workplaces, with incentives to learn the language. French is practically non-existent, even in those parts ostensibly located in Quebec.

Much of Akwesasne's character, mobility, and shape is defined by its rivers. Akwesasne sits at the confluence of the Raquette, St. Regis, and St. Lawrence Rivers. Early in my fieldwork, a chief told me that one can never get a sense of the territory without going onto the water. The rivers are beautiful, and some of my fondest memories involve spending time on the water with friends. Hundreds of residents own boats, from recreational canoes and kayaks to motorboats and larger vessels. People continue to fish in the waters, and in the summer much recreational time is spent on the river or the many islands dotting it. When Cornwall Island was cut off from the Canadian and US mainland in 2009, the community quickly organized a ferry system to get residents off the island to school or work. Some residents would like to see a permanent ferry in place between the island and "Canadian" portions of the territory, so that residents can travel quickly and easily without having to worry about going through American border controls.

Historically, the St. Lawrence River was a major source of subsistence and industry for Akwesasronon. Fishing and logging were big industries, though emissions from manufacturing plants in Canada and the United States have poisoned the waters and necessitated new forms of local industry. Johansen (1993) suggests that the rise of Akwesasne's cigarette trade and casinos (discussed in greater detail in chapter 4) can be directly attributed to the ecological decline of the river and the inability of residents to make a living by it. Despite the (now slowly improving) toxicity of the water, people still supplement their incomes and diets with fishing and occasional trapping.

Much as the river is an important natural resource, the border can also be seen as a sort of natural resource and important facet of Akwesasne's economy. Today, major industries within Akwesasne include the Akwesasne Mohawk Casino, one of the largest employers in the region, whose clientele are largely cross-border visitors. The casino is the place one is most likely to hear French in Akwesasne. Part of the appeal of having it in Akwesasne is the fact that it is one of the only places where an ambulance would pick up a patron in what is ostensibly the United States and drive them across the border where they can benefit from Canadian health care. Given the fact that many casinogoers are Québécois in their golden years, this is a bigger draw than one might initially think. Other local employers include Akwesasne's numerous (American and Canadian) government agencies, which have proven apt at successfully gaining funding from the many provincial and federal authorities that lay claim to Akwesasne.

Tobacco is another big business in Akwesasne. The community became famous (or notorious) for the clandestine cross-border sale of tax-free cigarettes, also referred to as "buttlegging," in the 1990s. While there is stigma associated with the cigarette trade, it is important to note that not all trade is illegal by either Canadian or American laws. Akwesasne hosts several large tobacco-processing plants that are licensed by New York State. Through agreements with New York, Akwesasne's businesses can also sell discounted tobacco and gasoline on reserve.

As in other Mohawk communities, many in Akwesasne are in steel or iron work, travelling to worksites and returning home regularly with income and interesting stories. This work is predominantly performed by men, and many of the men I spoke with had spent at least one summer trying out the occupation.

Unlike neighbouring towns in Canada and the United States, Akwesasne offers a wide range of jobs requiring high skill and high education and has not experienced a significant degree of "brain drain." Akwesasne is among the most well-educated Indigenous communities in North America, with a high-school graduation rate well above that of Indigenous and non-Indigenous communities alike. Many residents go on to university, and regardless of which side of the border they reside on, can apply to some New York State universities as a New York resident. Akwesasronon can also claim funding from various Mohawk, state, federal, and provincial governments, and a successful student can earn scholarships covering most, or all, of their student fees.

Much of Akwesasne's commerce is located along New York Interstate route 37. You may remember my discussion of route 37 from the prologue. Driving along 37, one encounters full-service gas stations selling discount petrol, with adjacent shopping marts. A couple, "The Bear's Den" and "Twinleaf," have expanded to several locations that include either their own restaurants or franchises such as Tim Horton's or Papa John's Pizza. They are popular lunch spots for people living and working within the territory. With a reward system in place, travellers often prefer one location over another (I have a Twinleaf rewards card, although little thought went into choosing which establishment to frequent).

In years past, these gas-station-resto-marts were a big draw, not just locally but for cross-border travellers interested in buying discounted gas or cigarettes. Purchases once included a bridge pass for anyone coming from Cornwall. These stores have become, to a certain extent, Akwesasne's ambassadors; in my years as a member of the Cornwall outdoor club, any trips southward to the Adirondack Mountains started and ended with a fill-up and coffee at Twinleaf.

There are other restaurants along 37, including makeshift chip stands that are open seasonally, a few sandwich shops (both franchises and locally owned), diners serving home-cooked daily specials, and a Japanese buffet serving pan-Asian cuisine.

Public buildings also dot 37. Driving east from the US port of entry in Massena (the direction one would take if coming from Cornwall or the island), one passes the Akwesasne Public Library and Museum, which in addition to an extensive library collection also hosts local archives and a cultural museum and shop. One then passes the Saint Regis Mohawk Tribe's administration building, with an LCD sign advertising events in Mohawk and English.

Driving past the Saint Regis Mohawk Tribe offices, one arrives at another focal point of local traffic – the intersection of route 37 and St. Regis Road. This four-way intersection with a traffic light is situated next to a US post office, several churches, and the American Legion, a popular site for drinking and social events. One can continue east or south into Hogansburg and other southern parts of the territory, or north, as I did daily in my commute, to St. Regis Village, part of Akwesasne's northern section.

I asked a friend to give me a broad overview of the differences between St. Regis Village, Snye, and the island. He told me that the village is the "urban" part of the community, where houses are close together. It used to be a fishing village and has the highest density despite its small size. The island is a bit more geographically detached from the rest of the community, and historically has the closest ties to the city of Cornwall located directly to the north. It is a bit more like the suburbs. Snye, he told me, laughing, "Snye is just Snye." Everyone at the table we were sitting at laughed with him. Snye is the part of Akwesasne I spent the least amount of time in during fieldwork. Swampy, with large plots of farmland, Snye is the largest and most dispersed part of Akwesasne located north of the borderline. It is also the easiest place to get lost in when driving at night. If the village is urban, and the island is suburban, then Snye represents the countryside.

There is little, if any, visible evidence of "the border" when driving into St. Regis Village or Snye. Snye has a road called "borderline road" that roughly lines up with parts of the borderline. The concrete on the road changes in St. Regis Village, and one sees a street sign in kilometres (rather than miles) per hour. But primarily, the first thing one notices is the lack of anything to notice. Houses straddle either side of the line, as do power cables. One colleague has a front door in one country and a mailbox in another (making it easier to do online shopping).

In the village, houses line up next to each other, with small yards in between. MCA administration buildings are located in the village, along with the Kanekwatseriio health centre, one of the few health centres in Indigenous communities to feature a traditional medicine clinic. The dual offices of *Indian Time*, Akwesasne's local newspaper, and the CKON radio station sit astride the borderline as well. There are a few multipurpose shops in the area, small grocery stores that may have soup or sandwiches available, but commerce is mostly located south of the borderline. This means that most shopping, or simply getting a bite for lunch, requires heading back to route 37 and, ostensibly, New York State.

In theory, non-Indigenous travellers coming from St. Regis Village or Snye to Hogansburg should first report themselves at the Massena or Fort Covington port of entry, and only then turn around to go back to the road and conduct their affairs. In practice, however, this rarely happens. While US border patrol monitors the corridor overtly or covertly, they typically will not pull over a car in the territory, and when they do pull cars over, it is typically outside of Akwesasne's limits.

Cross-border movement is much more heavily controlled for Akwesasronon travelling from Cornwall Island. Cornwall Island is, at present, sandwiched between the Massena (US) port of entry to the south and the Cornwall (Canada) port of entry to the north. Consequently, island residents must go through a port of entry any time they leave the island overland. When returning to the island via New York State, they are legally obligated to drive first into the city of Cornwall to report in to border officers before turning around and going back to the island. I discuss this reporting-in policy in much greater detail in chapter 5.

It is hard to overstate the extent to which this is an abnormal situation. I invite the reader to imagine what it would be like to wait in line and present yourself to a border officer any time you wanted to leave home to do grocery shopping, go to school, go to work, visit most friends or family, or simply visit another town or city. Further, imagine having to drive past your home any time you want to return to first let a border officer know what you were up to. Or having to go to another country to eat lunch or go to the store.

These "inconveniences" range from banal to infuriating but do not always map easily onto the legal discourse of settler colonialism. There has not been any court case over crossing a border to buy a slice of pizza, although someone in Akwesasne could get into trouble doing just that. And even if they do not typically get in trouble, the fear of doing so and the potential for an officer to intimidate them accordingly play into the "imponderabilia of everyday life" (Malinowski, 1922) at the border. I am grateful to one anonymous reviewer for pointing out that, because of their seeming insignificance, banality, or illegibility, these incidents do not receive the same political attention or theorization that one typically finds in the literature on Indigenous sovereignty and settler colonialism. At the same time, they represent the penetration of settler colonialism into local life in a way that may be microscopic in scope but is ubiquitous in scale.

Returning to our geography, Cornwall Island hosts the Peace Tree Mall, a gas station, and several smaller businesses. The mall, located on the main road connecting bridges to the mainland has lost many of the businesses that catered to cross-border traffic since the relocation of the port of entry in 2009. Whereas in the past someone could drive from the city of Cornwall onto the island to do some shopping and then drive back to Cornwall without having to report to a border officer, this is no longer the case.

At the centre of the island is a four-way stop, sometimes referred to as the crossroads. This is the former location of the now demolished Cornwall port of entry (visible on the map: figure 2.1). Also recently demolished at the four corners is the former site of "The People's Fire," a wooden building constructed to heat and support protesters during the anti-gun demonstrations, a site that remained a meeting point for local activism for several years. On the other side of the road are Jock's convenience store (selling groceries and sandwiches), several homes, and large fields where people have barbecues or play lacrosse in the warmer months.

You can head east or west at the crossroads and journey into the island – east to the lacrosse stadium, which hosts many matches and Akwesasne's annual pow wow, or west to administration buildings and a school. There are also houses on either side. Driving north from the crossroads, you pass the Peace Tree Mall and cross the bridge to the Cornwall port of entry and the city of Cornwall. Driving south, you head across a different bridge to the Massena port of entry and New York State.

While there are physically two bridges connecting the northern and southern spans of the island to Ontario and New York State, respectively, they are sometimes referred to by local governments as a single bridge with a "northern" and "southern" span. This piles confusion onto confusion, since officers sometimes ask "how many bridges did you cross" to ascertain whether someone totally unfamiliar with the territory has crossed the borderline. Thinking of these two structures as a singular bridge connecting Canada and the United States reifies the false image of a simple pathway between countries, and maintains Akwesasne as a "no man's land" – physically there but conceptually invisible.

I'd like to leave the island for now and head back south (of the borderline) and along route 37 for our final stop looking at religion (of course, we'll have to cross customs first). Next to the tribe's administration office is that of the Mohawk Nation Council of Chiefs, also referred to as "the Nation." The Nation is the more prominent of two Longhouses that claim traditional authority in Akwesasne, and is the one officially recognized by the Mohawk Council of Akwesasne. Though the Nation's administration building is located along 37, the Longhouse building itself is located north of 37, closer to the library.

The dominant religions in Akwesasne are the traditional Longhouse religion and Christianity, with different flavours of either available.

Though traditionalists tend to belong to one of two Longhouses, it is possible to attend ceremonies at either. The Catholic church, which residents proudly point out hosts a priest from the Philippines, is the dominant church, but several Protestant churches also dot the territory. Other religious affiliations can be found among residents who follow their own interpretation of Christianity, traditional religion, or other sorts of spirituality. I met many residents who attended both church and Longhouse services, although some voiced concerns that such dual affiliation was untenable in the long term, like having a foot in two boats.

I promised one person I spoke to that I would include an anecdote he shared about the Longhouse and the border. He told me that his Longhouse marriage was legally recognized in Canada because the Longhouse is situated south of the borderline. He said that while Canada does not recognize Longhouse weddings, the United States does. Canada also recognizes New York State-recognized marriages. Consequently, since he was married in a Longhouse south of the border, his traditional marriage was recognized north of the border. Had he been married in a Longhouse north of the border, Canada would not have recognized it.

A frequent source of frustration for Longhouse members is cross-border funerary logistics. As Canadian, US, and traditional interment practices differ, bodies brought to and from the Longhouse often have to cross several borders. Both Canadian and US ports of entry try to make special arrangements for funerary proceedings so that people paying their respects will not be held up at a port of entry. The initial expansion of the temporary port of entry in Cornwall in 2009 from two to three lanes was justified, in part, to expand service to Akwesasronon for a funeral.

The existence of multiple Longhouses is not unique to Akwesasne. The Mohawk community of Kahnawake, for example, has three. Questions or even simple statements involving the Longhouse(s) can get confusing. Even my statement that there are multiple Longhouses is not something everyone would agree with. Some would say that there is only one – whichever one they belong to. Others would say that there is only one – the confederacy. Others are more flexible.

Political Geography, Places of Interest

The map shown in figure 2.1 (and which also appears earlier, in the prologue) is one of several representations of the Akwesasne Mohawk Territory. It was created for me by Jutta Turner at the Max Planck Institute for Social Anthropology.

The Akwesasne Mohawk Territory includes land both north and south of the Canada-US border. Southern, "American" portions of the

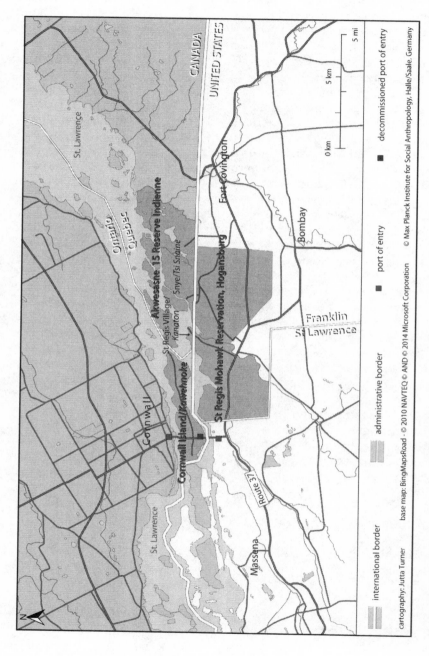

Figure 2.1. Map of the Akwesasne Mohawk Territory. Map courtesy of the Max Planck Institute.

territory consist of the "Akwesasne/Saint Regis Mohawk Reservation" in Hogansburg, New York, and are administered by the Saint Regis Mohawk Tribe (SRMT). Northern, "Canadian" portions of the territory are administered by the Mohawk Council of Akwesasne (MCA). They include Cornwall Island, St. Regis Village, and Snye.

Cornwall Island is often referred to as "the island" or *Kawehnoke*, meaning "island" in Kanienkehaka (Mohawk). St. Regis Village is often referred to as "the village" or *Kanatakon*, meaning "village" in Kanienkehaka. Tsi Snaine is almost always referred to as "Snye." "Tsi Snaine" is purportedly a Mohawk-ization of the French word for canal, *chenail*. There are also numerous islands along the St. Lawrence River where some residents live or have camps, or where the MCA leases land to a non-Indigenous occupant. While Cornwall Island is ostensibly located in Ontario, St. Regis Village and Snye are ostensibly located in Quebec.

Talking about This Map

I want to take a moment to give the reader a sense of just how daunting it is to discuss Akwesasne. Let us consider the few paragraphs in the last section. They are my effort at giving a concise overview of the territory that meshes with both the provided map and the way people in Akwesasne most commonly talk about the territory. Yet this seemingly simple task of describing a map is laden with political considerations and pitfalls.

Here are a few examples: (1) I state that there is land north and south of the borderline. In doing so, one could argue that I imply the legitimacy of that borderline, which can be viewed as an artificial imposition upon the Indigenous peoples of Akwesasne. Someone could reply, "But there is no border"; (2) I write that territories are administered by several Mohawk governments. But not everyone supports those governments. Someone could reply, "But those governments don't represent the people"; (3) I start off with English words for the territories, which can be viewed as privileging the language of settler colonialism. Someone could reply, "But you should use the Mohawk words"; (4) I use the term "Kanienkehaka" to refer to the language, and then include "Mohawk" in parenthesis – yet the term "Mohawk" is much more common locally. Someone could reply, "But most people in Akwesasne say Mohawk";[1] (5) I use the term

---

1 One anecdote that recently showed up in my Facebook feed: a friend from the community posted, "People should speak Indian!" Me: "You mean Kanienkehaka?" "I don't know what you mean." Colonization at its best.

"ostensibly" to suggest that even if these parts of the territory are in Quebec and Ontario according to settler-colonial legal norms, that is not a simple objective fact. Some Canadian and American politicians may disagree. Someone could reply, "But it's really Canada and the United States."

For each of these points of consideration, I described the territory in a way that has the potential to cause disagreement with politicians, scholars, academics, activists, border officers, administrators, youths, elders, and so on. There is no way around it. If I had written something different it could have upset someone else. There is no perfect way to describe the territory that is both comprehensible and pleases everyone at any moment. I have endeavoured to make my writing as inoffensive as possible, and I suspect that most people would not pick a fight with my terminology unless they had another reason to criticize my writing more broadly.

And this is my point – that Akwesasne (and Akwesasronon) can be described in many ways, and context is a big player in determining what Akwesasne and its people will be at the moment they are invoked. Whether a reader deems my terminology as brilliant, offensive, acceptable, incorrect, or whatever, will vary by reader, and by what they get out of their reading more broadly. The context (framing) plays as big a role as the text in determining how someone will respond.

Akwesasne the Community

Perhaps the least controversial way to describe Akwesasne is as a community. Yet even if there is near-ubiquitous agreement that Akwesasne is a community, what people mean when they use the term is less universal. People may disagree as to where and when Akwesasne starts and stops, what it means, what it should mean, what it does, or what it should do, and yet still agree that Akwesasne is a single community. In its polyvalence as a word, "community," like "Akwesasne," is multifaceted – it is one word used to convey many meanings, sometimes bundled together and sometimes separated, sometimes mutually exclusive and at other times mutually informative.

"Community" is the word Akwesasronon most frequently use to talk about Akwesasne – particularly when considering the border's imposition. A friend told me that as much as Akwesasne has its divisions and is often represented by local media as fractured, there is a wholeness to the community that transcends any schisms whenever outside challenges emerge. It was this spirit of community that brought people together in opposition to the CBSA's arming initiative on the island, and that drove relief efforts when the CBSA's withdrawal in 2009 caused the bridges to close, isolating residents of Cornwall Island with no overland transit to the American or Canadian mainland.

Speaking of Akwesasne as a single community is productive when highlighting the disruption caused by the Canada-US border's imposition. In my own writing, I often refer to Akwesasne as "a single Mohawk community straddling the administrative boundaries of Quebec, Ontario [...]." The Mohawk Council of Akwesasne's website title page also opens with this message: "Akwesasne is Home to a Strong, Vibrant Mohawk Community." The wholeness of Akwesasne as one community is frequently juxtaposed with the division imposed by the border – demonstrating that *despite* the border, Akwesasne is united *as* a community.

But what does it mean to call Akwesasne a community? When someone says, "Akwesasne is a community," what are they saying about Akwesasne?

For all its significance as a term depicting unity, the concept of "community" is not unitary. Warning against "conceptual slippage," Vered Amit (2002) argues that, within scholarship, the term "community" has referred to different things. It can be a collective (a particular type of social solidarity), a concept (a sense of belonging felt by members of a group), and a type of network (a set of shared connections), while simultaneously being a referent for a vernacular "taken for granted form as a unit of analysis, the location, rather than the object of research" (42). In other words, the term "community" has the potential to mean a lot of things all at once – while simultaneously referring to a physical location or place inhabited by a group of people.

This offers a useful way of thinking about Akwesasne, which also has the potential to mean a lot of things all at once – while simultaneously referring to a physical location inhabited by a group of people. Further, even if the word "community" is conceptually slippery, it is emotionally tactile. Community holds an affective worth for which people throughout history have been willing to fight and die (Anderson 2006).

Yet there are some common threads that permeate Akwesasronon uses of the term. One thread is the common valuing of community – whatever the community of Akwesasne *is*, it is something good, and something to be preserved. Another thread is the assumption that there is a core unity. Even in those instances in which Akwesasne is "a community divided," it is still *a* community. Furthermore, the ability to navigate Akwesasne's multiple meanings is something Akwesasronon have in common. Community in Akwesasne may be many things at once, but it is also about being many things at once. Multifacetedness is part of its *telos*, so to speak. To be part of the community, to be Akwe-sasronon, is to be multifaceted.

A Flexible (and Inflexible) Geography

Akwesasne can be described as a "flexible geography." Here, I draw upon Aiwa Ong's (1999) theory of "flexible citizenship" and Thomas Biolsi's (2005) theory of "imagined geography" (which itself draws heavily upon Ong). The complex geopolitical landscape engenders, and at times necessitates, a variety of spatial representations. A journalist may write about Akwesasne as an Indigenous space autonomous of settler authority. A border officer may only be satisfied if Akwesasne is described as the United States or Canada. Akwesasne can be one thing in one conversation and another thing in another. This is a theme that I return to throughout this volume – when I emphasize the role of context in determining "what is going on" at a given moment.

The way one approaches or represents Akwesasne is often contingent upon the context in which that representation occurs. This goes further than suggesting that Akwesasne is a "hybrid space." Sometimes Akwe-sasne may be represented as a hybrid – simultaneously A, B, and C. But it can also be represented as wholly A, B, or C, or even not A, not B, or not C – or any combination thereof. Akwesasne can be American, or Canadian, or both, or neither. When talking about Akwesasne, and hearing others talk about it, my mind frequently returned to a quotation from Walt Whitman's *Song of Myself*: "Do I contradict myself? Very well then, I contradict myself. (I am large, I contain multitudes)" (1892). Though Akwesasne is not vast, it contains multitudes.

Where Are You From?

One of the most problematic questions one can ask an Akwesasronon is, "Where are you from?"

As I drove with a friend in Akwesasne, he relayed a story of border crossing at a port some distance from the territory. He had driven up in a New York-plated car and presented a US ID card. The border officer asked him where he was from. He said, as he told me he always did, "Akwesasne." The officer told him that Akwesasne is in Canada. This surprised my friend, who, like the Facebook commenters at the start of this chapter, was simultaneously from Akwesasne and New York State. My friend told me that he calmly explained to the officer that while some parts of Akwesasne are in Canada, other parts are in the United States. The officer disagreed and continued questioning my friend until his supervisor stepped in. The supervisor, more experienced and familiar with Akwesasne, told the officer that indeed some parts of Akwesasne are in New York State, and allowed my friend to proceed. As he finished the story, my friend told me, as he had many times in the past, "There really is no border," and that Akwesasne was neither in the United States nor in Canada, but was simply Akwesasne.

How to make sense of my friend's statements – telling a border officer that Akwesasne is in the United States, and telling me that Akwesasne is not in the United States? One easy way to interpret this inconsistency is that when facing difficulties with the officer, my friend stretched the truth. He didn't *really* mean that some parts of Akwesasne are in the United States. He was just framing his situation in a way that the officer would recognize and accept. This meshes with what Audra Simpson talks about when she speaks of "feeling citizenship" (2014, 171–6).

Yet even if my friend truly feels, deep down inside, that Akwesasne is not in the United States or Canada, this does little to explain why the Facebook respondents at the start of this chapter described themselves as in New York. They had little to gain from doing so. Nor does it explain the many other times in Akwesasne when friends and colleagues have described themselves as American or Canadian – during a sports match, when talking about military (typically US) service, when the right country song comes on the radio, or on the fourth of July.

Let us set aside, for the time being, the extent to which there is a singular, "true" way in which residents understand the territory. The answers to "Where are you from?" are numerous. Some people say "Akwesasne"; some people say "Snye"; some people say, "It's complicated"; and some people (as I discuss on pages 52 and 88) say, "Fuck you." The same person's answer will differ depending on who is asking and in what context – whether it is a border officer, an anthropologist, a friend from out of town, or an annoying person in a bar.

This may be a productive space to highlight how my research approach differs from what is currently available in the literature. My interest here is not in how people feel at the core of their being but in how they present the territory (and in other chapters, how they present themselves) in different contexts and for different purposes. This is not to discount any claims to core beliefs but rather to change the focus of inquiry. In doing so, my approach is distinct from the study of how Mohawk nationalism offers a kernel or perennial ideology at the heart of every Mohawk person's perceptions of themselves and their territory. Such an approach is useful if one wishes to articulate and explore a core political ideology, or ontology, that is distinct from the expectations of Western settler states. It is less useful if one wants to map out how that ideology manifests itself, or fails to manifest itself, in different contexts. Though I look to both, I am more interested in how people act, and decide to act, than in how they feel. My research methodology involves collating a diversity of border experiences with an eye to the banal rather than diving deeply into one-on-one interviews with an eye towards the exceptional or memorable.

Talking about It

Many in Akwesasne are acutely aware of how important words are in talking about the territory, and the extent to which different ways of describing the same location or organization carry their own politically charged connotations. The terms one uses to describe the territory become understood, or misunderstood, outside the community, with consequences for border crossing.

Early versions of the MCA's cultural training materials for border officers included a map demarcating important community buildings. The only Longhouse depicted was the Nation's. As I note above, this is the Longhouse with the most adherents, and the one recognized by the Mohawk government. BSOs undergoing this training would have assumed that there is one Longhouse in Akwesasne, and that it is located in a particular location. Yet as I mentioned above, travellers may state that they are coming from a different Longhouse, or may argue with an officer over how many Longhouses exist. In this regard, even officers' efforts to incorporate cultural awareness into their work may result in confusion or suspicion. Asking "Which Longhouse?" may please the traveller by showing a familiarity with the territory, or it may offend the traveller who feels there is only one Longhouse.

One resident told me about his frustrations at efforts by BSOs to gain a deeper sense of Mohawk culture and traditions. He told me he hated it when officers try to chat with him about Haudenosaunee culture or history. As we sat talking in the library, he discussed one experience when an officer had asked him how many clans there were. He told me he had replied, "Who the fuck cares?" When she responded, "You don't have to be like that," he said again, "Fuck you, who the fuck cares?" He told me that she finally returned his passport and told him to have a nice day. He looked at me and said, "You ask ten of us a question, you get ten different answers. Say I gave her an answer, and the next person gives her a different answer. Who the fuck cares?" For him, efforts to understand Akwesasne's culture were more counterproductive than useful. Because Akwesasne can be depicted and understood in so many ways, officers may find themselves more rather than less suspicious if they begin to think that they understand the territory.

The Mohawk Council of Akwesasne, which governs parts of the community north of the borderline, was originally called the Band Council. The renaming of the organization represented a conscious effort on the part of local government to reframe Akwesasne as something greater than a band. Grand Chief Mike Mitchell explained the decision to me:

> We were known [back then] as the Saint Regis Band Council, we were known as the Saint Regis Reserve. We had a band administrator, band projects, everything in our projects was band, and I did a little bit of research. I said, there's no mention of tribe, there's no mention of nation. It's almost like a swear word, like the government won't allow you to say that you belong to the Mohawk Nation. When they figured the longhouse, because they always said nation was that it was one way to put a label on them, like it was something evil or bad. So, I introduced several things, a change of name for the council, a change of name for the community. And that's where the Mohawk Council of Akwesasne and the Akwesasne Mohawk Territory [came from]. We refused to refer to ourselves as a reserve or a band, and the example I gave was there is no group in North America that is Indigenous other than a small isolated family that could be considered as a band. And I saw the way to mentally keep your people suppressed and down is call them by the lowest standards that you can set. If the nation is up here [gestures high] and the band is down here [knocks low onto the table], and the tribe and everything else you can call is going up that way [gestures in between]. So, every time you refer to yourself as a band, you're admitting that you're no longer a nation. You're not thinking of a treaty, you're not thinking of your rights, or the nation [which] is proud. Everything you accept in the mind of intimidation, of saying, "Indian Affairs controls everything."

For Mitchell, the decision to rename the MCA and the territory was a recognition of the psychological impact of the naming schema of settler states. This is akin to what Michael Billig (1995) would call "banal nationalism," though in this context "banal colonialism" may be a more apt term. Exercising choice in naming the Akwesasne Mohawk Territory and Mohawk Council of Akwesasne represented a move toward enacting sovereignty in everyday life. It also highlights why such a simple thing as naming can have such controversial underpinnings.

The "who the fuck cares" resident I quoted above also claimed that the renaming of the band into the Mohawk Council was a mistake. He felt the fact that some people talked about a band and others a nation and others a council overwhelmed and confused officers. The officers, in turn, would see Mohawks as inconsistent when talking about their own territory and governments.

I also spoke with a small but vocal minority who felt that the renaming of Akwesasne represented a betrayal. They did not see themselves as Mohawks but rather as the descendants of many Indigenous groups in the area, and argued that, by changing the name of the community, the MCA risked abrogating treaties that had been made with the "Saint Regis Indians" or the "Band." I discuss Grand Chief Mitchell's role in politically reshaping Akwesasne more broadly in the next chapter. While this was a minority opinion, it demonstrates the extent to which "talking about" the territory can be rife with tensions.

When talking with border officers, Akwesasronon have a wide variety of words available to describe their point of origin or destination. This can get confusing. As one example, the "Saint Regis Mohawk Tribe" represents parts of the community located ostensibly in New York, but "St. Regis Village" represents a part of the community located ostensibly in Canada. I found that people coming from the village would typically say "St. Regis" (or simply "Saint") while people coming from the New York portions of the territory would typically say "Hogansburg" or "Hogan." Of course, others may refuse to say anything other than "Akwesasne" or may simply refuse to talk to the officers at all.

Initially, when officers asked me to explain where I was coming from, my answers were longer and more descriptive. I'd nervously say, "I'm coming from St. Regis, the village, the one north of the border," for example, thinking I was being helpful. Yet I found that the more I sought to give officers the information I felt they needed, the more I was scrutinized by them, as someone unfamiliar with the territory. I also got the sense that officers may have seen me as patronizing, as assuming (improperly, even if sometimes correctly) that they did not understand the territory well enough to ascertain which part I was coming from. It marked me as an outsider, and even more suspect.

Over time, I adapted my language to bring it more in line with what I heard from people in Akwesasne, providing short answers such as "St. Regis" or "Hogan" without providing additional explanation unless asked to do so. These interviews proceeded far more smoothly than the ones in which I imagined myself trying to be helpful. Border officers and Akwesasronon – like anthropologists – typically recognize language as meta-discursive, indicators of one's political orientations, comfort, discomfort, strangeness, belonging, or suspiciousness. When I became able to reveal my familiarity with the territory through speech, officers interacted with me differently.

Beyond the Territory

Akwesasne does not simply begin or end in the Akwesasne Mohawk Territory. Many Akwesasronon live in housing developments that, while technically off reserve/reservation land, are seen as part of the community. This housing is especially popular among families that have one or more non-status members. Further, many Akwesasronon live or work in neighbouring towns or cities in Ontario or northern New York State.

North of Akwesasne is the city of Cornwall, Ontario, where I lived when commuting to the territory for my fieldwork. With a population greater than 45,000, Cornwall is the most populous city in the region by a wide margin. Cornwall hosts numerous call and distribution centres, though it has one of the highest unemployment rates in Ontario, having lost much of its factory production in the past several decades. Cornwall is frequently cited as an unpleasant place to live, being ranked 167th out of 190 in a survey of Canadian cities by *MoneySense* ("Canada's Best Places to Live 2014: Full Ranking" 2014), and hosting the lowest-rated schools in Ontario ("Regional Schools in Decline?" 2015). Despite these challenges, many in Cornwall love their city and could not imagine living elsewhere. A recent public-relations campaign for Cornwall chose the slogan "You don't have to be rich to have a rewarding life in Cornwall" to advertise the city's merits and relative affordability.

Relationships between Cornwall and Akwesasne are mixed. In the aftermath of the 2009 port of entry closure, the then mayor of Cornwall, Bob Kilger, supported reconciliation between Akwesasne and the CBSA. At the time, it was viewed as a mark of solidarity, although this stance was likely motivated in part by a desire to bring a swift return to cross-border commerce from Cornwall. Indeed, Cornwall's public support of Akwesasne waned once the border crossing reopened, even though the new entry location crippled mobility within Akwesasne.

Many in Akwesasne live, work, shop, or study in Cornwall. Some residents seek social services there in order to avoid the scrutiny or stigma of doing so in their own community. Residents with a Canadian health card will typically go to Cornwall's hospital for major procedures. Friendships between Akwesasronon and non-Indigenous Cornwall residents may develop through these networks (and can be challenged by the logistical difficulties of cross-border travel). Prejudices persist as well, however. I was surprised when the kindly old man who invited me over for a pizza dinner with his family while I was moving into my apartment in Cornwall asked me if I was going to "put the Indians in their place."

Despite being one of Ontario's poorer cities, Cornwall is fiscally better off than its American neighbour to the south, Massena. The relationship between Cornwall and Massena was the subject of a comparative history by Claire Puccia Parham entitled *From Great Wilderness to Seaway Towns* (2004). Parham suggests that, though the two cities have comparable geography and access to natural resources, Cornwall managed to develop more successfully than Massena thanks to stronger support from the Canadian government. Cornwall's economy was also largely built upon opening itself up to polluting industries, resulting in environmental degradation that disproportionately crippled traditional practices in Akwesasne (something I discuss in chapter 4). Problematically, Parham's text contains few references to Akwesasne and falls into a troublesome trope of considering a land occupied by Indigenous peoples for generations as a "great wilderness."

Much of Massena's commerce is centred on large stores – BJ's, Walmart, and Home Depot – as well as a now-derelict shopping mall. Massena's historic centre has a few successful businesses, but many have closed down. In the 1990s and early 2000s, Massena counted heavily upon cross-border visitors to the shopping mall. A popular weekend trip for Cornwallers involved driving into Akwesasne, filling up one's car with cheap gas and getting bridge passes, shopping in Massena, and purchasing dinner in Massena. One Italian restaurant and bar, Trombino's, is nearly always filled with Canadians, and lost so much business during the 2009 border closure that its precarity made local news. Although the Akwesasne Mohawk Casino now attracts the majority of Canadian guests, Canadian commerce has shifted to Cornwall, which hosts its own shopping mall and Walmart.

As Massena residents do not have to traverse an international borderline to spend time in parts of Akwesasne other than the island, ties between Massena and Akwesasne are relatively unproblematic. Local New York State schools have made efforts to integrate Mohawk teaching and language into their curricula. Many Akwesasronon choose to live in Massena and the surrounding area, and non-Indigenous Massena residents find work in and around Akwesasne.

Conclusion

When I asked a chief how I should depict Akwesasne – as a nation, part of a nation, Canadian, American, both, or neither – he told me that he had a standard answer for such a question: "Akwesasne has been many things to many people."

My goal here has not been to point out inconsistencies but to show the consistent ways in which Akwesasne remains many things to many people. Throughout these permutations, Akwesasne is a community.

The flexibility of Akwesasne's geography does not undermine but rather defines the territory.

Above, I quote an Akwesasronon who did not like it when border officers tried to make sense of his community. He said, "You ask ten of us a question, you get ten different answers." It may be more complicated even than that – asking the same person a question ten times does not guarantee the same answer each time.

When asked, "Where do you come from?" an Akwesasronon can give any one of a dozen or so answers, some of which may not be mutually compatible. Someone can come from Canada, the United States, Akwesasne, "the Canadian part of Akwesasne," "the US part of Akwesasne," Cornwall Island, Hogansburg, St. Regis, the village, the reserve, Snye, Quebec, Ontario, or New York. If asked, "Where are you going?" the same is possible.

Driving along route 37, one would not notice much difference between the Akwesasne Mohawk Territory and another northern New York State township, except perhaps an above-average number of gas stations and tobacco stores; businesses named after bears, wolves, and turtles; and a few unfamiliar flags. Yet as one approaches a port of entry, these cosmetic differences become legal ones.

The nearly invisible distinctions between Akwesasne's "Canadian" and "American" "sides" become very important when a border officer asks a traveller where they have come from and where they're going. Travelling in and around Akwesasne often literally demands an accounting – or more accurately, a variety of accountings – for what it is, and where it is. Furthermore, the room for complexity in these accountings is limited. A complicated answer may be seen as patronizing or cause for suspicion. While Akwesasne may have radio stations for all, a driver can only listen to one at a time. Similarly, Akwesasne may be flexible, but the conditions of life in the territory often demand the appearance of rigidity.

Akwesasne has been many things to many people, and it continues to be so. As much as such a chimeric identity may frustrate those trying to render the community legible, it is part of what defines Akwesasne. Such variability may frustrate advocates for Akwesasne but also presents challenges: "technologies of border control and immigration penalty, including 'hard technologies' and 'innovations in social practices' [which] manifest an effort [by states] to tame uncertainty and know the unknowable" (Pratt 2005, 2).[2] My own depictions of the community

---

2 Though Pratt is here talking specifically of immigration, this assertion can be applied to all cross-border actors, especially as a cause and consequence of uneasy relationships with states.

as chimeric should by no means discount its claims – as I note above, Akwesasne contains multitudes, but it never stops being Akwesasne.

The story goes that when Hiawatha helped unite the five nations of the Haudenosaunee Confederacy,[3] he demonstrated the strength of union by bundling five arrows. While a single arrow could easily break, a bundle was far stronger. The story does not, however, ruminate on how difficult it would be to shoot a bundle of arrows while hunting. The bundle is not a permanent state, but rather one permutation of multiple strands – it can be unbundled and rebundled as need arises. Hiawatha's message may serve as an apt comparison for Akwesasne, burdened by and benefiting from its many strands. This bundle, I suggest, is flexible, with different strands added, subtracted, emphasized, or rejected as necessity, ideology, or law demands.

The flexibility and complexity of Akwesasne's geography are engendered by its unique position relative to the Canada-US border. But Akwesasne's relationship to the border has changed dramatically over time. In the next chapter, I try to offer a sense of how the border came to Akwesasne, or perhaps, how Akwesasne came to the border. Though often not a conversation *about* colonialism, the language of border interactions is inevitably one *of* colonialism. This history set the stage for both the demands placed upon Akwesasronon and the different permutations that have become available over time.

---

3 The sixth nation, the Tuscarora, joined in 1722, though at the start, the confederacy contained five nations.

Chapter Three

Doing History in Akwesasne

Introduction

The first time I risked illegally crossing the Canada-US border in Akwe-sasne was while sitting beside two CBSA officers. I was attending a pre-sentation of Akwesasne's cultural training, which would subsequently be provided to line officers. This also enabled me to watch Akwesas-ronon discuss the history of their own community, and how to present that history to border officers.

The Mohawk Council of Akwesasne offered me the opportunity to attend an early, unofficial presentation of the cultural training materials that line officers would be receiving over the next few months. Border officers did not want me to attend the official presentation itself – as one officer told me, they felt the need for it to be a "safe space" without any outside observers. While the materials I wrote would be included in the presentation, I, physically, would not. Instead, I was offered the chance to watch MCA present and revise a power-point conversation about the community's history, with administrators as the intended audience. We met for lunch at the casino, located on the southern side of the community (ostensibly in the United States), but the meeting was to be held in one of the administration buildings located north of the border (ostensibly in Canada).

Grabbing a ride with the officers from the casino to the administration building where the presentation was held, I expressed my concerns – Would I have to report in if I were crossing the border? After all, I'd be driving from the United States to Canada, as far as border control was concerned. The CBSA administrator thought about it for a moment and said that, as far as they were aware, the building was on both sides of the border, so as long as we stayed on the southern side of the build-ing, I'd be fine. I smiled in appreciation, figuring that my bases were covered. The smile wavered however when I realized that the forbidden part of the building included the bathrooms (as a brief aside, this is not the only time intertwined concerns over bladder control and border control are mentioned in this text). Fortunately, the meeting proceeded without incident. A few months later, I checked on Google Satellite to see where the borderline actually was relative to the building. It turned out nearly all of the building was north of the borderline, including both the office we sat in and the bathrooms. While our movement (or lack of movement) was here based on a misunderstanding, there are other residences and offices in the area that literally straddle the border. My concern was by no means unjustified.

Over the course of the presentation, my friends and colleagues at the Aboriginal Rights Research Office (ARRO) presented a history of the community. They are all very knowledgeable about the history of their community, and we had spoken about oral history, ethnohistory, and archaeology in the past. The presentation's depiction of Akwesasne's historical continuity was brief, however – presenters stated that Akwesasronon had been in the territory since time immemorial.

While the CBSA administrators nodded along with the presentation, Mike Mitchell, the grand chief at the time, piped up. Mitchell pointed out that the history was more complicated than that. He spent several minutes talking about the historical migration of people into and out of the St. Lawrence valley (a narrative that I present in detail in this chapter). Mitchell was especially versed in this narrative of Akwesasne's history, and in competing ones. A few years earlier, he had been the complainant in a Supreme Court case concerning whether Akwesasne had an Indigenous right to cross-border mobility. The court's decision turned largely on how the history of the community was understood. This is also something I discuss in greater detail in this chapter.

Mitchell was the boss, and his account of Akwesasne's history was undoubtedly more accurate and subtle than the initial presentation. The materials were revised accordingly, and quite a few more slides were added without objection. When I asked my friends who had designed the presentation about it afterwards, they were as aware as Mitchell of the complexity of the history. For them, however, the goal was to present something officers would sit through without rolling their eyes. In their initial view, it was more important to maintain the officers' attention, and for the officers to walk away from the training with a firm sense of Akwesasne's rights and legitimacy in the region. Ultimately, they accepted the grand chief's view that accuracy was more important than simplicity. Officers would listen to Akwesasronon tell their history, and unlike at the port, Akwesasronon would be responsible for saying when the conversation was over.

A few months later, I was called into the grand chief's office to help design materials for a visiting delegation of students from Columbia University. As I walked into the office, the chief asked me how my research was going and said, with a smile, "Do you have any new history for us?" This time, I was charged with telling a history of Akwesasne and determining what to include and what to leave out. I saw his question as half a joke – Akwesasne's history may be old, but what people say about it is often new.

This chapter provides a sense of the way people in Akwesasne engage with history today – and the ways in which history in Akwesasne is both new and old. I suggest that some historical narratives have assumed greater prominence because of their direct relevance in court cases related to Akwesasne's rights. Court proceedings, and specifically rights claims, have shaped which historical narratives are most prominent in local histories, and which versions of those narratives are most acceptable. This has a direct impact on what it means to do research in Akwesasne, and serves as a useful counterpoint to anthropological studies of the way "culture" functions in Canadian courts. Much as the previous chapter examined how the "where" of Akwesasne engenders and requires many possible framings, this chapter does the same with the "when" of the community.

In discussing the history of history in Akwesasne, I also provide my own limited history of the territory. My emphasis is specifically on questions of how "the border" came to Akwesasne and how Akwesasne came to the border. Whereas it would be easy to argue that Akwesasne, as an Indigenous community, simply existed astride the Canada-US border from time immemorial, such a description is only partially true. While Akwesasronon existed in the region in and across what later became the border, the shaping of Akwesasne into a permanent settlement in its current location was tied to the residents' own political manoeuvring and objectives.

Alongside numerous answers to the oft-asked question "Where are you from?," Akwesasronon navigate a plethora of responses to the question "When, and how, did Akwesasne come to be?" Much as, in the previous chapter, I offered both a spatial overview of geography and an ethnographic sense of how geography manifests in Akwesasne, in this chapter I do the same for history. In doing so, I talk about how one talks about history in Akwesasne and offer some explanation as to how a community can end up with an office building that has bathrooms in one country and a conference room in another.

Two Epochs

In chapter 4, I offer a recent history of how *this* border came to Akwe-sasne, emphasizing the past thirty years of enforcement. Here, how-ever, I focus on two epochs, loosely defined as "Akwesasne before Akwesasne" and "Akwesasne after Akwesasne." Generally speak-ing, narratives about "Akwesasne before Akwesasne," the first epoch, speak to the legitimacy of Akwesasne as a Mohawk community. They attest to Akwesasne's rights as a Mohawk territory with pre-contact claims to the area. Narratives of the second epoch, "Akwesasne after Akwesasne," speak to the legitimacy of particular forms of governance (councils, chiefs, Longhouses, etc.) within the community.

The first epoch, "Akwesasne before Akwesasne," encompasses the earliest known occupancy of the St. Lawrence valley by Akwesasne's ancestors. This is before the establishment of the singular permanent settlement of Akwesasne. As I explain below, this period, though the most chronologically removed from the present, has been among the most pertinent for Akwesasronon in its contemporary assertion of bor-der rights. It is a popular topic of conversation when Akwesasronon speak about the history of their community, especially with actors invested in the border (border officers, journalists, researchers). This period is also more prominent in the writings of professional historians (see, for example, Trigger and Pendergast 1978; Trigger 1987; Pender-gast, Chapdelaine, and Wright 1993; Abel 2002; Parmenter 2010).

The second epoch, "Akwesasne after Akwesasne," encompasses the period several hundred years later in which the permanent settlement of St. Regis/Akwesasne was founded in the late eighteenth and early nineteenth centuries, in the backdrop of the period historians call "from borderlands to borders" (Adelman and Aron 1999). Despite the fact that this period is more recent and better documented than the earlier period, it is less prominent in published or popular accounts of Akwe-sasne's history. An exception to this is work by local historians (among them Darren Bonaparte 2007, 2008, 2009), who have written about the community's early political history both independently and on behalf of the Mohawk government in well-researched publications in local periodicals. Such writings are often ways of commenting on contem-porary political issues such as the legitimacy of Akwesasne's elected governments (see, e.g., George-Kanentiio 2006).

As much as "the border" came to Akwesasne when settler states decided to impose their own spatial politics on the continent, Akwesasne intentionally developed in a border region as part of a long-standing Mohawk strategy of occupying such areas for diplomatic and economic benefit. Akwesasne's ongoing geopolitical existence brings into question the assertion by Adelman and Aron (1999) that the early 1800s marked a fundamental end to the existence of borderlands in America's northeast. Akwesasne continues to remain a marginal and semi-autonomous political entity despite long-standing efforts by Canada and the United States to monopolize sovereignty within national borderlines.

But before talking about the past, I wish to draw attention to the present – or, at least, to how the past matters in the present, and what this meant for me as a researcher trying to "do history" in Akwesasne.

History in Akwesasne Today

The grand chief's half-joke, "Do you have any new history for us?," contains a few seeming contradictions that get to the heart of how history can operate in Akwesasne. The first is the idea of a "new" history, and the second the idea of history "for" Akwesasne.

"New" history is nothing new in Akwesasne. Among many in the community, there is an ongoing sense of uncovering the past. News articles and Facebook posts often feature historical information presented as newly discovered. As one would assume, especially popular are narratives that portray the community positively. Akwesasne has also grown a serious body of local historians disproportionately more substantial than one might expect to find in communities of similar size. The Mohawk Council of Akwesasne's Aboriginal Rights Research Office, where I was based for my fieldwork, employs a full-time staff with skills in historical research and writing, who gather data for a wide variety of purposes, including local news and presentations, as well as documents for court cases. There is a simultaneous focus on preserving the oral histories known by elders and discovering local histories that have been overshadowed by more popular narratives.

Perhaps the most audible voice in Akwesasne's local history is Darren Bonaparte, whose blog "The Wampum Chronicles" (Bonaparte n.d.) and publications cited above represent a significant body of historical research. Bonaparte's writing has generated a resurgence of interest in Akwesasne not only as one of several communities that are part of the Mohawk Nation but as a past member of the "Seven Nations Confederacy,"[1] an association of missionized Haudenosaunee and non-Haudenosaunee Indigenous polities in the early nineteenth century

---

1 There are some in the community who assert that Akwesasne is still a member of this seven nations confederacy and not Mohawk at all. They argue that the current Mohawk Council is illegitimate. While numerically small, they have recently attained media attention for their protestations (see, e.g., A.S. Hale 2017).

(distinct from the five, and later six, nations Haudenosaunee Confederacy). Bonaparte's research has resituated a fundamental aspect of the way people talk about Akwesasne's history, an aspect that was all but ignored outside the community a few decades ago.

Despite exceptional local historical research, Akwesasne has long been overlooked in the writings of many university-affiliated historians and publications for a general audience (but see Wilson and Mitchell 1960). "Iroquois studies," the interdisciplinary study of Haudenosaunee peoples, has long paid little if any attention to Akwesasne and its past. This may be because Akwesasne was viewed, like Kahnawake, as not "traditional" enough to hold the attention of European scholars (Simpson 2014).

A definitive history of Akwesasne and the border has not yet been written, and I see it as a task better suited to professionally trained historians than to this anthropologist. Thus, my efforts here are a synthesis of existing secondary sources and oral histories rather than the result of archival or documentary scholarship. The packaging and arrangement may be new, but the product is recycled.

Beyond the idea that history can be "new," the idea that history can be "for" someone, though anathema to a purely scientific model of historiography, speaks to the way history has operated in the community more broadly. The legitimacy of authority, rights claims, and land claims has long hinged upon the emergence or dominance of one particular historical narrative over others. In the broadest of terms, it is about claiming the right to say, "We were here first." Battles have existed for generations as to whose claims to authoritative voice are more valid, with historical knowledge serving as munitions.

In recent years, the idea that history has sides has filtered through the courts (Clifford 1988). The adversarial system of the judiciary invites experts such as anthropologists, historians, and elders to present history as either "for" or "against" a given litigant. For rights cases, this is most commonly represented by the Mohawk government on behalf of Akwesasne, and a federal government minister on behalf of the crown. Different parties hire historians and anthropologists to present a narrative of the past that agrees with their claims. Both land-rights claims and the seminal "Mitchell case" (discussed in the next section) hinged upon particular readings of history. In this capacity, history in Akwesasne is rightly seen as "for" or "against" community interests.

As I remark at the start of this section, many in Akwesasne saw me as a historian or archaeologist. People frequently asked me whether I could look into historical archives to get a sense of why Canada refused to ratify the section of the Jay Treaty dealing with Indigenous border-crossing rights, or if I could look to the archaeological record to elaborate upon the earliest occupancy of the community. Why did these sorts of questions come to dominate people's interest in my historical research? The answer, I feel, has something to do with the ways in which such knowledge has recently functioned in Akwesasne's legal travails.

Ronald Niezen's article "Culture and the Judiciary" (2003a) argues that Canada's juridical standard for Indigenous rights, embodied most substantially in the "Van der Peet test," relies problematically upon "an unstable concept as the source of rights." The test, in brief, allows for an Indigenous group to claim a right if they can demonstrate that the practice is integral to the culture, existed at the time of contact, and continues to be important. Though seemingly a positive move toward granting or recognizing the rights of Indigenous peoples, Niezen's article also suggests that juridical testing and definition of Indigenous "culture" is problematic. It risks reifying notions of the culture concept that have been rejected by contemporary social scientists as insufficient at best and misleading at worst. These tests ultimately embrace an ossification and essentialization of what constitutes culture.

Mike Mitchell and the St. Lawrence Iroquois/Iroquoians/Peoples

Mitchell v. the Minister of National Revenue (MNR) – or "the Mitchell case," as it's referred to in Akwesasne, or "my case," as it's referred to by Mitchell – served as the test case for Indigenous border-crossing rights. Akwesasne Grand Chief Mike Mitchell refused to pay duty on personal and community goods as he drove across the Cornwall port of entry, then located on Cornwall Island, in 1988. Mitchell and his lawyers argued that there exists an Aboriginal right to cross-border mobility as a central cultural practice that has existed since contact.

This was the second time Akwesasne had challenged mobility restrictions in the courtroom. A prior case, *Francis v. The Queen* (1956), had argued not for an Aboriginal right, but for a treaty right, to border crossing.[2] Under the provisions of the Jay Treaty, Indigenous peoples have the right to traverse the border unimpeded when carrying "traditional

---

2 A brief anecdote about the Francis case was shared by an elder: One of the goods Francis was attempting to bring across the border was a washing machine (Mitchell would similarly bring a washing machine when attempting to cross the border). When Francis lost the case, he was unable to bring the washing machine home. Whenever his children would ask, "Where's our washing machine?" he would reply, "The Queen took it."

goods." Though American courts recognize the Jay Treaty, Canadian courts ruled against Francis, arguing that Britain, and not Canada, had signed the treaty, and that while Canada ratified most provisions of the treaty, they did not ratify the one concerning Aboriginal border rights. The Van der Peet test opened a new avenue for Akwesasne to pursue border crossing as an Aboriginal right rather than a treaty right.

Niezen's article focuses on the ways in which the culture concept has operated within the Canadian judiciary. While the Mitchell trial has served as a case study for Aboriginal rights, and the limits of Canada's recognition of those rights, it can also serve as a case study for the ways in which a juridical context forces different narratives of history into an adversarial framework. In other words – the way the court framed history affected the ways in which the community was able to frame its own history in the courtroom. Yet this history reverberated beyond the courtroom. It set the tone for the dominant, if not the only, conversation one could have about Akwesasne's past. This became the history people talked about. A dominant popular narrative of Akwesasne's history emerged as a counter-narrative to that proffered by the Canadian state in its efforts to deny Aboriginal rights to the community.

I suspect that the Mitchell case had a direct bearing on my presence as a researcher. My first point of contact in Akwesasne was Grand Chief Mitchell, who was eager to discuss the case with me. Many of the people I interviewed were connected with the case, as lawyers, witnesses, or simply deeply interested parties. Akwesasronon who watched the trial continue to speak of it emotionally, praising the well-reasoned testimony of their witnesses and condemning the bitter antagonism of the opposing council and its witnesses. My reading of Akwesasne's history has served as a sort of shibboleth for my anthropological work with Mohawk populations both in Akwesasne and in and around Kahnawake.

As I sat with Mitchell – he vetting me over dinner – I found myself having two conversations at once. I spoke at length about my interest in interviewing border officers and learning about contemporary border issues impacting the community. Mitchell answered my questions, but frequently brought the conversation to a discussion of Akwesasne's history and treaty rights. While I saw those two spheres of knowledge as distinct at the time, eventually I saw how they were inextricably interwoven. The border today cannot be taken out of historical context; that history and competing understandings affect the ways in which Akwesasronon, and to a lesser extent border officers, talk about and understand the border.

Mitchell and his lawyers had to prove that trade and mobility across what is now the Canada-US border was a central practice of Mohawk peoples at the time of contact. To do so, they called historians and elders as witnesses to attest to that fact.

The crown countered with historians of their own, suggesting that cross-border trade was not a facet of Mohawk society because, at the time of contact, Mohawks were based south of what is currently the border, in the Mohawk valley. They argued, in contrast, that trade was something all Indigenous peoples participated in and was not a practice distinctive to Mohawks. Finally, they suggested that any trade which occurred took place within the confederacy on an east-west rather than a north-south axis – so even if trade was a traditional practice, it did not traverse what later became the border.

The debate hinged upon what has been referred to as "the St. Lawrence Iroquoians" controversy. In brief, the first written accounts of the St. Lawrence valley's inhabitants come from Jacques Cartier in 1535. Cartier encountered an Indigenous population living in the valley, with a large village settlement called Hochelaga where Montreal currently stands. Historians have long referred to this population as "the St. Lawrence Iroquoians," privileging the term "Iroquoian" in reference to the small syllabary Cartier documented from his exchanges, which showed that the inhabitants spoke something within the Iroquoian language family. Archaeological evidence and Cartier's depictions demonstrate that, like other Iroquoian- language-speaking populations, the inhabitants of the St. Lawrence valley lived in longhouses within palisaded villages, and took part in the corns-beans-squash, or "three sisters," agricultural complex.

The controversy began, in part, when Samuel de Champlain visited the river valley in 1603. The permanent settlements were gone, with little immediate explanation as to where their residents had moved. The unexplained absence resulted in a debate and controversy in the archaeology and ethnohistory as to the reason. The main question, as Trigger and Pendergast succinctly put it, was "What happened to the St. Lawrence Iroquoians?" (1978, 360).

At present, the dominant theory is that population stresses, such as disease and military aggression by Mohawk nations to the south and west, were too much for the river-valley occupants to bear. Many village inhabitants were absorbed into the Mohawk nations, while others, heading north and northeast, were absorbed into Algonquian or Anishinaabe and Wendat (referred to in earlier literature as Huron) villages.

The history of the "St. Lawrence Iroquoians" frames local claims to Indigeneity and legitimacy in several ways. By asserting shared heritage with the earliest recorded populations of the valley, Akwesasronon reify the fact that "they were here first," a presence in the region since time immemorial – Indigeneity with a capital "I." Doing so also reasserts the right of Akwesasronon to transmit their own history, in opposition to those who may wish to delegitimize their claims.

Even the term "Iroquoians" is a controversial one, as it distances the population from the more specific "Iroquois" peoples to which Akwesasronon belong. "Iroquois" refers to the political confederacy; "Iroquoian" refers to the language group of the Iroquois and also the Huron peoples. I spoke with several who privilege the term "St. Lawrence Iroquois" for this reason. Others suggest omitting the term altogether in favour of a more neutral way of talking about the archaeological record that references region rather than language or nationality.

Asking "What happened to the St. Lawrence Iroquoians?" risks becoming another iteration of "the myth of the vanishing Indian." It relies heavily upon the trope of an Indigenous population's disappearance, and reasserts an especially Western notion of population dynamics in which populations rise and fall or appear and disappear. A more complete reading of "what happened" requires more nuance.

Drawing predominantly on work with Wendat informants, Trigger suggested adding oral testimonies to the reading of the archaeological record. This complements Raymond Fogelson's (1974) call for an "ethno-ethno history" in which researchers must recognize that history is rooted and that temporalities and values vary among populations.

If we assume that the St. Lawrence population was depleted at least in part because of warfare with Mohawk peoples, the question of what happened to them is not difficult to answer. Warfare by Mohawks, and by Haudenosaunee in general, helped them replenish and expand their own populations through absorbing and adopting enemy combatants (Richter and Institute 1992; but see also A.F.C. Wallace 1970; Parmenter 2006). Unlike popular notions of Western warfare, the goal was to expand and increase one's own population rather than simply to decrease one's enemies' population. There is no reason to suggest that warfare in the St. Lawrence valley was any different. Even if some young men died in warfare, the majority of the population would have been absorbed into the neighbouring nations. Those captured by Mohawks would have become Mohawk. What happened to the St. Lawrence Iroquoians? Whether by choice or by force, they became Mohawk.

One can frame the history of the Akwesasne Mohawk Territory in two seemingly contradictory ways. One can say that the original inhabitants were "wiped out" due to aggression by Mohawks. One can say that the original inhabitants were Mohawks. These permutations have dominated legal claims and contestations to rights over the territory.

The first history can be used to delegitimize Mohawk claims to regional Indigeneity, representing the current occupants as latecomers. There is something appealing in the simplicity of this history. It relies on a less-nuanced understanding of the past, and one in line with a historically "Western" conception of history. To a non-Indigenous Canadian audience, it serves the added benefit of allaying, at least in part, potential guilt, suggesting that Indigenous politics were no less brutal than European ones. It may also support the "terra nullius" trope that the land was uninhabited at the time of European occupation and therefore acceptable for legitimate European settlement. This is a good history for Canada, but not for Akwesasne.

The second history, similarly, can be used to legitimize Mohawk claims to regional Indigeneity and, consequently, bolster their claims to Aboriginal rights. It speaks more soundly to history as it exists locally, and recognizes that population dynamics in North America up to the time of contact followed their own particular flows, adhering to Trigger and Pendergast's (1978) admonition that we should not retroactively place national identity upon populations for whom such identity had, and still has, its own meaning. Yet this narrative may be less appealing than the simpler one. It is harder to grasp and requires several additional logical steps to make sense. Its implications continue to de-legitimize non-Indigenous claims to the territory. Yet simply suggesting that the original inhabitants of the valley were Mohawk, full stop, also lacks subtlety, as I discuss in greater detail at the end of this section. This is a better history for Akwesasne.

During the Mitchell case, Mitchell's arguments relied upon the assertion that, as far as the Van Der Peet test was concerned, Akwesasronon continue to represent the "time of contact" civilization dwelling in the valley. As a result, trade and movement across what later became the border were a fundamental aspect of their exchange during that period, and therefore must be recognized as an Aboriginal right.

The crown's arguments hinged in part upon the notion that the St. Lawrence Iroquoians were a distinct population from the Mohawks. At the time of European contact, the Mohawk Nation was centred in the Mohawk valley in upstate New York. By arguing that the Mohawks were located south of the borderline at the time of contact, the crown argued that there was no "prior cultural practice" related to border crossing. The minister suggested that because Mohawks were based in the south, their mobility lay from east to west in what is now New York State.

The courts needed to know whether the St. Lawrence Iroquoians were Mohawk, or at least Mohawk "enough" to justify Mitchell's claim.

After winning in lower courts, Mitchell lost when the Supreme Court of Canada drew favourably upon the crown witnesses in 2001:

> In the present case, the evidence indicates that the Mohawks travelled north on occasion and trade was a distinguishing feature of their society. The evidence does not show, however, an ancestral practice of trading north of the St. Lawrence River. Mohawk trade at the time of contact fell predominantly along an east-west axis. (*Mitchell v MNR* [2001] 1 S.C.R. 911, 2001 SCC 33)

The court's decision came down to, or, as many see it, was justified by (see Garfinkel 1967) "whose" history they chose to uphold. Ultimately, the court claimed that it was a matter of the scale and shape of Haudeno-saunee trade. While east-west trade existed, north-south trade did not. They also denied claims that Mohawk peoples resided in the St. Lawrence valley at the time of contact. As Niezen writes, the Mitchell finding suggests that "pre-contact aboriginal practices are therefore subject to the criterion of compatibility with the Crown's sovereignty as a central prerequisite of cultural rights" (2003a, 10).

Akwesasronon responded indignantly to the assertion by the crown's expert witness, University of Toronto professor Alexander Von Gernet, that they were "confused about [the past]," as a local Cornwall publication remarked:

> Canadian-based Mohawks are not really Mohawks but Iroquois/Huron hybrids confused over their true identity, a border-crossing rights trial was told here on Tuesday. And because their true ancestry lies within the Huron culture, their historically-recorded faith is not the traditional native longhouse teachings but rather Catholicism as taught to them in the 17th and 18th centuries by French Jesuits. (Hrabluk 1996)

This reading of history cut at the community's "face" (see, e.g., Goffman 1959; Goffman 1967) – that is, the way the community represents and, here, understands itself publicly. The above testimony went beyond suggesting that Mitchell's claim was unfounded in suggesting that Akwesasronon are mistaken about their own past. Members of the community were understandably upset by this argument.

History in Akwesasne, at least as it relates to local government, is often, if not legal history, a history that relates to law. The MCA website's "our history" section features eight linked pages on the community's past. More than half of these subsections, and nearly all the text, are directly concerned with court cases and treaty rights. The telling and retelling of history are an active part of what the government of Akwesasne does.

I found my own understanding of Akwesasne's history was one of the ways in which people sought to engage with and understand me as a researcher. By seeing how I dealt with this history, Akwesasronon could get a preliminary sense of how I would approach other questions in my study. It was a seminal aspect of local claims to legal rights, and continues to be a part of how Akwesasne represents itself to itself, to the media, and to outsiders such as border officers. As much as the Canadian judiciary's efforts to define rights in terms of culture and history reshaped judicial expectations, the juridification of Indigenous culture and history matters in communities as well.

In the next section, I discuss another origin story of Akwesasne and the border. I look at the geopolitical events in North America that led up to the establishment of the permanent settlement of Akwesasne/ St. Regis, and the imposition of the border on that location. I attach this historical narrative to the broader questions of North American borderland studies. Though Haudenosaunee peoples, and especially Mohawks, have occupied a central role in the history of the border, Akwesasne, despite its location astride the borderline, has long been a blind spot in this literature – referenced, if at all, only briefly and in passing (see, e.g., White 1991; Adelman and Aron 1999; Taylor 2002; Johnson and Graybill 2010).

Akwesasne and the Border Meet

Here I consider the ways in which "the border" and "borderlands" became a focal point for Mohawk territorial sovereignty and enterprise from 1600 to 1812, the period leading up to the formalization of the Canada-US border into something resembling its present shape. Though the borders distinguishing French, British, and US North America had yet to ossify when the St. Regis/Akwesasne mission settlement was founded in the mid-1700s, the founders were capitalizing on a long-standing practice of articulating, occupying, and profiting from a strategic location at the intersection of powers. I argue that Akwesasronon have always been a "river people," but they have also long been a "border people."

At the time of early European settlement in North America, the five (and later six) nations of the Haudenosaunee Confederacy, the Seneca, Cayuga, Onondaga, Oneida, and Mohawk,[3] had recently joined into the

---

3 The sixth nation, the Tuscarora, joined in 1722.

most powerful political alliance in their region. In the eastern woodlands, corn, the confederacy, and wampum played the role that "guns germs, and steel" (Diamond 2005) did in Mesoamerica. A strong constitutional system of governance and laws, strong alliances, and a highly productive agricultural base (Pleasant 2010) enabled the confederacy to dominate Indigenous politics in the region, eventually spreading from the Great Lakes in the west to the Atlantic Ocean in the east.

The territorial apex of the confederacy came following the "Beaver Wars" of the mid-1600s. The Mohawks, as one of the senior, "big brother" nations served as "guardians of the eastern door," fortifying and expanding eastward.

This expansion served several purposes. Firstly, military expansion replenished the nation's population at a time when disease had devastated the Indigenous landscape. Through adoption, the Haudenosaunee were able to grow rather than shrink in power, population, and influence while others struggled to survive. Secondly, by pushing from the Great Lakes to the coast, the Haudenosaunee were able to enjoy a de-facto position as middlemen between European and Indigenous powers (see Taylor 2002). Of paramount benefit was control over the lucrative trade of beaver skins in exchange for manufactured goods such as metal tools, beads, cloth, and rifles, as well as the opportunity to form alliances with new European settlers.

By controlling the east-west corridor of the eastern woodlands, the Haudenosaunee could regulate any north-south trade between the fur-trapping Algonquian-speaking populations to the north (recent evidence has shown that the Haudenosaunee were also very productive fur trappers) and European trade centres to the south. The "Longhouse" of the Haudenosaunee Confederacy became a sort of border, or borderland, between Indigenous and European spheres of influence and production. Haudenosaunee diplomats actively fostered this formation – discouraging outside alliances and incentivizing Europeans to set up trade in their territories.

Cornell historian Jon Parmenter (2010) has convincingly argued that Haudenosaunee spatial sovereignty, especially during this period, was not about access to bounded territories but about control over trade and transport routes within a given territory. Thus, the confederacy encouraged European trading posts and even small settlements as long as it held the monopoly over the legitimate means of movement through the landscape. I discuss the protocols for movement within Haudenosaunee territory at the end of chapter 4.

By the mid- to late 1600s, some Mohawks, choosing to embrace the Catholicism spread by missionaries, decided to form separate communities in newly established missions in and around the Montreal area. The first of these settlements was Kahnawake (previously spelled Caughnawaga). Though maintaining a Mohawk identity, Kahnawake was a melting pot, with many Indigenous residents from all over the region. Early masses were held in Mohawk, but also in Huron and other languages. It is from this fact that the crown's expert witness came to describe Akwesasronon as "Iroquois/Huron" hybrids, though such a claim is built on the assumption that nationality is transmitted through blood rather than practice and self-identification. This is an idea rejected by many anthropologists though all too frequently embraced by states employing legally delineated status for Indigenous populations (Sturm 2002).

Overcrowding, internal divisions, and environmental degradation in Kahnawake encouraged some residents to form a new community, Akwesasne, at the confluence of the Racquette, St. Regis, and St. Lawrence Rivers in 1754. The choice of Akwesasne was bolstered by its convenient location in well-known hunting, logging, and fishing grounds, and at a nexus point for French and British trade, as well as Catholic and Protestant spheres of influence. In this regard, the earliest Akwesasronon continued the long-standing enterprise of forming settlements in footholds between European states. Akwesasne, at the time more often referred to as St. Regis, joined Kahnawake, Kanesetake (Oka), and four other Catholic Indigenous nations to form the Seven Nations Confederacy of Canada – the predominant political association of Catholic Indigenous polities. In this capacity, Akwesasne was not only part of the Mohawk Nation but a nation in its own right.

Shortly after the founding of the Akwesasne/St. Regis Mohawk community, the American Revolution redrew political boundaries in North America. Phillip White-Cree has referred to the revolution as "the most traumatic times for the Haudenosaunee" (2014, 28). Though the Haudenosaunee confederacy maintained an official stance of neutrality leading up to the American Revolution, the Mohawk Nation was divided in its support, and many individuals chose to fight. Mohawks still residing in the Mohawk River valley supported the British, with whom they held stronger ties. Akwesasronon, and other northern Mohawk communities still tied to French interests, sought to aid the American colonies (ibid., 30). Ultimately, in the face of insurmountable pressures to take sides, the Haudenosaunee Confederacy decided to let nations decide for themselves. Akwesasne strove for neutrality and became a place of refuge for Mohawks and other Haudenosaunee living close to battlegrounds (ibid., 31). The American Revolution claimed the lives of many Haudenosaunee peoples fighting in support of European settler states that would soon push for the eradication of their sovereignty.

Following the revolution, Britain and the newly formed United States established a border dividing the continent. Haudenosaunee peoples were promised exemption from "Washington's treaty line," an exemption that was recognized in article III of the Jay Treaty at the conclusion of hostilities. The interest of Britain and the United States in excluding Indigenous peoples from border regulations was as much a matter of practical trade as of appeasing military allies. Indigenous Americans effectively became mobile duty-free traders, ensuring that the lucrative north-south trade would continue.

Though the first inscription of the border came following the American Revolution, the line only ossified following the War of 1812. Tensions between the British and newly independent Americans rekindled the possibility of playing the two dominant European powers off against one another. For a brief period of time, the Haudenosaunee were able to return to the comfortable role of middlemen, securing trade and gifts in exchange for positive relations and neutrality. Yet the benefits of the strategy were short-lived. Their land base continued to erode rapidly, as private land developers in the United States played the states and federal government off against one another while flooding into Iroquois territories. Mohawk leaders such as Joseph Brant sought to create, delineate, consolidate, and defend territorial bases for their peoples (while securing a bit extra for themselves as well) (Taylor 2002). As the Iroquois nations' land base became defined not by access to and mobility throughout a large territory but by occupation of small areas, the confederacy's sphere of influence waned.

This period, according to popular historiography, marked the transition of North American political geography from "borderlands to bordered lands" (Adelman and Aron 1999). Adelman and Aron define this period solely in terms of the emergent monopolization of power by European settler states on the North American continent. As Indigenous populations became politically and militarily marginalized (both figuratively and literally), North American politics transitioned, they argue, to a contestation between European colonies with more clearly delineated boundaries. In drawing this distinction, Adelman and Aron sought to dissociate borderlands from frontiers, the former representing consolidation and the latter expansion.

Adelman and Aron have been praised for their efforts to offer some sort of structured periodicity to the history of early North American settlement and their ability to push the paradigm beyond Turner's frontier thesis (Turner 1893; but see Johnson and Graybill 2010). They can also be criticized, however, for downplaying both the ongoing role of Indigenous agency and the ways in which Indigenous nations had pre-existing notions of spatial ordering. Akwesasne stands, at the very least, as proof that borderlands remain in North America. It remains a space where both Canada and the United States have been unable to monopolize the legitimate exercise of power. This distinction defines "the border situation" in Akwesasne today, but is inexorably rooted in the community's early history.

The situation of Akwesasne in the War of 1812 is a complex one, deserving more space than I allot here. If the American Revolution marked the most traumatic time for the confederacy, the War of 1812 brought this trauma home to Akwesasne. Though the confederacy sought neutrality in the conflict, Akwesasne, located along the newly created Canada-US borderline, was strongly affected by the war. Battles were fought between kin in different communities, including an early battle in St. Regis Village on October 1812 when American troops, including some Mohawk warriors, led a sneak attack on the British-controlled village. While some Akwesasronon chose to join the British in response to the sneak attack, others fought for the Americans, with the community itself divided over whom to support (Bonaparte 2012). After the war, British and American troops remained stationed in and around the Akwesasne Mohawk Territory, signifying the beginnings of the border's militarization as far as Akwesasronon were concerned. The map of Akwesasne in 1817 (figure 3.1) shows the location of both British and American military encampments. Fortifications on some islands remain to this day. Also worthy of note is the fact that the houses within St. Regis Village disappear south of the new borderline, as seen in the lower right-hand corner of the map, effectively erasing the community's contiguity of occupation across the line, while the treeline continues. This map was created prior to the redrawing of the borderline by the border commission to emplace islands solely within the territory of Canada or the United States.

Simply suggesting that the border came to Akwesasne in either 1776 or 1812 diminishes long-standing Mohawk strategies of creating and dominating border regions. The Canada-US border was shaped by those strategies. Although they did not imagine the shape it would take, Mohawks were active participants rather than passive actors in reshaping the continent's political geography following the arrival of European settlers. They returned to the St. Lawrence valley amid a period of religious and political uncertainty and opportunity. As much as the border came to Akwesasne, Akwesasne came to the border.

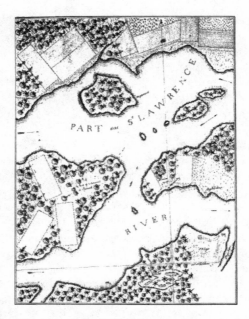

Figure 3.1. Map of the Akwesasne Mohawk Territory, 1817. Credit: Thompson and Adams, 1817. Image courtesy of Chicago's Newberry Library.

While the Canada-US border divided Haudenosaunee nations, one could also argue that the earliest border between European powers in the region comprised the Haudenosaunee themselves. It was impossible to easily move, trade, or conduct diplomacy or warfare through much of the north-eastern woodlands without the support of the confederacy, bolstering their position as power players in the region. Though this boundary ultimately proved divisive and deadly, the border was, and remains, a resource to Akwesasronon and other Mohawk peoples.

As in the past, Akwesasronon still economically and politically profit from their ability to dominate trade through a border corridor. They continue to profit from travellers who go through the territory to cross the border, and they continue to sell goods at discounted prices. They also continue to leverage their position in a major commercial corridor to exert influence on political and economic endeavours. These advantages are part of why Akwesasne was such a desirable location for settlement in the past.

The border can be used for profit, but it can also be exploited. Many in Akwesasne see "borderland vice industries" (Carey and Marak 2011) such as tobacco and gambling as putting the community at risk and stigmatizing it. During the Mitchell case, attorneys for the crown repeatedly argued that if Akwesasne became a true duty-free zone, it would give them an unfair commercial advantage. The economic consequences of open cross-border trade were used as one justification for the limitation of mobility rights. The border is a resource, but one whose extraction is regulated both within and without.

Conclusions

A lot of history is missing from this account. I have focused on a narrative of the territory's founding as a Mohawk community; while "[o]ral tradition ... suggests that there were already people here when this first Kahnawake migration occurred[,] these people may have come from either the Mohawk valley or the Onondaga/Oneida mission at Oswegatchie" (Bonaparte n.d.). Indeed several of the elders I spoke with told me that Akwesasne was initially two communities, Oswegatchie and St. Regis, which became unified into one.

While I mention the origins of the Canada-US border's inscription upon the Akwesasne Mohawk Territory, I do not talk about the earliest measures to enforce the borderline. I have neglected the story of Saiowisakeron (John "Jake Ice" Fire), who died attempting to rescue his brother while resisting the British imposition of government upon the community in 1899. Jake Fire has become a symbol for Akwesasne, a martyr signifying Akwesasne's resistance to the external imposition of settler sovereignty. A statue of him stood in front of the port of entry in Cornwall until recently; during protests the statue held a sign reading "Your gun killed me."

In emphasizing the Mitchell case, I also did not discuss Akwesasne's ties to the broader history of border-crossing rights for all North America's Indigenous peoples, or the confederacy in general. I have not discussed the mission of Cayuga Chief Levi General ("Deskaheh") to the League of Nations on a Haudenosaunee passport in 1923 – an early precursor to the international movement of Indigenous peoples (Niezen 2003b). Deskaheh was denied re-entry into Canada and died in the home of Tuscarora Chief Clinton Rickard – the first, and arguably most successful, Haudenosaunee border-rights activist. Rickard raised funds for the defence of Paul Diabo, a Mohawk steelworker born north of the borderline and deported from the United States. The court ruled in favour of Diabo's claim to a treaty right to live and work in the United

States in 1927, and since then, the US government has recognized a limited right of Indigenous North Americans to work, live, and move between Canada and the United States. I discuss the consequences of this decision for American border enforcement in chapter 4. Following the trial, Rickard established the Indian Defense League of America, and began an annual border crossing demonstration that continues to this day (Rickard 1994).

The history of Akwesasronon and the border is inexhaustible, and potentially exhausting. Like Akwesasronon themselves, the history traverses and challenges the lines that have come to define the territory. Identifying clear lines of demarcation in this context, such as "from borderlands to bordered lands," is not simply a challenging task; it is a counterproductive one. It defeats the fluidity of boundaries that are themselves at the heart of Akwesasne. My current treatment has been cursory, seeking to exemplify and examine those historical narratives that relate directly to Akwesasne's claims to Aboriginal border rights and their establishment. History in Akwesasne is as much about the present, and one's orientation to the present, as it is about the past. When history becomes a matter of law, that same history becomes a different matter for community interest.

There are overlaps between the conceptual significance of Akwesasne's geography and that of its history. Both are invoked, provoked, and revoked by different people and at different times. They exhibit a polyvalence both chosen by and imposed upon Akwesasronon, often in relation to the broader history of colonialism in North America. Akwesasne's history, like its geography, is complex in ways that enable and demand the construction of different narratives, without ever diminishing the fact that Akwesasne is a whole far greater than the sum of its parts.

This chapter has attempted to do two things with Akwesasne's history. Firstly, I offer a description of key moments, epochs, and transitions that came to form the community's current situation – particularly vis-à-vis the border. Secondly, I provide an account of history's role in the present, and the ways in which history is something that is "done" (and "doing") as much as it is lived, recorded, and remembered. This effect is observable in microcosm by an ethnographer's attempt to "do history" in the community, but also in the ways people "do history" at the dinner table, the port of entry, or even in the courtroom – in other words, history as (1) "what happened" and (2) "what we do with what happened."

While I can present these as two separate threads for analytical purposes, in the day-to-day experiences of the border this is not possible.

Both permutations are mutually informative and constitutive. History, as many scholars have argued, is a palimpsest; and in Akwesasne history is a palimpsest that is folded into beautiful (or ugly) shapes, used to cover one's head in a storm, or even rolled up and used to whack people over the head.

The border is not something that simply "happened" to Akwesasne. It is something that has happened in different ways and that is continuing to happen. Any account of the border that strips Akwesasronon of agency, not just in the present but as a long-standing, politically conscious, thoughtful, history-making, and strategic community, leaves too much out. Akwesasne came to the border, just as the border came to Akwesasne – even if the terms of what all that should, or does, mean remain contested.

In the next chapter, I jump ahead more than a century and look not at how Akwesasne came to the border (or vice versa), but at how *this* particular border came to Akwesasne. In other words, I look at the local particularities that define the relationship between Akwesasne and border enforcement and render Akwesasne unique along the borderlands. Focusing on the period from 1969 to 2009, I look at how the contemporary relationship between Akwesasronon and border-services officers has changed in the face of a restructuring of the economies and border enforcement of Akwesasne, Canada, and the United States.

Chapter Four

The Changing Face of the Cornwall-Akwesasne Border

Introduction

On 21 January 2018, a resident of Akwesasne posted a video on Facebook showing an encounter with a CBSA officer at the port that was widely shared online. The resident, whom I have called "BT," had a bag of plant matter confiscated by a port officer. She claimed it was tobacco. The port authorities claimed that it was marijuana. While the initial posting and conversation refer solely to the bag as containing loose-leaf tobacco, subsequent conversations on Facebook referred to the bag as a "medicine pouch," and its confiscation as an even more egregious violation of her rights as an Indigenous person.

She went to secondary inspection to voice a complaint as a friend taped the exchange (and subsequently publicly uploaded the video to Facebook). The lens focuses on an older officer standing with both hands on a desk, leaning forward while talking with her, with his shoulders hunched – panning out a few times to show the half-dozen other officers in the facility as they did a poor job of pretending not to be paying attention to the exchange while working on computers or taking a bit too much time to make a cup of coffee while surreptitiously listening to what was going on.

I include a transcription of her conversation below, changing the participants' names – although in the video, the names are publicly available to a reader who wishes to dig for them, this offers a degree of anonymity for participants. It is also worth noting that while I present the conversation in dialogue form, participants were frequently speaking over and interrupting one another.

I regret that I am unable to depict the officer's body language in a way that would not claim authorial privilege to frame the exchange. I showed the video to several colleagues and asked their opinions. Those who identified as tending to the conservative side of the political spectrum were sympathetic with the officer. They interpreted his body language as showing that while he was physically stressed by her provocations, he maintained a professional composure. Those colleagues who identified as tending to the liberal side were sympathetic with her. They interpreted his body language as an effort to physically intimidate her from across the counter.

BT: [The video starts mid-sentence.] [...] shake of marijuana. So did you test that, that it's tobacco?

OFFICER: The officers tested that, yes.

BT: So you have the report.

OFFICER: I have the results, yes.

BT: So I want a copy of those results.

OFFICER: No.

BT: Yes. There's no way that you can say that this is marijuana, unless proven, right? This would be like me coming in here and saying, "You're under an arrest, this is vodka [holds up a water bottle]" this [indicates the bottle], is water. The same with the bag of tobacco, that was tobacco, not marijuana. So I need a report that says [...]

OFFICER: I don't have to give you a report, I'm not going to give you a report.

BT: Yes, you do. I will file for it.

OFFICER: Then file for the report.

BT: And so, I also want to have a meeting with you and your director.

OFFICER: [Nodding] You can do that at your next leisure.

BT: Okay, so one thing is that I looked online and there's no phone for here. So how do I get ahold of you? I have my calendar here.

OFFICER: You have a paper and pen? I'll tell you what it is right now.

BT: Well, actually, when are you available? For a meeting?

OFFICER: [Shakes head] It doesn't work that way, I'll give you a phone number, you can call the office.

BT: You want me to call the director, or do you want me to call Ottawa?

OFFICER: I'll give you the number for the chief, that's the number you'll get from me.

BT: Okay.

OFFICER: It's [Gives number].

BT: And his name?

OFFICER: Martin Lasalle ... Lacole, sorry.

BT: What is it?

OFFICER: Martin Lacole.

BT: And what is his title?

OFFICER: Chief of Operations.

BT: And what about your director of the port?

OFFICER: The director of the port is Jeff Smith.

BT: Okay, should he be there?

OFFICER: Nope, the director of operations is my direct superior.

BT: And your name is Chauncy? [Points to name tag]

OFFICER: Chauncy.

BT: I remember you quite clearly.

OFFICER: I remember you as well.

BT: So anyways, there's no way I'm filing for this. But it wasn't marijuana, you do know that, right? It's tobacco?

OFFICER: I saw ... not the results, a printout. It's a spray that's used. It turns a different colour whenever the cannabis is exposed to it. And it turned that.

BT: It's not even cannabis.

OFFICER: [Shrugs] Okay, if you say so.

BT: Okay, so I want you to retest it, and I want it filmed.

OFFICER: No.

BT: Okay, so when we file for this, we get it back, right?

OFFICER: You do whatever you have to do.

BT: And do we have to go to court for it?

OFFICER: I don't know.

BT: You should know.

OFFICER: You want to file an appeal. That's your right to appeal.

BT: You should know how it gets back.

OFFICER: No.

BT: You don't know that?

OFFICER: No, I know you have a right to appeal.

BT: Because you're just here for taxes, right?

OFFICER: No. [Shakes head]

BT: You're not cops.

CAMERAMAN: [Also from Akwesasne] So you're not qualified for your job then.

BT: You're not even qualified to even check that.

OFFICER: I'm not going to answer you, sir.

CAMERAMAN: [Chuckles]

OFFICER: [To cameraman] Your question has no merit.

BT: Shouldn't it be the RCMP then? Should the RCMP [Royal Canadian Mounted Police] or the OPP [Ontario Provincial Police] confirm that that was marijuana or tobacco?

OFFICER: Are you done making your requests?

BT: No, I just want to know.

OFFICER: No, they don't have to do the testing on it.

BT: But you're just tax collectors?

OFFICER: Anything else you'd like to know?

BT: You're here to collect the taxes.

OFFICER: Anything else that has any relevance to this case?

BT: I'm just making sure that you know.

OFFICER: Anything else you'd like to know that has any relevance to this matter?

BT: You know what, I will call your supervisor, whoever, and I'll have a meeting with him.

OFFICER: Please do. Thank you. Have a good day.

In the previous chapter, I discussed some of the implications of "doing history" in Akwesasne, while offering a brief account of the community's early history vis-à-vis the Canada-US border. I suggest that as much as the border came to Akwesasne, Akwesasronon had a long-standing engagement with the boundaries of Indigenous and settler spheres that began long before the American Revolution. In this chapter, I look at the current state of border enforcement in Akwesasne, and how it came about. In doing so, I try to get a sense of how *this* border came to Akwesasne. Doing so sheds some light on the minutiae of what took place between "BT" and "Officer Chauncy" in the preceding exchange. It helps us get a sense of how a conversation about tobacco turned into the insistence by two Akwesasne residents that the officer was really a "tax collector," "not cops," and "not qualified" for his job. It also explains why an Akwesasne resident suspected of illegally bringing marijuana into Canada had the bag confiscated rather than face arrest at the border, and why they felt it would not be abnormal to open up their agenda in the port office and try to schedule a meeting with the supervisor. This exchange was the product of decades of change in the ways in which Akwesasronon and CBSA officers thought about one another.

Three Snapshots

To consider the ways in which Akwesasne and its relationship with border enforcement changed during this period, we can look at three events as snapshots, each taken twenty years apart.

In 1969, Mohawks from Akwesasne gathered on Cornwall Island to protest the island's customs house and the charging of duties to members of their community. The protest took the form of a bridge blockade, which was filmed in the documentary *You Are on Indian Land* (Mitchell 1969), co-produced and directed by Mike Mitchell, then a young filmmaker. Border officers are conspicuously absent from the film. Prior to their arrests, youths and elders join hands and sing "We Shall Overcome." It was a moment that invoked the emergence of Native American activism and the "red power movement" more broadly, local resistance to long-standing impositions of the Canadian government in Akwesasne, and a broader spirit of peace and protest associated with the 1960s.

Twenty years later, in 1989, a visitor standing in the same spot would have heard not singing but gunshots – some of them volleyed between those same people who had been holding hands in 1969. Nineteen eighty-nine marked what some journalists have called Akwesasne's "civil war" (Hornung 1991; but see Johansen 1993), when "pro" and "anti" gambling forces eventually took up arms against one another, leading to several deaths, a Canadian military intervention, and the temporary imposition of martial law upon parts of the community. The conflict, though framed in terms of a community division over gambling, was inexorably tied to the rise in clandestine cross-border commerce, or "smuggling," that flourished in and around Akwesasne in the 1980s. Border officers were again absent from the conflict, continuing to process international travel and charge duties while ensconced in Canada's first bullet-proofed port of entry.

Another twenty years on, in 2009, protests came back to the island. This time, Akwesasronon were again united in opposition to Canadian border enforcement. Unlike in the 1969 protests, border officers were placed at the forefront of local concerns. Protesters demanded that the port of entry on Cornwall Island exempt itself from the CBSA's universal arming initiative, holding up signs reading "No guns on the Island." Ultimately, the protests resulted in the evacuation of the Cornwall port of entry officers by the midnight deadline for arming. Once officers packed up and left the island, the bridges leading to and from Cornwall Island were closed, isolating all overland travel off the island until a "temporary" port of entry opened in the city of Cornwall months later. The aftermath of that move is an ongoing concern for Akwesasne, which I discuss in detail in the next chapter.

What happened between 1969, 1989, and 2009? How to account for such disparity in Akwesasronon's attitudes toward the border and one another?

This chapter offers a corollary to Karine Côté-Boucher's "The Micropolitics of Border Control: Internal Struggles at Canadian Customs" (2013; but see also Côté-Boucher, Infantino, and Salter 2014; Côté-Boucher 2015, 2018). Côté-Boucher's study is the most exhaustive to date of the ways in which national policy resituated Canadian border work, particularly in the formative period of "the 1990s." (I explain later on why I put the decade in quotation marks here.) Côté-Boucher argues that a combination of neoliberal practices, new enforcement technologies, and the simultaneous expansion of CBSO powers and limitations of discretion resulted in a "disembedding" of border work, in which officers saw their role transmute from that of autonomous state agents to parts of a vast, often invisible machinery of border intelligence and enforcement. Though drawing on interviews at ports of entry, Côté-Boucher's view is national, and focused on the perspective of officers. She also focuses on commercial traffic.

Here, I look at how these changes were felt locally, by both the border officers themselves, and the travelling public interacting with them in non-commercial processing. As much as a national process of disembedding defined border work in the 1990s, at the Cornwall port of entry this accompanied depersonalization. Akwesasronon travellers and border officers began to feel themselves in a less personal relationship vis-à-vis one another, as mutual understanding and flexibility at a local level became replaced with non-negotiable national policy regimes.

My interviews with border officers affirmed Côté-Boucher's case for taking a "generational" approach to the study of border work (2018). While officers come and go with regularity, they frequently see themselves as belonging to particular generations, each with its own set of normative understandings about how border work operates. In the 1960s and early 1970s, the stereotypical generation of border officer consisted of military veterans seeking the promise of a well-paying, comfortable government job after army service. Their primary objective, according to retired officers, was to simply stay out of trouble. From the mid-1970s to the early 1990s, the stereotypical generation consisted of baby boomers seeking a good salary and the opportunity to stay close to home in Cornwall. These officers saw themselves as hired tax collectors rather than policing officers, and took on a more proactive role in local policy. From the late 1990s onward, but especially after the year 2000, the stereotypical BSO was younger and motivated to act as a law-enforcement officer.

Local knowledge of border officers, acquired through first-hand experiences with Akwesasne residents, was replaced with decentralized knowledge gathered from other state and private organizations. This knowledge was centralized in computer databases rather than in the unique institutional memories of CBSA personnel.

The "agency" of agents was challenged by new policies. Their responsibilities and powers grew, but their leeway in choosing how to exercise those powers diminished. In the aftermath of the 2009 protests, officers left the island entirely, refusing to negotiate an exception to Canada's universal arming initiative for border officers. Some officers maintain relationships with people from Akwesasne, and many are genuinely interested in getting to know travellers. However, this relationship-building is no longer a defining facet of what it means to be a successful border officer in Cornwall.

Depersonalization

In subsequent sections, I will look at the factors that resulted in a deper-sonalization of border work in Akwesasne. Here, however, I wish to elaborate on what I mean by "depersonalization." I use the term to draw attention to the changing relationships between Akwesasronon and CBSA officers.

"Personal," in this context, should not be confused with favourable, although the two have often gone hand in hand. Rather, when I suggest that relations between officers and travellers became depersonalized, I mean that the ways in which BSOs and Akwesasronon connected with one another became increasingly divorced from a shared local context.

Though typically not living in same geographic space, officers and Akwesasronon could previously have been seen as belonging to the same community, by some definition of the term (see chapter 2). Even non-Indigenous officers belonged in many of the same networks, interacting face-to-face on a daily basis, often eating and shopping in the same spaces, and at times developing friendships and other relationships. While some officers never set foot on reserve land when they were not working, many did. Several told me stories of playing sports in and around Akwesasne with mixed teams of residents and non-residents; one, a farmer, said he knew the community well because he often sold and traded with farmers on the reserve. The territory was Akwesasne's, but access and exchange were regularly shared.

The shared assumptions and space that defined officer-Akwesasronon relations had, until "the 1990s," resulted in mutually constitutive local knowledge and interpersonal intelligence. Networks of friendship and business extended into officers' work. They were essential facets of offi-cers' intelligence-gathering operations. They were how officers knew whom to stop and whom to let go, who was from Akwesasne and who was an outsider.

This also impacted the ways in which Akwesasronon talked to offi-cers. Even when relationships were not friendly, Akwesasronon and BSOs were often named and known. An Akwesasronon traveller would engage differently with an officer depending on their personal (or second-hand) experiences of that officer.

In time, this changed, as officers increasingly divorced their professional persona from their personal persona, and Akwesasronon increasingly divorced their image of officers from their image of people in general. To Akwesasronon, officers became less "people" and more "officers," and to border officers, Akwesasronon became less "people" and more "clients" or "travellers."

One BSO's response to a questionnaire I circulated is revealing of this changing relationship. In response to the question, "Do you feel you have a relationship with the community of Akwesasne? Please elaborate as possible," they wrote:

> I feel that my relationship with Akwesasne has nothing to do with me, and everything to do with what my uniform represents. I feel that to the clients that I encounter, I am simply another person in a uniform. By the time I deal with the clients, they have already spoken to a primary officer, and are now either inside at the counter, or in secondary awaiting an exam. Whether I am friendly, rude, polite, demanding, etc., has no bearing on how they see me. To the clients I am simply another officer "wasting their time." The CBSA and MCA do have a relationship that has developed over years of trying to work out kinks. We have a job to do, and they have lives to live, and our paths do have to cross from time to time. I feel that the relationship has evolved over time due to necessity and that it is often strained by the various incidents and circumstances that arise. We as officers perform our duties as best as we can and always in good faith, and that often leads to issues and concerns from the Akwesasne community because of it.

The officer's assertion that their uniform and what it represents play a central role in how they are seen by the community is affirmed by my discussions with Akwesasronon. When I asked an Akwesasronon living in Cornwall what she did when she ran into BSOs in town, she said that she honestly could not recognize them out of their uniforms. Other people I spoke with at times described officers as interchangeable nonpersons, frequently referring to them as "robots."

This depersonalization is not simply in one direction. Officers mentioned the responsibilities they took on once wearing the uniform, which is symbolic of their authority and responsibilities. A uniform is not just a uniform; wearing it transforms officers' notion of their powers and responsibilities. If I can be forgiven a Goffman-inspired digression, a uniform, like a mask, impacts the actor as much as the audience.

Much as the uniform can be a symbol of the office to an officer, officers in uniform can be viewed as symbolic of the Canadian state, the border, and everything in between. This is especially the case for those Akwesasronon most strongly opposed to the border's imposition. In not recognizing – in Simpson's terms "refusing" – an officer, one can refuse the border, or Canada itself.

One traveller, known for his outspokenness, spoke of refusing to say anything other than "Fuck you" to officers, "What is your name?" "Fuck you." "Where are you coming from?" "Fuck you." An officer I interviewed mentioned having to close their booth to cry after one such interaction, suggesting that some officers continue to care much more than others about their relationships with Akwesasne residents.

For some travellers, there is often a wilful desire not to look beyond the uniform, because the uniform represents a fundamental rights violation. In corollary, for some officers, there is a wilful desire not to go beyond the uniform, because the uniform encapsulates their border work. This may be mediated by a recent mandate that CBSA officers wear name tags, which the CBSA unions resisted, though it is too early to tell at this point. Here, uniforms and uniformity, a uniformity sown by national and local policy changes in the 1990s, go hand in hand.

The officer's assertion that "Whether I am friendly, rude, polite, demanding, etcetera, has no bearing on how they see me" falls short of what I observed. It is certainly the case that, once brought to secondary inspection, a traveller's negative impression of the first officer who sent them will likely affect their impressions of a second. However, in both personal experience and my discussions with Akwesasronon, I found that officers can, and often do, make and change impressions among travellers. As I mention in the introduction, the way an interaction is framed matters. The depersonalization of border enforcement at the Cornwall port of entry is neither complete nor inevitable. In the remainder of this chapter, I try to get a sense of how depersonalization resulted from a combination of national shifts in Canadian border enforcement and local shifts in Akwesasne's politics and economy.

Notes on/of Contention

Before considering the recent history of CBSA-Akwesasne relations, there are two points of contention I wish to highlight here. These are the term "smuggling" and the Akwesasne Warrior Society. Both terms are used – and misused – frequently by local actors and media, and my own choice in how to present them offers yet another micro political danger zone to map in contours but avoid dwelling on in the long term.

Concerning "smuggling": Akwesasne has long been a zone of international trade, some regulated and some unregulated by American and Canadian customs regimes. In the coming sections, I discuss the ways in which Akwesasne's reputation as a "smuggler's alley" (Sallot 2002) has shaped both public perceptions of the community and local border enforcement.

Webster's dictionary defines "to smuggle" as "to import or export secretly contrary to the law and especially without paying duties imposed by law" (Merriam-Webster n.d.). It is certainly the case that some trade in Akwesasne is clandestine, actively seeking to avoid the imposition of duties or other restrictions by any government. Yet the extent to which this trade is contrary to the law is less easy to establish with certainty.

Many in Akwesasne see themselves as subject to their own laws as Indigenous, Haudenosaunee, treaty, and/or Mohawk peoples, rather than to laws imposed by an illegitimate settler state. I spoke with one group which stated that they are only subject to "natural law," and thus not to the rules of Canada, the United States, or Mohawk governments. Thus, to call clandestine trade in Akwesasne "smuggling" is to invoke a particular understanding of how law operates, or should operate, in the territories – an understanding that is not universally shared. It is to render contested law normative. Yet to refrain from calling this trade "smuggling" offers the same risk, of discounting the views held by many, including individuals within the Mohawk government and border officers charged with regulating cross-border trade.

There is also a local distinction held between the clandestine trade in tobacco, a traditional product, and a large enterprise, and the clandestine transportation of weapons, illegal drugs, and people. While many do not see the cigarette trade – "buttlegging" – as smuggling (Simpson 2008) but rather as an exercise in sovereignty, many of those same actors would look down upon trade in cocaine, for example.

So how do I talk about this trade without labelling it – without framing it in a particular way? Whatever words I choose will privilege one interpretation over others. For my purposes in this chapter, I try to be specific about what is being traded, with the implicit understanding that what I term "clandestine" cross-border or international trade is considered illegal by the Canadian state.

Another sticky topic is the Mohawk Warrior Society of Akwesasne. Even my grouping of a discussion of the society with a discussion of clandestine trade is a problematic one. The society is often associated with clandestine trade, yet many within the society recognize such an association as problematic, undermining the genuine political concerns and ideologies held by the members. Indeed, distinctions are often made between "warriors" defined as the manifestation of a set of political ideals concerning sovereignty, autonomy, and protection of their communities (Alfred 1995; but see also Hornung 1991), and "warriors" defined as opportunistic power-grabbers relying upon the idiom of sovereignty to protect their own interests (Elliott 1996; but see Johansen 1993). The extent to which this represents two sets of people, or two interpretations of the same set of people, is equally contentious.

In Akwesasne, as elsewhere, political organizations hold both dogmatic and self-interested members. In my own limited discussions with members of the Warrior Society, I saw them as respectful adherents to a strong sense of ideology concerning Mohawk sovereignty. Without seeking to interpret the Akwesasne Mohawk Warrior Society in either a particularly positive or a particularly negative light, the coming sections discuss the ways in which Canadian border-enforcement policies in Cornwall were reshaped by a particular set of beliefs concerning the Warrior Society. CBSA officers were largely concerned with the society; some were afraid of it. They often associated the society with illegality. These beliefs led the CBSA to treat the society, and at times Akwesasne more generally, as a hotbed of militant political activism and clandestine trade.

The 1960s to 1980s: Akwesasne Challenges the Status Quo

Let us return to our first image of community protest in Akwesasne. The 1969 documentary film *You Are on Indian Land* depicts an Akwesasne Mohawk protest at the establishment of a customs house on Cornwall Island. The film opens with a young Mike Mitchell, sporting a greaser haircut, standing in a packed town hall. He is speaking to a government officer who is wearing a three-piece suit and puffing lightly on a "father knows best" pipe:

> There's been many wrongs done to us in the past, and today we don't even trust the white man coming into this reservation. You cannot blame us for that. We don't want to be a Canadian citizen. We don't want to be an American citizen. They told us a long time ago that we were North American Indians and today we feel this way too. We feel this way because we think this reservation is ours. And it does not belong to the white man. It's the only part we still have left.

Mohawk protesters blockaded the international corridor, putting up notices reading, "You are on Indian Land." The film was co-produced by Mitchell, then a young Akwesasne Mohawk studying film in Montreal. With the fashions, protest songs, and (surprising) projection of a sense of optimism, the film feels like a product of the 1960s.

You Are on Indian Land depicted a call for the recognition of Akwesasne's sovereignty and rights directed at the Canadian government and public. However, in historical hindsight, it may be more indicative of internal matters within the community than of a changing relationship between Akwesasne and Canada, heralding the coming transition in local governance toward traditionalism and autonomy, and away from puppet council control. Though the police physically remove protesters, by twenty-first-century standards they appear impossibly pacific. The most negatively portrayed individual is the band council chief, who asks the police for a firearm to protect himself from protesters. The film's narration states that though he represents himself as a kindly old man, he was not elected by the people of the community. Within a couple of decades, Mike Mitchell, a traditionalist, had been elected chief, the Band Council of Akwesasne had been replaced by the Mohawk Council of Akwesasne, and what was widely viewed as a puppet of Canadian governance became a formal platform for its challenge.

The 1960s represented an era of renewed Indigenous activism in North America, with Akwesasne at the forefront of the growth of both the "red power" movement, and the Mohawk Warrior Society (T. Alfred and Lowe 2005, 11). Alfred and Lowe differentiate between the red power movement and the Warrior movement by suggesting that whereas the former focused on transnational Indigenous alliances and had a more urban focus, the latter was a grassroots movement focusing on local, on-reserve issues. Whereas some in Akwesasne worked within state structures of power to reform community governance from within – as with Mitchell's successful run to be elected chief – others emphasized working outside those institutions. Akwesasne can be viewed as a testing ground for both models, models that are, in practice, not mutually exclusive – one can partake in some facets of governance (such as services, or even working for government) while refuting others (such as voting).

The 1980s marked a period of transition in Akwesasne's governance, with the restructuring of the Akwesasne Band Council by Longhouse traditionalists. The predominantly Christian band council came to be replaced with a predominantly Longhouse council. This is not to say that the two are mutually exclusive – Ernest Benedict, a leader of these reforms and a traditionally condoled chief, was also a fluent speaker of Mohawk, knowledgeable elder, and member of the church. Mitchell, the first traditionalist elected to council in recent history, spoke to me about being the object of tremendous ill-will from many old-guard Christians within Akwesasne until he placed a picture of himself shaking hands with Pope John Paul II in his office.

Several of Mitchell's former allies saw his refusal to disband the council as a betrayal of trust – thinking that Mitchell had been elected to devolve power to the Longhouse rather than reform the band council. This division revealed a larger schism among Akwesasne's traditionalists that coincided with a split of the Longhouse into two Longhouses, the rise of the Akwesasne Warrior Society, and the emergence of clandestine trade as a distinct political and economic force.

1980 to 1990s: Clandestine Trade and the Changing Border Economy

Changes in North American border enforcement opened the way for a successful business in clandestine trade, which many in Akwesasne embraced – both out of a profit motive and as a means to practise sovereignty. The 1980s marked a deeper shift in Canadian policy away from protectionism and toward greater trade with the United States (see Konrad and Nicol 2008; Bowling and Sheptycki 2012). The 1987 Canada-United States Free Trade Agreement (CUFTA), a predecessor to the North American Free Trade Agreement (NAFTA), heralded this shift, though the deregulation of cross-border commercial vehicles had begun years before (Côté-Boucher 2013). In the 1970s, Canada had also begun strengthening taxes on cigarettes, petrol, and alcohol. These two factors increased both the ease and the profitability of trading in clandestine tax-free goods. Many in Akwesasne took advantage of this newly opened market. Early forms of on-reserve trade, such as the sale of tax-free petrol, were not illegal until Canada closed loopholes; I spoke with one trader who made a large profit and then exited the business as soon as it became illegal.

Devastation to the local environment also fostered clandestine trade. The river, a long-standing source of sustenance, was poisoned by local paper-processing and other heavy industries. Unable to rely on historically available natural resources, residents had ample motivation to look to the border. Though cigarettes, tobacco, and petrol were initially viewed as relatively innocuous and, as noted above, were not necessarily illegal from the onset, a very small minority of residents transitioned to more lucrative but also controversial contraband such as firearms, drugs, and people. These trade goods also connected some Akwesasronon to organized crime networks in Canada and the United States. It is important to note that the large-scale trade in tax-free tobacco – "buttlegging" – which involved a much more substantial segment of

Akwesasne's population, did not blossom until the 1990s. Thus, in the 1980s, clandestine trade, though lucrative, involved a small percentage of Akwesasronon.

As Timothy Winegard writes, "Estimates revealed that the cocaine ring through Akwesasne to Montreal and Toronto during the late 1980s was worth $40 million per month" (2009, 10–11). Trade in guns had the added effect of heavily arming participants in the enterprise, many of whom had formal military training in North American armed forces. A few residents became extremely wealthy from clandestine trade and were able to invest capital into other ventures. One of these ventures, gaming, became a major source of controversy in the late 1980s when the federal 1988 Indian Gaming Regulatory Act codified the potential for legalized gambling in Indigenous communities.

While this did not, strictly speaking, legalize casinos in Akwesasne, some local business owners either interpreted it as such or at the very least saw this as an opportunity to open up their own gambling operations. It was not until later that the Saint Regis Mohawk Tribe formed an agreement with the state to begin legalized gambling operations in New York State. Regardless of the letter of the law, casinos arrived in Akwesasne in the late 1980s, and with them, controversy, opportunities, and challenges.

With the development of tribal gaming came internal debates across Indigenous communities as to whether to embrace this form of enterprise. Many saw this as a golden opportunity for profit, but others were wary of the moral challenges posed by gaming. Many Longhouse people in Akwesasne opposed gambling, which is condemned in the Code of Handsome Lake (although, as in Kahnawake, not all Longhouse people in Akwesasne look to the code to guide "traditional" practice). Others were not opposed to gambling, per se, but wanted to ensure that revenue sharing was collective, rather than privatized.

Akwesasne's proximity to the border made it an extremely convenient location for customers from New York State, Quebec, and Ontario. Ultimately, several gaming ventures were opened in Akwesasne; initially limited operations controlled by the Saint Regis Mohawk Tribe were replaced with large-scale ventures controlled by private members of the community. Regulation of these enterprises was hampered south of the borderline where the Saint Regis Mohawk Tribal police had been disbanded following corruption scandals, leaving a power vacuum. The general consensus within Akwesasne was that the start-up capital for gaming machines, facilities, and staff had come from the "ill-gotten gains" of clandestine trade and relationships with off-reserve organized crime. Conflict between the "pro" gaming interests of private casino owners, supported by the Akwesasne Mohawk Warrior Society, and "anti" gaming forces, led by Longhouse members, elected Mohawk councils, and opponents of the Warriors or of casino owners (Winegard 2009), came to a head in armed conflicts in 1989 that claimed the lives of two Mohawk men.

Several books have been written about what took place in 1989. Some were largely in sympathy with the "pro" forces (Hornung 1991; Busatta 2009) or the "anti" forces (Johansen 1993; George-Kanentiio 2006; Winegard 2009), and many in Akwesasne told me that none of these accounts gets it completely right. At the forefront of critiques is the notion that this conflict was simply about gambling. Rather, as I hint above, gaming was the spark that lit a powder keg consisting of a long-standing dispute within the community about more fundamental questions of Mohawk sovereignty, self-determination, and the future of the community. Rather than attempt to retell in a few words an event that has required several books to discuss, I wish to keep this discussion attuned to "the border," both the role that Akwesasne's cross-border location played in the conflict, and the ways in which this conflict impacted local enforcement practices.

Several facets of Akwesasne's location at the borderline rendered the casinos especially feasible, profitable, and difficult to combat. Cross-border trade facilitated the capital and connections used to get casinos off the ground. Clandestine trade in firearms also armed Warriors, providing martial support for casino interests. Once built, casinos could rely on a cross-border clientele. Akwesasne's unique location astride the borderline made it extremely difficult for American or Canadian police forces to maintain any monopoly over the legitimate use of violence within the territory. American and US officers had to respect the borderline and refrain from pursuing suspects across national boundaries. The "jurisdictional nightmare" of Akwesasne made it an ideal environment in which different forces could manifest and oppose one another.

The border also offered Akwesasne two models for revenue distribution – one typically linked with American capitalism, and the other linked with a more Canadian idea of wealth sharing. Whereas pro-casino forces represented themselves as job creators and intrepid businessmen in an idiom that would have done twenty-first-century Fox News proud, anti-casino forces expressed a communitarian revenue-sharing model that meshed with the Canadian liberalism of the 1980s. This is not to say that Akwesasronon took cues from either their northern or their southern neighbours; rather, the border represented an open space for exploring, and exploiting, not simply commerce but ideologies.

While some in Akwesasne challenged the Canadian imposition of sovereignty at the border by undermining it with clandestine trade, the Mohawk Council of Akwesasne sought to do so in the courts. In 1988, Mike Mitchell, then grand chief of the Mohawk Council of Akwesasne, refused to pay duty on goods he had brought across the border. The incident, like the 1969 protests, was planned as a media event, to which journalists were invited, and for which children were taken out of school to join Mitchell. The port of entry took part in planning the event, and the "arrest" had been rehearsed the day before.

"The Animals Running the Zoo": Changes in Akwesasne and Border Enforcement

Between the 1960s and 1990, Akwesasne experienced a substantial shift in local governance, a rise in two distinct models for resisting the settler state, and a change in the local economy characterized by a rise in clandestine trade. Members of the community whose political and economic activities were rooted in a belief that the Canadian state was illegitimate at best and anathema at worst were also increasingly well-armed. Border officers stationed at the Cornwall port of entry sat at the centre of these changes looking out. They began to feel these changes as Warriors threatened to take over the port and new directives from above and within were issued in an attempt to manage the cigarette trade and other facets of the clandestine economy. Officers' responsibilities and understandings about their own work shifted alongside changes in Akwesasne and changes in Canada in general.

Things began to change at the Cornwall port of entry and Canadian borders nationwide in the 1980s and 1990s. The state increasingly pressured border officers to simultaneously regulate and facilitate the booming trade that resulted from intergovernmental agreements with the United States. In local enforcement practices in Cornwall, this resulted in two major concerns regarding Akwesasne.

The first was how to process regular travellers coming from Akwesasne. Prior to the establishment of a remission order, which exempts Akwesasronon from paying taxes on personal and community goods brought from the United States into Canada, residents were constitutionally subject to the same regulations as non-Indigenous Canadians. Local enforcement strategies alternated between unofficial policies of a wider threshold of tolerance for Indigenous-carried goods and institutional efforts at standardizing services.

The second concern was contraband trade, particularly the large-scale movement of cigarettes, alcohol, firearms, and drugs. BSOs relied on local intelligence and cooperation between themselves and local Mohawk and US governments to develop successful "anti-smuggling" practices. As I remark above, prior to the 1990s, this trade was dominated by a smaller, identifiable percentage of the population, and as a result, the distinction between "bad guys" and "good guys" was relatively straightforward in the eyes of BSOs. Yet when an increasing number of Akwesasronon, especially youths, came to view the tobacco trade as a viable form of employment, this proved difficult for enforcement. The goal was to identify "bad guys" and limit their ability to transport contraband, but many young people bringing cigarettes across the border were only "bad" by a very limited interpretation of the term.

Tensions on the Rise – Within and Without

Though the oldest officer I interviewed recalled shots being fired at the port of entry as early as the 1970s, those incidents decreased with the hiring of an unarmed Mohawk security service at the port facilities, before rising again in the late 1980s. Officers told me of a Molotov cocktail thrown at the port and of an angry Akwesasronon who smashed equipment with a baseball bat. Work stoppages occurred several times during this period, as the threat of "calling in the Warriors" expanded.

At that time, border officers were unarmed, and would remain so until 2009. If a traveller was perceived as dangerous, the protocol was to let them continue past the port, to be subsequently intercepted by local police. Tensions and security concerns became an increasingly important factor in port operations. One officer I interviewed described his job as "long periods of boredom interspersed by sudden periods of terror." Another told me that the port officers were "this close" to withdrawing from the island until the port facilities were redesigned and bullet-proofed in the 1980s, making the Cornwall port of entry the first bullet-proof port in Canada.

Tensions were on the rise. Port officers were made to formally apologize in 1988, when a local newspaper revealed they had created a T-shirt saying "I survived Canada Customs" that featured an officer under attack by arrows and tomahawks with a torn copy of the Jay Treaty at his feet (Hooper 1988). A former port administrator, speaking at a human-rights tribunal in 2013, remarked that he felt the defensive reinforcement of the port of entry led to a feeling of complacency among officers. Among Akwesasronon this contributed to the image of the port as a Romanesque Canadian outpost upon their own territory.

One month later, following a successful large-scale raid in Akwesasne on twelve warehouses containing drugs, and the arrest of seven

community members, Mohawks identifying themselves with the Warrior Society staged their own raid on the port of entry, when roughly
200 Warriors and supporters arrived at the port, surrounding it in
protest. They then "ordered" Mohawk security personnel to leave
and evicted roughly a dozen non-Indigenous persons from the island.
Border officers withdrew voluntarily, citing a refusal to work. Some
officers remarked that they feared for their lives, while others stated
unequivocally that "We were safe. They made no threats on us at all"
(Staff 1988; but see also Karon 1988).

Notwithstanding all the growing conflict between border services
officers and Akwesasronon in the 1980s, several officers I spoke with
suggested that friction was far greater between front-line officers and a
revolving door of administrators who were seeking to bring those officers
to heel. The primary cause of these conflicts was the disjuncture between
the letter of the Customs Act and the unofficial policy regime that dominated enforcement practices in Cornwall in the 1970s and 1980s.

Officers were pressured by an imperative to maintain peaceful relationships with Akwesasne alongside a contradictory imperative to
treat Indigenous and non-Indigenous persons equally under the law.
For some, the special status afforded to Akwesasronon challenged their
sense of liberalism and the feeling that all Canadian citizens should
be equal under the law. Others recognized the need to treat Akwesasronon distinctly, but lamented the lack of formal legal support for
doing so. This resulted in contradictory desires to treat Akwesasronon
with greater and less scrutiny. In Akwesasne this vacillation was felt as
increasing uncertainty and volatility at the border.

The focus of officers' scrutiny at that time was solely on the movement
of goods, not the movement of bodies. Mohawk travellers could typically enter Canada without any sort of identification, even if this right
was never formalized in documentation. Once familiar with a traveller's face, officers typically waved them through without demanding
ID, and Mohawk security services and experienced officers could help
junior agents identify which travellers truly came from Akwesasne.

One officer relayed an anecdote suggestive of both the internal
stresses of enforcement in Cornwall and the disproportionate strength
of officers in comparison with other ports:

We had this reputation of, in Cornwall, the staff don't take shit from nobody.
And it was because of the environment out there, and we had this one idiot
[new supervisor] come into town, and they always come in with the same
chip on their shoulder that they were going to put us in our place once and
for all, and it was the department that was running the zoo. And we always

took the impression that it was the animals running the zoo. [...] and this guy came out after he was here a month, and he gave us a rule on alcohol. Specifically, on how much alcohol he would allow the Natives to proceed with. And it started at ten bottles. [...] and he was putting this in writing, which we couldn't believe. This was the first idiot that put something in writing. Ten bottles of liquor. So that means he crosses every time and he gets ten bottles of liquor, and we say, he can't do this ... And a white person is allowed none. You've got two sets of rules, and you just can't do that. So one of our officers, one of our quieter, more laid back guys said, "I'm not taking this from you anymore. I'm no longer taking orders from you." And the chief, this guy was the chief, he said then, "Fine, you and your friends here, you've got your good friend in Ottawa" – we got along tremendously at that time with one of our superiors, he recognized the predicament we were in and he felt sort of a connection with us, and we with him – he said "You get along so well with him, then you go to Ottawa and get your orders from him." He [the officer who complained] was gone. He jumped in a car, and he went to Ottawa and said, "You've got to get this guy out of here, there's going to be a war in Cornwall, and it's not between the Natives and staff, it's between the staff and your chief." And he was right. They [the new chiefs] were yanked all the time. They could not deal with it. They were sending raw, non-uniformed people into our midst. And that didn't work. And we have history on our side, we went through, on average, one a year.

Power struggles between officers in Cornwall and the administration in Ottawa played a larger role within the port than struggles between officers and Akwesasronon. Officers' fears were tied to their security – physical security, but also legal security and job security. The above-quoted officer informed me that officers took to recording supervisors surreptitiously in order to protect themselves in the event that they were arrested or fired for failing to uphold the Customs Act. In this regard, the earliest surveillance technologies in the Cornwall port of entry were those used by border officers on one another rather than on the travelling public. Successful administrators were those prized for their ability to look out for the best interests of port staff while still fulfilling Ottawa's expectations.

The 1991 Remission Order – "Put That in Writing"

The Mitchell case shed a light on inconsistencies in regulation that had previously been kept in the shadows. Officers' testimonies pointed to the disjuncture between the letter of the Canada Customs Act and the customary practices of border enforcement at the Cornwall port of entry.

It is worth noting that when Mitchell won in the lower courts, part of his team's argument concerned the unfeasibility of requiring residents of Akwesasne, as a cross-border community, to pay taxes every time they crossed the border. This argument was no longer available with the passage of the Akwesasne Residents Remission Order, a 1991 order-in-council that renders Akwesasronon exempt from duty on "personal" and "community" goods. By the Supreme Court case, representatives of the crown could point to the order as offering a compromise for Akwesasne residents who were crossing the border.

The motivations behind the order's passage are multifaceted. Some in Akwesasne claim that it was the result of successful pressure on their part. My own reading is that the order offered a way for Canada to justify denying broader border-crossing rights to Akwesasne in the Mitchell case. One officer informed me that the Akwesasne Residents Remission Order was a response to officers' own pressuring of their administrators. Officers were tired of risking unemployment, and possibly arrest, for doing what they had always been doing – exempting Akwesasronon from paying taxes on most goods. He explained, as follows:

> And don't let the Mohawks or the department fool you. The only reason that there is a remission order, the Akwesasne remission order, is because we, the officers, said to our department and to our government, we said, we're drawing a line in the sand, and after this date, we will not allow any Native to cross this border without paying full duty and taxes. There's going to be one law here. Because you guys are telling me, I'm breaking the law. And you guys, meaning our department. We didn't trust our department. Because they could come back to us and say, Why did you allow that particular individual with that car to go down the road? Why did you allow them in with this, that, and everything else down the road? What do I have? I'd say, Well, put that it writing. They'd say, I can't put that in writing, it goes against the law. I can't tell you as a superior to do anything that goes against the Customs Act or contravenes the law. And we find, our ass is hanging out in the wind here, believe me, and we finally said after a certain date, and here is the date, no more.

Though the remission order ostensibly sought to provide wider institutional support for the free movement of Akwesasronon throughout their territory, it can also be interpreted as a movement away from regulation tied to interpersonal relationships and customary practices and towards inflexible regulation tied to legal statute. The idea behind the remission order was that, if the CBSA tweaked the rules sufficiently, officers would no longer have to exercise discretion in regulating travel from Akwesasne. Personal knowledge, relationships, and ties to the community would be unnecessary if policy did its job correctly. Officers saw this as a way to protect themselves legally, though a visible long-term impact was a shift in their relationships with the community.

By the 1990s, as discussed in the next section, border work transitioned nationwide toward an increased emphasis on security and policing. The form this transition took at the Cornwall port of entry was bound to the historic relationship with Akwesasne and to a tremendous rise in the clandestine trade in cigarettes, particularly among Mohawk youths. The distinction of "bad guys" and "good guys" lost much of its relevance, as did the capacity for officers to treat Mohawk travellers on an individual basis.

"The 1990s": From Tax Collection to Law Enforcement

"The 1990s" were a formative period in Canadian border work's transition from revenue generation to law enforcement. I refer to the period in quotation marks to highlight that while this change began in the 1980s and continued into the new millennium, both officers and Akwesasronon identify the 1990s, or "the nineties" with the change as a whole.

It is during this transitional period that border work started to become "diffused" (Côté-Boucher 2013; but see also Côté-Boucher 2008). A wide variety of institutional actors became responsible for tasks that had previously been the sole province of port-of-entry personnel. Intelligence gathering, data collection, and data analysis were increasingly handled by public and private agencies that were often located offsite. The daily work practices of officers became further entwined with new policing technologies such as computers, scanning devices, surveillance technologies, and, later on, biometric identification.

The diffusion of border work along the Canada-US border was felt in Akwesasne through the depersonalization of border officers. This was a gradual process by which new enforcement strategies, policies, and technologies diminished the extent to which interpersonal connections framed local border work. One retired officer spoke as follows about the changes he experienced between beginning in the 1970s and retiring in the early 2000s:

Oh, it's changed 100 per cent. It's changed dramatically from when I started. You went from basically not asking questions, just sitting in the booth with the window closed to actually searching the Natives, and it all changed along the lines when the smuggling became really huge with the cigarettes. That's when, back in the nineties, and when the Bingo palace opened, and when the casinos started to open, that everything changed. You went from not even asking questions to making people identify themselves, make sure they are Native, to now, there's the Akwesasne remission order. You're only allowed this much. You're not allowed anything to the accommodation of others. Then we started searching them and started charging duty when it was applicable.

The remission order was designed to protect the communal interests of Akwesasronon and the legal work of local border officers. In effect, it set up a new regulatory standard that justified reduced officer discretion built upon interpersonal relationships between port personnel and Akwesasronon.

From Trust Management to Risk Management

Computers also played a role in this depersonalization. Networked with diffuse intelligence-gathering institutions, computers could generate referrals based on intelligence that officers might not know about, or even agree with. Computers also generate random referrals that mandate secondary inspection on randomly selected travellers. New enforcement technologies and modes of analysis also helped bring an institutional focus on "risk management" (see, e.g., Zureik and Salter 2005) to the Cornwall port of entry, replacing a long-standing emphasis on what could be called "trust management."

BSOs throughout Canada have long relied upon local intelligence to scrutinize travellers. This is a greater necessity in Cornwall, where approximately 70 per cent of travellers are "frequent flyers," travellers from Akwesasne moving across the borderline to go about their daily lives. Knowing the person who is crossing is more possible and more desirable. Older officers I spoke to emphasized the importance of positive relations with Akwesasronon. One, who also had a farm, spoke about trading with Akwesasronon. Another told me he made efforts to attend funerals and public events – doing so in uniform so that people would not feel he was "under cover." Marriages between BSOs and Akwesasronon were not uncommon as well. Trust, or good "face work," in the words of Erving Goffman (Goffman 1967; but see also Sheffer 2009), was at the heart of good border work.

The institutional memory for local port operations was thus contingent upon oral transmission. Officers told me that friends in Akwesasne would often give them a "heads up" about illicit shipments, either out of friendship with officers or out of animosity toward the shippers. Officers

I spoke to told me that their training had been useless in relation to the particularities of working in Akwesasne, and they relied heavily on advice from "old-timers." One officer offered the following anecdote:

> When I started, we didn't have the computerization we have today, and our lookout system was maybe written on a piece of paper. But I remember older officers, when an individual would come through now they'd say you know that guy who went through such and such a car? You keep your eye on him, because we nailed him twelve years ago. Well, I was keeping my eye on that man for more than thirty years, and that's my point. If you had an issue with that guy, and it happened ten years ago with an older officer, that older officer is training this new officer, and I was telling that to people when I was going out the door. You see that guy there, that old bastard, keep an eye on him. Well, Christ, he was about ninety years old by then. So that guy went through his life getting screwed at the border, and that wasn't because of the computer, that was because of what I was told …

Prior to the introduction of computers, intelligence gathering consisted of orally transmitted information built upon trust, or at the very least, interpersonal relations with Akwesasronon.

While officers recognized that digitized risk management could be effective in curtailing clandestine trade, they also saw that it could sour the relationships between officers and travellers. A retired officer was questioned in the courtroom about his decision to inform travellers from Akwesasne when their referral was randomly generated by the computer.[1] The officer expressed an ambivalence about the referrals.

> And I had no problems telling people it was a computer-generated referral because I personally didn't believe in them. On my training from 1990 onward, that was the policy of the CBSA, which has changed. I don't agree with the fact that there don't have to [be] … indicators or probable grounds to do a search, so you could be searched because the computer told me to search you. I'd always been trained that I had to make the decision. You do get enforcement out of that, but it's like going to the casino. You roll the dice. It's to make sure that the frequent fliers are being truthful. Sometimes a random referral might catch something an officer may otherwise miss. When you deal with 400 cars an hour, you miss a lot.

---

1 I discuss this incident and computer-generated referral in greater detail in "Don't Blame Me, It's Just the Computer Telling Me to Do This" (Kalman 2015a).

Officers were now obligated to refer travellers not solely based on their own suspicions but also when flagged by their computer systems. Random referrals stood out as a point of contention among those working in Akwesasne, where many "frequent flyers" had been known to officers for decades. Another retired officer explained his problems with the policy, and the irritation it caused:

> And even when the computer system came in, they had random referrals. The computer would just pick a number at random and that vehicle would be sent to the back. And we just go, "Are you crazy? We know who it is. We've seen the same person four times today, and it's this little grey-haired old lady that's going back and forth to see her kids." "No, you've got to send them to the back, you haven't got a choice." We're going, "Guys, it's February, there's a freaking storm, the lady's eighty years old, are you out of your freaking mind?"

While line officers have no direct say in randomly generated referrals, administrators have the capacity to set the threshold for each port. A former port administrator testified that the threshold for randomly generated referrals at the Cornwall port of entry was lowered during his tenure in order to account for the high rate of commuter traffic from Akwesasne. This suggests that as much as randomly generated referrals deny some discretion to line officers, administrators still exercise choice as to how much discretion they will deny officers through those programs. Thus with "random referrals," the people being stopped may be random, but the number being stopped is not.

The most common sort of computer-generated referral occurs when a vehicle or a particular profile is "flagged" by an outside agency, computer database, or other officer. A retired BSO with long-standing ties to Akwesasne expressed his frustration at the ways in which these referrals impacted his relationship with the community.

> Sometimes it's shitty, because it's like "You know me," [...] and the car's flagged. And you're like, "I've gotta send you in," and they're like "Fuck you." "It's my job, bro. I've got to send you in." If I was [still] doing an enforcement job, I'd rather not know anybody.

Prizing himself as a "chill guy," the officer was incapable of reconciling that self-image with the requirements of his work. Ultimately, he decided that border work was not for him.

The officer went on to say that computer-mandated referrals were also enforced by new surveillance technologies within the port. While these technologies were used to document travellers, they also ensured that officers complied with policy. He remarked,

> Everything's on camera, everything's recorded. You'd be fucked. I'd be in the office in an hour [if I didn't send a flagged traveller to secondary inspection].

Whereas most travellers think of cameras in a port of entry as recording them, officers recognize that they are being watched as well. This surveillance is overt and, since 1990, officers working in Cornwall have feared risking their jobs based on something recorded by their supervisors. This stands in contrast to the previous decade, as mentioned in the previous section, in which officers covertly recorded their supervisors in order to protect their jobs.

In May 1998, an amendment to the Customs Act expanded the powers of border services officers to arrest travellers for violations of Canadian law unrelated to the Customs Act. In effect, it placed much of the authority and responsibility previously held by police officers on the shoulders of border officers. The amendment also mandated that any interagency intelligence gathering between Canadian and American border services be done through formal channels – ending the days an officer in Cornwall could simply call Massena if they had a problem. Border work transitioned from high-autonomy low-responsibility revenue generation to low-autonomy, high-responsibility policing.

Expanding Powers – Combating Clandestine Trade

One Akwesasne chief told me that this expansion of BSOs' powers was the beginning of the end for positive relationships between Akwesasronon and port officers. He argued that the Canadian government had come to Akwesasne framing this expansion of powers as an effort to help protect against the cross-border abduction of children. While this was not a problem specific to Akwesasne, Akwesasronon swallowed the pill without argument, recognizing the importance of protecting children anywhere. He went on to say that once granted these powers, officers began exercising greater authority during primary inspection, particularly in targeting youth for greater scrutiny. Though the expansion of officers' powers accompanied a national directive, in Akwesasne it was often viewed as a direct response to local matters. It soon became clear to the community that the aim of the expanded powers, as far as it concerned Akwesasne, was not to curtail child abduction but to curtail the exploding cigarette trade coming from Akwesasne.

Clandestine trade in tax-free tobacco, or "buttlegging," became a major industry in the 1990s. Cigarettes would be purchased for export in Canada without incurring Canadian taxes, brought into the United States, and then surreptitiously brought back into Canada without declaration. As a result, Akwesasne could bring tax-free Canadian cigarettes into Canada and make a substantial profit doing so. Though much of this trade was conducted at the behest of the non-Indigenous owned and operated R.J. Reynolds Tobacco Company, Akwesasne became internationally known as an epicentre for smuggling (Cockburn 2008; Simpson 2008; Busatta 2009). Many in Akwesasne, especially youths eager to make easy money in a location where jobs are not easy to come by, would travel with a trunk full of cigarettes, earning a big payoff for a few hours' work. People caught transporting cigarettes into Canada were fined rather than arrested, which simply became the cost of doing business. Additionally, as Audra Simpson and Sandra Busatta point out, the tobacco trade was viewed by many participants not as an illegal or immoral practice but as an exercise of sovereignty. When I presented my research to an adult-education course in Akwesasne filled with students in their mid-thirties and early forties, one student's response to her classmate's complaint that officers had profiled Indigenous youths was "Come on, we were all smuggling back then."

The trade was so substantial that Canada established an anti-smuggling task force with the Royal Canadian Mounted Police that operated from 1993 to 2000 and was revived in 2010. Many lead figures in the task force were "old guard" border services officers, who brought their years of rapport and contacts in the community into the service of anti-smuggling efforts.

While BSOs in Cornwall did not go so far as to associate all Akwesasronon with illegality, as officers in other entry ports may have done, local work practices began to emphasize increased scrutiny in efforts to curtail buttlegging. As much as enforcement targeting youths and people driving expensive cars may have helped "risk manage" the tobacco trade, it weakened ties with Akwesasronon, whether or not they were affiliated with the trade. It also demonstrated an assumption by officers that any visibly wealthy young Mohawk is likely engaged in illegal activities.

It was at this time that another technology came to influence the significance of border work – electronic complaint forms.[2] Observing

---

2 For an in-depth discussion of the ways in which technologies such as computerized databases for border enforcement are influencing face-to-face interactions between border officers and travellers, see Kalman, 2015a.

an uptick in community complaints toward the CBSA, the Akwe-sasne Justice Department began compiling a folder detailing officer complaints. The internal handling of complaints renders the CBSA especially opaque, even among law-enforcement bodies, which are frequently characterized by a "lack of transparency" (Côté-Boucher 2013, 27), and was a tremendous source of frustration among Akwe-sasronon, who saw officers as discriminating without any conse-quences. Common complaints focused on the profiling of young Mohawks but also noted that officers were unreasonably aggressive in their exchanges with Akwesasne residents.

Though conflict between the CBSA and Akwesasronon came to a head in 2009, The majority of the stresses that led to protests at the arm-ing of border officers had their roots in the reshaping of the agency in the 1990s. While this period was characterized by economically moti-vated efforts targeting the movement of goods across the border, the next decade would be characterized by politically motivated efforts targeting the movement of people across the border.

From 2001 to 2009: From Protecting Revenue to Protecting People

By the late 1990s and early 2000s, the "old guard" of border services officers from the 1970s and 1980s became the demographic minor-ity. The institutional changes that characterized "the 1990s" were no longer a set of new, highly controversial practices but a defining and taken-for-granted facet of the job. A new generation of officers who saw themselves, from the start, as law-enforcement personnel came to the forefront of local operations. In interviews, these younger officers emphasized pride in nationalized training in Rigaud, Quebec, rather than on-the-job informal training by local staff knowledgeable about Akwesasne. Alongside this generational shift was an institutional shift in enforcement emphasis, from regulating the movement of illegal goods to regulating the movement of "illegal" people. Though counter-smuggling operations were still a priority, "border security" increas-ingly referred to protecting Canadian and American society from illegal immigration and/or potential terrorism rather than to protecting the economy from contraband.

The most cited cause for this transition in border policing is the ter-rorist attacks of 11 September 2001 (9/11), and their aftermath. Before it was revealed that the hijackers had arrived in the United States with American visas, fingers were pointed at Canada as their point of ingress. Akwesasne received international media attention as a possible entry point for the terrorists (The Mohawk Council of Akwesasne 2007). The idea that the Canadian border was a weak spot for American security encouraged the United States to push for continental agreements on border security, and emboldened Canada to expand the powers of its officers. The idea that Akwesasne was a weak spot within a weak spot led to increased pressure within the Cornwall port of entry to conform to national, rather than local, enforcement standards.

Three major legislative actions reshaped Canadian border enforcement in the wake of 9/11. First, in 2003 the Canada Border Services Agency (CBSA) was formed out of three previous agencies – Canada Customs and Revenue, Citizenship and Immigration Canada, and the Canadian Food Inspection Agency. Second, the Universal Arming Initiative announced in 2006 sought to arm and train all BSOs in firearm use by 2016. Finally, the 2007 Western Hemisphere Travel Initiative (WHTI, pronounced "witty"), an international agreement spearheaded by the United States, set a standard for "smart identification" and intelligence sharing by border-regulatory agencies throughout North and South America.

In itself, the reorganization of Canadian border agencies into the CBSA did not cause as substantial a change in day-to-day enforcement practices as the transition towards policing and diffusion of border work did in the 1990s. The daily work practices of officers had already changed, although the extent to which the CBSA is in fact a "service agency" has been contested by the agency itself, seeking to distance itself from the legal requirements of publicly funded service organizations.

WHTI sought to standardize cross-border identification documents in North and South America by mandating "secure" documents. By standardizing documentary requirements for cross-border travel, states could place a greater emphasis on intelligence-gathering processes well before a traveller gained the documents that they would present at the border. Embedded with intelligence information and registered on shared databases, "smart" travel documents carry a great deal more information about travellers than their antecedents. Borders increasingly became the last, rather than first-and-only, lines of defence for security operations and intelligence gathering.

Yet WHTI did not address the fact that both Canada and the United States had a long-standing history of accepting Indigenous status documents rather than passports as international travel documents. Though both states have sought to integrate security features into these status documents, this has been a slow process, resulting in a disjuncture between the requirements of WHTI and on-the-ground acceptance of documents lacking WHTI-compliant security features.

The Haudenosaunee passport, a travel document printed by the Haudenosaunee Confederacy, has been especially problematic for WHTI's implementation. These passports have been produced since the 1920s, and are indicative of the confederacy's efforts to articulate and enact its own sovereignty at the border. Many surveyed in Akwesasne stated that they would prefer to travel using a Haudenosaunee passport but do not do so because they are often not accepted, especially by Canadian officers.

A few instances of passport use and refusal have received media attention in recent years. One traveller from Akwesasne had her passport confiscated as a "fantasy document," which is the CBSA's official designation for documents that are not recognized by the Canadian state. The passport was subsequently returned, with an apology, to the Mohawk Nation Council of Chiefs. Many eyes were turned to the travails of the Iroquois Nationals lacrosse team whose travel to the lacrosse world championships in the United Kingdom was denied in 2010 (Price 2010; Kaplan 2010). The United States argued that the passports lacked the security features required in WHTI-compliant documents, refusing the passports on security rather than sovereignty grounds. Lacrosse players, several of whom were from Akwesasne, refused any offer of visa assistance from the United States, wishing to play "as Haudenosaunee." Though the team could not play, international media attention brought Haudenosaunee sovereignty and border issues to public attention worldwide. The confederacy has responded by designing future passports that match, or surpass, the security requirements of WHTI-compliant passports – a long and expensive process.

Though WHTI clearly distinguished between valid and invalid travel documentation, its implementation at the Cornwall port of entry was not absolute.[3] At the time of my arrival in Akwesasne in early 2012, many Akwesasronon still entered Canada without showing any identification. Yet this unofficial policy of non-carding was irregular. Some officers always asked for ID; others only asked if they were unfamiliar with the traveller. It was customary for many in Akwesasne to present ID only when asked for it – some without complaint, others asking, "Why do you need to see my ID?" When I drove with Mohawk travellers, officers often looked at me before asking my passengers for their identification. Once, while sitting in the backseat of a full car coming

---

3 I discuss document requirements and exemption in greater detail in my article *Proofing Exemption* (2018).

from a birthday party at around 3:00 a.m., I was surprised that the officer on duty simply waved us across. I discuss this practice of not ID-ing Indigenous travellers in much greater detail in chapter 6. The practice, which was never a policy, was officially ended in 2014 with a policy of "universal compliance verification." The move caught many in the community by surprise, resulting in long lines to get across the border, as some travellers had not bothered to bring documents, and others were forced to produce non-scannable documents, each of which had to be entered manually by officers.

The CBSA's arming initiative was the most influential factor in reshaping border work in the early twenty-first century, and represented a triumph for the CBSA unions in placing border officers on an equal footing with other Canadian law-enforcement officers (Côté-Boucher 2013). The arming initiative sent an international message that Canada was serious about border enforcement, and brought more than $100 million of additional funding to the agency. Drawing on her own interviews with border officers, Côté-Boucher shows that arming had a multifaceted impact on the ways in which BSOs conceptualized their own work, one intimately tied to the association of guns with masculinity in the wake of feelings of emasculation caused by the loss of discretion in the 1990s.

The arming initiative also furthered the generational divide between BSOs who began their jobs as law-enforcement officers and those who came into their positions as revenue collectors and were then told they had to change roles. For comparison, suppose that the Canadian government were suddenly to mandate that all census takers must carry a hand gun. Many senior officers preferred early retirement to arming, furthering the generational demographic shift in ports of entry. In the next section, I discuss the local impact of the arming initiative at the Cornwall port of entry and the 2009 protests and port closure.

The Protests of 2009

On the evening of 31 May 2009, a large group of protesters from Akwesasne gathered around the Cornwall port of entry, then located on Cornwall Island. They had been present for weeks, and some for longer, protesting the port's implementation of the CBSA's Universal Arming Initiative, which was slated to commence on 1 June. Protesters held up signs reading "No guns on the Island," "Guns make it easy to kill," and "This is Mohawk land." Prior to the midnight deadline for arming, port-of-entry personnel packed their belongings and left the port. Claiming concern for their security, instead of simply heading north into the city of Cornwall, personnel drove south via New York State before turning north into Canada and looping back to the city of Cornwall.

In the aftermath of the port closure, the Seaway International Bridge Corporation immediately closed road access between Cornwall Island, the city of Cornwall, and the southern bridge connecting Cornwall to the United States. The island and its residents were subsequently marooned. Shortly thereafter, the bridge connecting the island to New York State was blockaded, but only in one direction, making it possible for island residents to leave but not return. Though the US port of entry serviced few if any travellers, it remained open during this period. Regular traffic through the island recommenced more than a month later when a temporary CBSA port facility was opened in the city of Cornwall, north of the island, on 13 July 2009, and bridge access was fully restored. Arriving alongside the new port facility was a "reporting-in policy" obligating anyone going to the island to first report themselves to the city of Cornwall. I discuss this policy at length in the next chapter.

What took place in the hours leading up to the withdrawal is still contentious. Representatives of the CBSA have blamed Akwesasronon for threatening the port, while Akwesasronon accuse CBSA officers of overreacting to peaceful protests. Below, I quote at length from the proceedings of the Federal Court of Canada in the case brought by Grand Chief Timothy Thompson, the Mohawk Council of Akwesasne, and the Mohawks of Akwesasne against the Minister of Public Safety and Emergency Preparedness, the president of the Canada Border Services Agency, and the Minister of Transport, Infrastructure and Communities. Thompson and the MCA sought a judicial review of the activities of the CBSA in the wake of the protests and the institution of the reporting-in policies.

It is interesting to note that the court used the first person "I" in its findings on the protests, something it had avoided for all other parts of the proceedings. Though striving for neutrality, and representing undisputed facts, the choice of facts presented aligns with the court's ultimate finding in favour of the Minister of Public Safety, the CBSA, and the Minister of Transport.

The Protests on 31 May 2009 and the Closure of the CBSA Facility

[41] There is also a disagreement between the parties as to the nature of events which took place on May 31, 2009. The applicants submit that there was a peaceful political demonstration against the arming of CBSA Border Services Officers scheduled to take effect the following day. The applicants point to the fact that no one was ever arrested for actions occurring on that

evening as support for their position that the protest remained peaceful. On the other hand, the CBSA witnesses state that the protests on the evening of May 31, 2009 presented a threat to the safety of the CBSA officers on duty.

[42] While the two sides place a very different spin on what happened at the CBSA facility on Cornwall Island on the evening of May 31, 2009, I do not, however, understand there to be any dispute about the fact that several hundred protesters gathered at the facility. Some of the protesters were wearing combat fatigues, and some wore balaclavas or bandanas obscuring their faces. A large backhoe was also brought to the site.

[43] At approximately 8:00 in the evening, Grand Chief Thompson and others presented Mr. Markell with the "third and final notice" of the MCA resolution. Mr. Markell had a discussion with Chief Cheryl Jacobs who asked if the implementation of the arming of the Border Services Officers could be postponed. Chief Jacobs also advised Mr. Markell that she was doing her best to control the protesters, but that "there was a group of angry men prepared to take matters into their own hands."

[44] Over the course of the evening, individuals wearing "Warrior" insignias on their clothing shone lights at surveillance cameras on the site, making it difficult to monitor the area around the CBSA facility. Bonfires were also set at several locations surrounding the CBSA facility.

[45] At around 11:00 p.m., Mr. Markell spoke to Jerry Swamp, the Chief of the Akwesasne Mohawk Police Service. It is uncontroverted that Police Chief Swamp told Mr. Markell that he was worried that his officers might not be able to control the crowds, and that it may be in the CBSA's best interests if the CBSA staff left Cornwall Island.

[46] Approximately 40 minutes later, Mr. Markell was advised that SIBC [Seaway International Bridge Corporation] employees working at the toll booths on the north end of Cornwall Island were being evacuated out of fear for their safety.

[47] Richard Comerford, the Regional Director General for the CBSA's Northern Ontario Region, was monitoring the situation by video feed. Just before midnight, Mr. Comerford spoke by phone to Police Chief Swamp, who advised him that there was a large crowd gathering at the CBSA facility on Cornwall Island, and that he could not guarantee the safety of the Border Services Officers. The applicants do not dispute the fact that Police Chief Swamp suggested to Mr. Comerford that CBSA employees should leave the facility.

[48] Mr. Comerford then instructed Mr. Markell to evacuate CBSA personnel from the Cornwall Island facility and the port of entry was closed.

The 2009 protests and their aftermath represented a sort of "epito-mizing event"[4] for the changing relationship between Akwesasronon and Canadian BSOs. More important than what may have occurred is what different actors think occurred, and the way they talk about it. I discuss this in greater detail in chapter 6's "border stories." How-ever, in brief, it is worth noting the variety of framings of the event that have been presented. Akwesasronon are at times represented as uncontrollable (invoking, and sometimes even employing the "wild Indian" or "savage" tropes); border services officers are represented as spiteful and inflexible; and leadership on either side as either fool-ishly ineffective or cunningly Machiavellian. Fire was a common met-aphor invoked by both Akwesasronon (with bonfires seen as a symbol of community togetherness) and border officers (with fire seen as a symbol of lawlessness and danger). The protests made it possible for people on either side of the protest lines to justify the stories they tell themselves about both themselves and the people on the opposite side of the protest lines.

In the month following the CBSA's withdrawal, Akwesasne's commu-nity solidarity was at an all-time high, as residents developed makeshift ferry services to support the suddenly isolated Cornwall Island resi-dents. Shortly thereafter, when service returned to the city of Cornwall, residents were annoyed by the long wait times but appreciated the new freedom of movement onto the island without the need to go through customs. Though the CBSA demanded that travellers report to the city of Cornwall whenever arriving on the island, this policy, which I discuss in detail in chapter 5, did not become implemented in practice until Sep-tember 2009. Many I spoke with in Akwesasne suggested that officers blamed Akwesasronon for the port's relocation, and that they were not shy about sharing this feeling. Several told me that officers made gun signs with their hands at Mohawk travellers as they drove by. Many feel that the reporting-in policy and vehicle seizures are collective punish-ment directed towards Akwesasronon.

---

4 The term "epitomizing event" is here drawn from Raymond Fogelson's "The Ethnohistory of Events and Nonevents," in which he writes,

> Plot-generated "events" may be constructed for purposes of narrativity, for "telling the story." Yet, surrounding the "real" or constructed events is a residuum of cultural data critical for historians and ethnohistorians. These include values, meanings, symbolism, worldviews, social structural principles, and other variables of cultural analysis without which any event, real or imagined, cannot be adequately interpreted. (1989, 141)

By securing support for the arming initiative, the CBSA union was able to position itself as a law-enforcement agency on equal standing with the RCMP and other police services. Many in Akwesasne are quick to point out that it was the union, rather than the local administration, that most firmly refused to budge on the arming issue. While the CBSA union stated unequivocally that officers would not return to the island, Ottawa responded that the union did not have the authority to make that call.

The 2009 standoff between Akwesasronon and BSOs epitomized their relationship following decades of change in both the community and the port. It simultaneously represented the culmination of long-standing conflicts and set the tone for the future relationship between the two entities. Both CBSA officers and Akwesasronon suggested that while the arming initiative spurred the protests and withdrawal, it was simply the straw that broke the camel's back – a capstone on decades of increasing antagonism, difference, and loss of trust between officers and community members. Though Akwesasronon and CBSA administrators both suggest that rapport between the two has begun to be re-established, they also accept that the relationship is far from positive.

Conclusion

As I write this, nearly a dozen years have passed since the 2009 protests that resulted in the closure of the CBSA port of entry on Cornwall Island. The protest fires have been reignited a few times, recently in support of the nationwide "Idle No More" movement, and in opposition to local enforcement policies.

Looking at a recent history of CBSA-Akwesasne relationships, one cannot point to a "golden age" in which officers and Akwesasne residents got along swimmingly. The existence of "the border" remains a perennial point of contention. There has always been friction, although the quality of the friction has changed. By some measure, relationships between the CBSA and the community are less heated now than they were in the 1990s and 2000s. While anti-smuggling activities still remain a concern for CBSA line officers, their autonomy in dealing with these matters has been diffused to other law-enforcement agencies. Many of the most controversial officers no longer work at the port of entry, replaced by a younger and more uniformly trained generation who have never seen themselves as anything other than law-enforcement personnel.

In a sense, there is more "distance" today, both physical and social, between border enforcement and the community. Today, few CBSA officers find themselves in the Akwesasne Mohawk Territory unless they are en route to someplace else in New York State. Officers are not playing hockey at the Turtle Island Arena with Akwesasne residents, nor are they socializing with them during their off hours.

This distancing can be understood as a consequence of the depersonalization of border work at the Cornwall port of entry. Local enforcement, and what defined "the local," transitioned from a shared context in the 1970s and 1980s to an increasingly disparate divide between local concerns and national policy by the 1990s. A combination of technologies, policies, and practices redefined the space of "the border" for both Akwesasne residents and BSOs.

As Akwesasronon and border officers increasingly saw themselves as strangers to one another, the terms by which they understood one another, and the border itself, were rendered both more distinct and less familiar. Not only did officers and Akwesasronon come to experience the space of the border differently, they came to understand its meaning differently. What "the border" means to a Mohawk traveller and what "the border" means to a CBSA officer are two different things, and there are fewer opportunities to share these interpretations than there were in the past.

Even if the social and physical distance between officers and Akwesasronon has increased, the necessity of cross-border travel has not. Akwesasronon still move across the border daily and account for the clear majority of international (and now domestic) travel through the port. Akwesasronon travellers not only go through processing when driving across a port of entry but are also targeted by "reporting-in" policies that obligate them to bring themselves to the port when crossing a borderline.

In the next section, I transition from an account of how this border came to Akwesasne to a discussion of the policies, laws, and logics that bring Akwesasronon to the border, often against their wishes. These policies are built around a disjuncture between an "ideal type" of border and the geopolitical realities of the Akwesasne Mohawk Territory. The definition of borders simply does not work in Akwesasne as it does elsewhere along the Canada-US border. To get a sense of the variety of definitions officers and travellers employ, I ask, "What sort of line is a border?" and explore what happens at the Cornwall port of entry post-2009 when the site of the borderline and the site of border enforcement fail to correspond.

Chapter Five

"Reporting in" to/from Akwesasne

Introduction

In summer 2014, the Seaway International Bridge Corporation (SIBC) decommissioned the derelict high-level bridge connecting Cornwall Island to the city of Cornwall to the north and replaced it with a sleek, smooth, substantially shorter low-level bridge (figure 5.1). The old bridge had been designed decades earlier in accordance with the dream of a Canadian commercial corridor along the St. Lawrence River. Ultimately, it was never used for cross-river commerce, as another high-level bridge connecting the island to New York State to the south became the preferred means for seaway trade, with ships passing under it rather than the northern bridge.

Yet the northern bridge remained the only way to travel overland between the island and Canada. Drivers had no choice but to travel along its massive rickety frame, which swayed and creaked when high winds hit the St. Lawrence.

During my year of fieldwork, the bumping of my car against the bridge's potholes became the theme song to my daily commute. At the foot of the bridge was the third incarnation of the "temporary" port of entry, located in the city of Cornwall since 2009.[1]

With line-ups to the port of entry leading directly onto the bridge, I, and many in Akwesasne, might spend twenty minutes to more than an hour every day waiting in line at the bridge in order to get into Canada. Some travellers would proceed to the city of Cornwall, though many – residents of Cornwall Island – were obligated to report themselves to

---

1 This is still the case with the current, newer, low-level bridge. However, the discussion in this section emphasizes the long wait times associated with the older, high-level bridge.

Figure 5.1. Cornwall bridges. Photo courtesy of the author.

the port of entry at the foot of the bridge only to double back and return to their home on the island, which they had just passed.

The bridge had become a part of the landscape, and like many in Akwesasne, I was mostly glad to see it go, despite the memories. In celebration of a new bridge's construction and remembrance of the old bridge's history, the SIBC held a "Day of the Bridge" on 8 July 2014, when the old bridge would be open to foot traffic (figure 5.2). Tables dotted the bridge, displaying photographs from its history – a newspaper clipping from 1962 read, "Cornwall-Massena Bridge opens July 3, another great bond between two nations!" – and with volunteers handing out bottled water and souvenirs. One extended family from Cornwall Island gathered for a group photo overlooking the island.

As I was in town for a few days, I decided to meet up with some friends living on Cornwall Island. Since the bridge would be open, I decided to walk from the city of Cornwall south to the island, meet my friends there, and then walk back to my car in the city of Cornwall. I had walked along the bridge several times in the past as part of political

Figure 5.2. Bridge foot traffic on "Day of the Bridge," 8 July 2014. Photo courtesy of the author.

demonstrations that closed down the cross-border corridor, first in solidarity with the Canada-wide "Idle No More" movement, and later on in protest at Canadian border enforcement policies.

When I reached the terminus of the bridge on Cornwall Island, I found myself unable to continue onto the Akwesasne Mohawk Territory. A barbed-wire fence blocked any foot traffic from the island (figure 5.3) with signs, facing the island, reading "BRIDGE IS ACCESSIBLE FROM CORNWALL ONLY. S'IL VOUS PLAIT NOTER QUE LE PONT SERA ACCESSIBLE A PARTIR DU COTE (SIC) DE CORNWALL SEULEMENT." The French translation was comical, as practically nobody in Akwesasne speaks French, and everyone speaks English. Akwesasne residents who wanted to join in "the Day of the Bridge" would have to drive from Cornwall Island, Canada, traverse a toll booth, report themselves at Canadian customs, and then proceed into the city of Cornwall (without having set foot off "Canadian" soil). Then, walking to the point where the bridge reached their home, they would have to turn around, walk back along the bridge into the city

Figure 5.3. Barbed-wire fence on the bridge. Photo courtesy of the author.

of Cornwall, and drive back across the toll booth once more before heading home.

Before encountering the fence, I had looked forward to writing about the event. I had the image in my head of Akwesasronon walking from Cornwall Island, and residents of the city of Cornwall walking from Cornwall, and the two groups meeting halfway. I could discuss the border as bridge, and two populations sharing their own unique memories of time spent on the bridge. Yet the image I found was a barbed-wire fence rather than a bridge. This provoked two questions: First, why was it necessary for the SIBC to block travellers from Cornwall Island, Ontario, from walking into Cornwall, Ontario? And second, how did "the border" come to manifest as a bridge for some and a barrier for others?

"The border," like Akwesasne, can be different things to different people at different times. Above I provide an anecdote in which, over the course of a single event, "the border" was a site of both nostalgia and frustration – a bridge and a barrier. What constituted "the border" on the "day of the bridge" depended largely on which side of the bridge you found yourself on, and which direction you were going.

The past several chapters have tried to bring context to the contemporary border in Akwesasne – looking at the histories, ideologies, and motivations that feed into many of the interactions between border services officers (BSOs) and travellers. This chapter engages more critically with the question "What is a border?" in Akwesasne – suggesting that Akwesasronon and border services officers employ very different conceptual models when engaging with "the border." The same word has a different meaning and history among the various actors.

I also look at the underlying logics of local border-enforcement practices specific to the Cornwall port of entry. These practices have resulted in the designation of Cornwall Island as Canada's only officially regulated "mixed traffic corridor" (space in which both individuals who have not left Canada and individuals who have crossed the border from the United States but have not yet been processed at a port of entry circulate simultaneously). I suggest that "reporting-in" policies created by both Canada and the United States to regulate the movement of bodies across the borderline in and around the Akwesasne Mohawk Territory are the consequence of the physical disjuncture between the site of the borderline in Akwesasne and the sites of border enforcement.

An "ideal type" of border is one in which travellers, after crossing a line, are directly filtered into a port of entry for processing. In Akwesasne, the reality fails to mesh with this ideal. There, one can cross the border without being processed, or traverse a port of entry without having stepped across a borderline. State efforts to force a particular vision of how borders *should* work in a site where the reality is far different have had mixed but largely negative consequences both for Akwesasne and for relations between Akwesasronon and local, particularly Canadian, BSOs.

This chapter looks at the various things "the border" can be to various people, and the consequences of these conceptions. Different understandings of borders and their purpose are responsible for the events that brought "the border" to Akwesasne and Akwesasne to "the border." They are responsible for the policies that regulate movement within and across the territory and bring travellers into contact with officers. These understandings are also responsible for the assumptions both officers and travellers bring to those interactions. This in turn influences what takes place when the two meet, and the ease, or difficulty, of cross-border encounters. Here, I examine what a border means to different people, and how those meanings play out in interactions between border officers and cross-border travellers. In doing so, I point to border crossing as a moment in which two often conflicting sets of ideas about "what is going on" must find some sort of resolution.

Borders as Lines, Lines as Borders

Different definitions of borders necessitate different ways of engaging with them. Across academic disciplines, scholars have presented borders in terms of metaphors (Anzaldúa 1999), as the territorial embodiment of a bundle of ideas (Johnson and Graybill 2010, 2), as an ideal type representing the limits of national sovereignty (Weber 1958; Gellner 1983, 1), as an essential facet of state ontology (Torpey 2000), and so on. Border studies has also offered windows into the ways in which a variety of disciplines privilege particular understandings of borders (Van Houtum 2005) with the recognition that a scholar's conception of "border" influences their study.

Anthropological approaches to bordering range from examinations of borders as sites and instantiations of state power and resistance to more localized explorations of borders as symbolically rich conceptual objects (Donnan and Wilson 1999, 1–4). Borders and borderlands are of particular interest to political theorizations of the state, as "an anthropology of the margins offers a unique perspective to the understanding of the state, not just because it captures exotic practices, but because it suggests that such margins are a necessary entailment of the state" (Das and Poole 2004, 4).

While many border scholars, especially in anthropology, recognize borders as "meaning making, and meaning carrying entities" (Donnan and Wilson 1999, 4), less attention has been paid to the ways in which actors involved with borders, such as cross-border travellers, policymakers, and BSOs, understand them. Such a gap makes sense considering how rarely and reluctantly these actors theorize what constitutes a border. "The border," as it relates to everyday practices, tends to be taken for granted by people who cross and enforce it on a regular basis. It may be a banal facet of one's engagement with the nation state, but it is by no means benign (Billig 1995). Anthropology, with its emphasis on long-term research engagement and ethnography, and its focus on the taken for granted, offers a useful methodological tool set for examining how different actors orient their activities along different understandings of "what is a border."

When people talk about borders, they are often talking about lines. Tim Ingold (2007) has suggested a movement away from thinking of lines in terms of boundedness and toward an emphasis on lines of movement – that is, trails or pathways. Though Ingold may be correct that imposing lined boundaries on essentially dynamic organisms (his examples are organic, but states are, I think, parallel here) can constrain, suffocate, and damage, if not destroy, it is at the intersection of lines of movement and borderlines that border policy takes shape. Indeed, the expectation of linear travel is a necessary facet of state regulation of borderlines.

"The border" is often understood as a combination of two objects: (1) the borderline and (2) the port (the site of enforcement). Further, the act of "border crossing" is frequently understood not in terms of geospatial traversal of either the borderline or the port but in terms of an interaction between a traveller and an officer. While most border actors do not reflect upon conceptual facets of borders and border crossing, they nevertheless unconsciously incorporate them into their practices.

Generally speaking, the port, the borderline, and processing, are spatially and temporally contiguous. As an "ideal type" for overland cross-border travel in North America and much of the world, as soon as a person traverses the borderline, they reach a port of entry where they are processed by border officers. As a result, even if the borderline, port, and processing can be conceptually distinguished, they are, for all intents and purposes, bundled. In most cases, the port may be conceptually distinct from the borderline, but such a distinction matters little.

The bundle of borderline, port, and processing comes undone in and around Akwesasne. On reserve land, one can cross the borderline at various points without encountering any sign of US or Canadian customs enforcement. Ports of entry are located at great distances from the borderline, and travellers are often processed by border services officers even if they have never crossed the line. At present, thousands of Akwesasronon live sandwiched between American and Canadian ports of entry. Because the port, line, and processing are physically and temporally separated around Akwesasne, their disparity as distinct and not necessarily interwoven ways of conceptualizing the border is rendered starker. In this case, the port is distinct from the borderline, and this distinction matters greatly.

Around Akwesasne, local border-enforcement policies require travellers to "report in" at a port whenever they cross a borderline, even if this requires a great deal of time and effort. These policies represent efforts on the part of policymakers and enforcement officers to artificially bring port and line together, even if they are physically separate. In practice, the policies have added new wrinkles for enforcement practices, have isolated Akwesasne, and have caused great difficulties for the community. When Akwesasronon do "report in" to customs, they bring their own set of assumptions about the border, which often conflict with those of officers.

Broadly speaking, BSOs tend to consider "the border" in terms of the borderline, and they orient their enforcement practices accordingly. Travellers, on the other hand, tend to consider "the border" in terms of the port, and they orient their travel practices accordingly. These different emphases as to what constitutes a border play out in interactions between officers and travellers. They impact the sorts of questions officers ask and the sorts of answers they may receive, as well as the efficacy of enforcement practices and resistances to those practices.

A worthwhile undertaking for border scholarship across disciplines would be to investigate the ways in which border actors organize their activities and interactions around different concepts of what constitutes a border. Because of its geopolitical situation, Akwesasne offers a useful opportunity to examine the ways in which seemingly indistinguishable facets of borders are in fact distinct, and the ways in which this distinction matters. Further, the case study of Akwesasne offers a window into the underlying logics and consequences of policy innovations designed to bring the reality of borders in line with the political and policy ideal. When policymakers try to force a geographically separated borderline and port together, as they do in Akwesasne, it has severe implications for the population residing in between.

When Do You Cross a Border?

In the introduction to this book, I invite readers to imagine themselves driving from Canada into the United States (or vice versa). I repeat this thought exercise once more in the context of the three facets of borders that I wish to emphasize at present: borders as lines, as sites of enforcement, and as exchanges with border officers.

Imagine yourself driving south from Montreal into New York State. You would most likely cross at the Champlain-Lacolle crossing. Your car follows a Quebec highway south until you see a large sign, "United States of America," and several lanes of cars leading into a primary inspection lane (PIL) booth. You choose to queue up at one lane and immediately regret your decision as the other lanes seem to be moving much faster. After waiting on line (New Yorkers wait "on line" rather than "in line") for an interminable period of time, you reach a booth housing a border services officer. Assuming you do not have any problems with processing, the BSO takes your travel document, asks several questions, and after returning your document says, "Have a nice day." Your car moves forward and heads onto a New York State highway.

If friends or family members called you along the way, at what point in your journey would you say, "I am at the border," "I am crossing the border," or "I just crossed the border"? You traversed the border-line separating the United States from Canada more than one hundred metres before seeing the large "United States of America" sign. By the time your car queued, you were within the legal jurisdiction of the United States. In that vein, the officer who spoke to you was not so much determining whether or not you could *enter* the country. From their perspective, you already had; you had crossed the borderline. They were instead determining whether, and under what circumstances, you could *proceed* within the United States. However, most members of the travelling public, myself included, would not say "I've just crossed the border" until after completing their interaction with the officer.

In this context, crossing the border was not the same as crossing the bor-derline. The border, in our example, can be thought of in three ways: (1) as the line differentiating states (what I refer to as the borderline), (2) as the site of the port of entry (POE) for processing travellers who cross that line, and (3) as the act of processing at that POE. These different understandings of the border (borders as lines, borders as sites of enforcement, borders as enforcement practices) are not simply conceptual tools for understanding borders. Rather, when officers and travellers talk about and negotiate the border, they employ those aspects and act accordingly. In the following section, drawing on ethnographic work with BSOs and Akwesasronon travellers, I offer examples of two different orientations towards what "the border" means and some implications of these orientations.

Asking Border Officers, "What Is a Border?"

I first considered the disparity between my own notion of the border and that of officers when "reporting in" to US customs following a day's work at the MCA administrative building in St. Regis Village. As always after leaving the village, I drove without stopping to the US port of entry in Massena. I parked my car, grabbed my passport, shut off my mobile phone, and walked into the port office. I waited for a seated offi-cer to look up, and told him, "I'm reporting in." He replied, "Where are you coming from?" I told him, "St. Regis." This dialogue represented a script I repeated hundreds of times over the duration of my fieldwork. The officer asked me, "What were you doing there?" I told him, "I study the border there." He looked up from his desk, and asked cynically (and off script), "Is it any different from the border here?"

I was surprised by the officer's question. How could he equate the heavily visible, highly militarized Massena port of entry, with body armour, automatic weapons, fences, barbed wire, and high-tech sur-veillance (figure 5.4), with the largely invisible "border" in Akwesasne,

Figure 5.4. Massena port of entry. Photo by Michael Moran, Michael Moran Photography, Inc.

with its totally unregulated fields, farmland, and roads (figure 5.5)? The photograph shown in figure 5.4 was taken by Michael Moran Photography and can be found on the website belonging to the architecture firm of Smith-Miller and Hawkinson, which designed the port. While there are many images of the Massena port of entry online, members of the public are prohibited from taking photographs there. At one protest during my research, journalists were detained for photographing protests at the site of the port. The figure 5.5 photograph is one of several I took of "the border" in Akwesasne, this one standing out because of the overgrown post marker. These two representations of the border are so markedly distinct I had difficulty understanding the officer's incredulity in asking whether the border was any different between the two sites. How could he have imagined any situation in which "the border" was the same in both places?

The answer came from my realization that the officer and I had fundamentally different ideas of what "the border" was. When I said, "I study the border," I was thinking about the port, border posts, signs (or lack thereof), the laws, and the interactions I could see and study.

Figure 5.5. "Border" with overgrown post marker. Photo courtesy of the author.

When asking me if the border was any different, he was thinking in terms of the borderline. From that perspective, there really was no difference between the border in Akwesasne and the border at the Massena port of entry. An invisible line looks the same wherever one draws it.

This helped me make sense of an exchange with an American port-of-entry (POE) supervisor weeks earlier in which I asked the supervisor, "What is the border?" I expected a philosophical or legalistic answer, but he looked at me quizzically and pointed to the location of the borderline at the southern span of the Three Nations Bridge, saying, "It's just over there."

Officers are often sensitive to the fact that the border means different things to different people, especially around Akwesasne. When I asked a retired CBSA officer, "What is the border?," he replied, "It depends on who you ask." When I remarked that I was asking him, he replied, "What's the border to me? It's the line that divides Canada and the United States."

Although I found the officer's perspective representative of that of BSOs more broadly, the Canada Border Services Agency (CBSA) informed me that I could not ask their current employees, "What is the border?" I was told that for BSOs, the border is exactly what the government defines it to be, and as far as performance of their duties is concerned, BSOs do not have their own perspectives on what constitutes a border. This prompted me to search for the Canadian government's definition of the border, though with little success.

Broadly speaking, Mohawk, Canadian, and US government actors tend to consider the border in terms of a line of demarcation. When I asked officers "what" the border is, their answers typically focused on "where" the border is. As they described it, "the border" created enforcement, and not the other way around. This conception of the border, favoured (though by no means exclusively) by border officers, affects their practices and the assumptions they bring into interactions with travellers, who often have disparate views as to what constitutes a border.

Looking for "What Is the Border?" in Legal Documents

Since officers told me that their definition of "border" was whatever Canada defined "the border" to be, I thought it would be useful to search for Canada's definition of the border in legislation. This proved more challenging than I had expected. Apart from the word "border" in the acronym CBSA, the Canada Customs Act – the legislation responsible for Canadian border regulation – contains only one explicit use of the term "border." Otherwise, the document details regulations concerning people and goods "entering Canada," and not people or goods "crossing the border into Canada."

The one section that explicitly mentions the border was added in 2012, to "designate as a mixed-traffic corridor a portion of a roadway or other access way that (a) leads from an international border to a customs officer [...]" (Customs Act 11.6). The term "border" in this context refers solely to the international borderline. It should be noted that Akwesasne is the only so-designated "mixed-traffic corridor," and this section of the Customs Act was almost certainly added to address enforcement problems following the removal and relocation of the Cornwall Island port of entry. This suggests that the only explicit mention of "the border" in the Customs Act, the act dealing with the entirety of Canadian border regulation, was added very recently and in response to difficulties over border regulation in Akwesasne.

Both Canada and the United States have gone to greater lengths to define "where" the border is, rather than "what" the border is. The

International Boundary Commission (IBC) offers a more direct engagement with the term "border" than the Customs Act, but ultimately emphasizes the "where" rather than the "what." As the commission's information brochure states,

> The proper definition and demarcation of that boundary [the Canada-US border] is as essential today as it has been throughout history for law enforcement, land administration, customs and immigration [...] the story of defining the boundary starts with the Treaty of Paris in 1783, which described the border between British North America and the American states. (International Boundary Commission n.d.)

"Definition," when it comes to the border, refers more often to its shape than its meaning – delimiting rather than describing.

This emphasis on the "where" of borders was not unique to US and Canadian state actors. The Mohawk government also emphasized the location of the borderline when circulating a press release concerning the possibility of moving "the border." In this release, "the border" referred to the line of demarcation, and not the port of entry.

Though many government actors I spoke with privileged the borderline when considering the border, I do not want to be too stark in this assertion. Border officers, especially those serving the ports of entry around Akwesasne, are often sensitive to a variety of ways of thinking about "the border" and aware that the term means different things to different people at different times. In the same vein, many in Akwesasne are acutely aware of the location of the borderline. Even if the line is largely invisible within the territory, the location of a person's residence vis-à-vis the borderline can affect their access to a wide variety of services. Yet at the same time, in the everyday lives of many travellers both within and outside Akwesasne, "the border" is defined not by *where* it is, but rather, by *what* it *does*. The site of the border is frequently understood as the site of border enforcement, most pertinently, the port of entry.

Borders as Ports

Many travellers conflate entry ports with borderlines. Whereas borderlines may be invisible, entry ports are highly visible manifestations of their presence. One could argue that such a view is false, that entry ports are not borders, and that the travellers are mistaken. However, rather than suggest that this is a case of massive misunderstanding, that anyone who conflates "the port of entry" with "the border" is simply wrong, it is instead worthwhile to examine why and how cross-border travellers understand "the border" in these terms, and the consequences of such an understanding.

When driving with passengers from Akwesasne or off the reserve, I often asked them to notify me when we reached "the border." Without fail, passengers would do so when we reached the port of entry. Akwesasronon would also point out the borderline when conducting community tours of the territory, but this was for the benefit of outsiders. Though travellers are aware of the distinction between the borderline and the port when stopping to think about it, in everyday practice it is the port that constitutes "the border" and not the line.

Most non-government officers I spoke with referred implicitly to the port of entry when discussing "the border." Akwesasne's grassroots "Idle No More" demonstrations to "move the border" offer a useful counterpoint to the MCA's press release concerning moving the border. When the Mohawk government talked about "moving the border," as mentioned in the previous section, they considered moving the line. However, when community activists talked about "moving the border," they considered moving the port. The relocation of the port of entry in 2009 was, as far as many residents were concerned, a de-facto relocation of "the border."

Even if officers I spoke with referred to the borderline when talking about the border, in much of state signage "the border" refers to the port rather than the border. In this way, the state reproduces among the citizenry a conceptual model of "the border" that does not entirely mesh with that of its own officers. Warnings by American border officers not to photograph "the border" in fact forbid travellers from photographing the port. The CBSA's "border wait times" website refers to the wait time for processing at a port of entry and not the wait time to cross the borderline. The MCA and CBSA jointly designed an electronic sign on the highway notifying travellers of "wait time to the border," again referencing time to the port and not to the borderline. One sees a corollary in many international airports worldwide, where the word "border" is located at the site of processing, even if the airport is far from the international borderline – a phenomenon Chalfin (2006; 2008) identifies as part of the telos of globalized, contemporary, sovereign statehood. As far as travellers are concerned, it is the port that they see and the port that they have to traverse in order to proceed on their travels.

This disjuncture between border policing's notion of border-as-line and a (state-supported) citizenry's notion of border-as-port can lead to tension when officers interview travellers. Both in Akwesasne and elsewhere, officers sometimes confuse travellers when they ask, "When did you cross the border?" or "When did you enter Canada/the United States?" One officer got flustered when a friend I was travelling with did not know how to answer a US border officer's question, "How long have you been in the United States?" From my friend's perspective, they had not even entered the United States, while the officer was trying to ascertain whether they had engaged in any activities after crossing the borderline but before reaching the port.

Whereas among BSOs and policymakers "the border" (understood as the borderline) engenders border enforcement, among travellers border enforcement often constitutes "the border" (understood as the site of enforcement). This disparity in perceptions is practically unimportant in locations where the line and the port are contiguous but has a substantial impact on border crossing in Akwesasne, where the two are separated in time and place. There, residences, businesses, homes, schools, libraries, government buildings, and more lie between the sites of borderlines and the sites of ports of entry. In the following section, I consider border crossing as it relates to different understandings of the border on the part of travellers and officers.

Different Perspectives

"Border crossing" is typically understood not in terms of traversal of either the line or the port but rather in in terms of an interaction between BSOs and travellers. It is in this interaction that various perspectives on the border come into direct contact. The question "When does someone cross a border?" elicited different responses from "What is a border?" For many, "border crossing" is rarely about moving across a line of demarcation but instead is about processing. A retired officer suggested as much in our interview:

> ME: When has someone begun crossing the border? When have they finished crossing the border?
> BSO: By the rules I was taught, they cross the border the second they present themselves to me. You must present yourself to a customs officer upon arrival in Canada. Well, you've arrived in Canada. Yes, the line's halfway across the bridge, but by law, that's no man's land. So you report. And you're done doing that, and you're in, once I say, "Have a nice day," and let you go.

Regardless of where a traveller is physically, there is a sense they have not finished crossing a border until they hear "Have a nice day," and have been released by the officer.

Because border crossing is defined in terms of an interaction between BSOs and travellers, the perspectives that those actors bring to the interaction are a central factor in determining what goes on during processing. "What is a border?" influences what goes on when someone tries to cross a border.

In processing, different definitions of borders are brought to bear. As Van Houtum remarks, "the representation of the border as a line of difference is making a difference" (quoted in Wilson and Donnan 2012, 411). I began a previous section discussing an interaction in which a BSO and I had fundamentally different ideas of what constituted a border. There, the impact was slight, a moment of confusion and rolled eyes. In the long term, the officer may have been frustrated or annoyed rather than bemused by my misunderstanding of something as seemingly obvious as what constitutes a border. He may have thought of me as purposefully antagonistic, or simply stupid, and processed me accordingly.

The exchange can also be problematic if an officer asks a traveller, "Have you crossed the border?" What does such a question mean? Have they crossed a line? Or a port? Have they been processed? The answers depend on how both the traveller and the officer view the border. And if they are employing different definitions of the term, things can get messy.

A useful term to describe the situation in Akwesasne may be "border confusion," in which a variety of actors employing disparate notions of what constitutes a border are forced to negotiate those notions in face-to-face interactions mandated by the state. I spoke with one visitor to Akwesasne who fell deeper and deeper into confusion when a border officer asked her whether she had crossed the border. She assumed that she was in the process of doing that, as she was at the port of entry. The officer tried to clarify by asking how many bridges she had crossed before talking to him, though this only made things worse when she, her passenger, and her child all guessed a different number. Though my friend was unaware of this at the time, the bridges connecting the northern and southern ends of Cornwall Island are often referred to as the "northern" and "southern" spans of a single bridge – furthering complications and at times erasing the thousand-plus Indigenous residents of the island from conceptual maps of the region.

I spoke with other visitors to Akwesasne who panicked after being accused of crossing the border illegally without first reporting to Canadian customs. When one friend called me from the bank on Cornwall Island where he had stopped to pick up money for the toll booth, I told him to head to the port of entry immediately. These visitors did not see themselves as crossing any borders, because they had not crossed any ports. Officers saw them as crossing borders because they had traversed the borderline.

This is further complicated in Akwesasne, where ideology can account for additional discrepancies in terms of how people understand "the border." If a traveller arrives at the port of entry with the perspective that "there is no border," this can prove challenging to the customs officer. The CBSA has painstakingly reworked the questions asked of travellers coming from Akwesasne in order to account for some of these discrepancies, but confusions persist. In the incidents I encountered, officers were forgiving of this confusion among non-Indigenous travellers unfamiliar with the territory but less so with Akwesasronon, who they felt should know better.

In the following sections, I contrast the US and Canadian policy innovations created to mediate the disparity between the borderline and the port around the Akwesasne Mohawk Territory. These policies are broadly referred to as "reporting-in" policies and require travellers to drive themselves to ports of entry after crossing a borderline, regardless of where they are located. To paraphrase the old saying, if you can't bring the border to the Mohawks, bring the Mohawks to the border. By forcing travellers to move in a certain way throughout the territory, these policies have had a largely negative impact on local circulation, relations with nearby officers, and economic and social exchanges with neighbouring non-Indigenous communities.

US "Policy"

There is an "unofficial" policy at the US port of entry in Massena that requires all non-Indigenous travellers to "report in" to customs after visiting Snye or St. Regis Village. People coming from these Canadian portions of the territory are told to drive, without stopping, to the nearest port of entry, walk inside, and report themselves to officers. This could be either the port of entry in Massena, New York, west of the reserve, or the much smaller facility in Fort Covington to the east. Because the Massena port is closer to the city of Massena and the bridge to Canada, the vast majority of "reporting in" takes place there. This requires driving through a minimum of nine kilometres and up to twenty-plus kilometres of homes, shops, schools, and businesses. I reported in daily in my yearlong commute to St. Regis Village.

The reporting-in policy produces an artificial filter that requires travellers to behave as if they were in any other cross-border corridor, driving directly to the port as if they had no choice in the matter. The term "filter" or "funnel" is a useful one for considering the ways in which flows of traffic are redirected in cross-border enforcement (I consider the conceptual metaphor of streams and flows in border travel in the next chapter). This corridor is a densely inhabited community, yet it becomes a quasi-no man's land through tacitly accepted legal fictions of border enforcement.

I use the term "unofficial" when describing this policy, as there is no written policy or signage justifying or explaining travellers' obligation to report. Border-patrol administrators explained the policy to me as a means to enable the circulation of Akwesasronon throughout their territory while keeping track of people who may be taking advantage of the community's unregulated cross-border corridors. According to US Customs and Border Protection (CBP), "If you are entering the US through the Northern or Southern border you must enter through an open Port of Entry staffed with CBP Officers" (US Customs and Border Protection n.d.). By the letter of US law, there is no legal way to move from Snye or St. Regis Village into American portions of the reserve, because there are no ports of entry there. As you may recall from previous chapters, this would also mean no legal way of crossing the street, or moving from one end of a house or backyard to another. Border officers recognize the community's unique geographic and historical situation. Officers were also quick to stress that they reserve the right to stop anyone traversing the borderline within the territory, but choose to do so sparingly, typically targeting only those they feel seem out of place in the territory.

There is no written legal statute officers can cite when requiring travellers to report in, and the authority of officers to mandate travellers to do so is unclear. BSOs at the port typically tell travellers they have to report in after leaving Akwesasne. Once officers got to know me, they stopped doing so. When I interviewed a port supervisor, he insisted that I should report in. When I pressed him on the matter, informing him that his colleagues in border patrol told me that the policy was not grounded in any written law or policy, he told me again, "You should report in." I let it drop. In chapter 6, I discuss the implications for this sort of language in the context of "policing by consent."

Many in Akwesasne vastly prefer the US "reporting-in" system over the Canadian one, discussed in the next section. It makes their lives easier and tacitly acknowledges that they belong in the territory and have a special legal status in accordance with that fact. American BSOs typically enjoy a better relationship with the community, and because of the Indigenous exemption from reporting, many members of Akwesasne do not even know about the policy.

Though the government of the United States legally recognizes an Indigenous right to cross-border travel, US border officers justify the non-invocation (also discussed in chapter 6) of border regulation for Akwesasronon along the lines of their discretionary powers rather than rights discourse.

One negative consequence of the Indigenous exemption is the potential to isolate non-Indigenous persons from the Akwesasne community. It makes it difficult to do business in Akwesasne, or meet with friends, if one has to drive to US customs every time one moves across a given part of the territory. I found myself organizing my days around minimizing reporting in, especially when visiting friends after work. I could not simply go from the office to my friend's house down the street and across the border – I had to report first, and then turn around and go back.

An op-ed piece from Akwesasne's *Indian Time* newspaper discussed one Akwesasronon's frustrations at the harassment of a non-Indigenous friend. The article highlights the ways in which the ambiguities of the US reporting policy can prove difficult for non-Indigenous travellers, and the extent to which the border permeates everyday life in the community.

Life on the Border: *Indian Time* – Vol. 22, Issue No. 41 – 14 October 2004

A friend of mine from Cornwall (non-Native) was coming to visit me in Snye. As she got to the US Customs the guy asked the usual questions, including the $10,000 question. All answers no. She is in the process of moving out of her apartment and into a new place in Cornwall. She had 2 empty cardboard boxes in her back seat in plain view to the guy. Well when he saw them you would have thought he thought he hit the seizure of all time. She was pulled in and sent inside.

"Why do you have empty boxes in your car? Are you picking up a load somewhere? Where are you hiding your guns?"

She drives a small compact car, with the usual in it: empty soda bottles, socks and sneakers, a sweatshirt. You know, the stuff some people carry around. Well it took SIX US custom officers to search her car and when she looked out the window to where they were taking apart her car, one of the officers was smelling her clothes. YUK! (I won't say what piece of clothing). When they found nothing inside her car they came in and started on her, asking her the same questions over and over again. Then they asked her if she knew she had to report back into the US Customs before she returns to Cornwall. She stated that "no" she didn't know that. They asked her "Well why don't you know that?" She said, "Because no one ever told her that?" "How would I know that?" She was then told that if she didn't stop and report in she could and would be arrested! During this whole process the officers were mostly yelling at her. And for what? Having 2 empty cardboard boxes in her back seat. Needless to say in the future (if she ever comes to see me again after this) she will be cleaning out her car. So for all you people who are Non-Native that work in St. Regis or Snye, this means teachers, nurses, contractors, anyone that visits these areas for whatever reason YOU MUST REPORT BACK INTO US CUSTOMS BEFORE crossing back to Cornwall or you will be ARRESTED!! As the one custom officer phrased it, "Oh and have a nice day." I have to wonder why ALL of the new officers at US customs are such major @$!%@#. So far we all know this: IF you're Native and drive a nice car, then you must do something illegal. If you're a non-native going to see someone native then you're doing something illegal. If you have empty boxes in your car you're doing something illegal. If you have clothes in your car the customs guys are going to smell them, and with that I'll end here. Signed, A box is a box.

The above exchange could be considered a simple instance of harassment in which rude officers exerted an unreasonable amount of authority against an innocent woman. After all, complaints of overzealous border officers are by no means limited to Akwesasne. Yet by other measures, this exchange was particular to Akwesasne. The woman was held under greater scrutiny because she was a non-Indigenous visitor to the reserve. The officers' threats to arrest her if she did not report in were framed in terms of policies unique to the region and her ignorance of those policies. Finally, the article serves as both a public condemnation of BSOs who abuse their powers and a warning to fellow Akwesasronon about the difficulties their non-Indigenous friends and colleagues may face when moving within the territory.

Canadian Policy

In September 2009, after relocating the Cornwall port of entry into the city of Cornwall, the Canadian government began enforcing an obligation to report in. This policy and its enforcement are regularly cited as the most pressing concern for Akwesasronon moving about the territory.

Though transit between Snye, Quebec, and St. Regis, Quebec, and New York State has always been possible (there have always been roads connecting these places), it is physically impossible for travellers to report overland to a Canadian port of entry after travelling to those parts of the territory. There are currently no ports of entry in northern portions of the territory. The only way to go to Snye and St. Regis over-land is through New York, and the CBSA has no presence in these por-tions of the territory.

A customs house was once located at the entry to St. Regis Village. Several residents enjoyed telling me humorous stories about officers lying in the booth half-asleep with feet up, waving travellers past using their foot. Now, both the booth and the pole that had once been used to mark the borderline are long gone. No such enforcement exists in Snye, either, where there are numerous roadways leading across the borderline.

With only one exception, in my year of commuting to St. Regis Vil-lage, Canadian officers did not expect me to have "reported in." That exception occurred within my first few weeks in Akwesasne. At the time, I didn't recognize the officer. He asked me where I had spent my day. I told him (honestly), that I was at the Mohawk Council of Akwesasne, "in Quebec." He asked me if I had reported in "over here." I thought perhaps he was talking about reporting in before going to Cornwall Island, in Ontario. I told him, "I didn't go to the island." He said, "No, but you went to Quebec ... right? [He did not pause to hear my answer.] That's in Canada ... right?" I began to worry. I didn't want to say "no," but there was no way I could have reported in over the course of my journey. I told him (urgently and exasperatedly) that I had gone there from Canada, and that I lived in Cornwall, and that I had at no point stopped in the United States. Implicit is the fact that it was physically impossible to do what he was suggesting – report myself to a non-existent port of entry upon arrival in St. Regis Village. Pausing for a second that seemed like more than a second, he said, "Okay," and then returned my passport. The tollgate arm opened and I breathed a sigh of relief, stepping on the gas and heading home to write.

This incident occurred within my first weeks in Akwesasne and was the only time I was given a difficult time for coming from the reserve. I had suspected that telling the officer I came from the Quebec portion of the reserve would have expedited the customs interview. After all, I hadn't left Canada except to transit through New York State. Instead, saying I had come from Quebec opened me up to further questioning as to why I hadn't reported in. In subsequent interactions, the officer seemed to recognize me. He would silently flip to my student visa, return my passport, and wish me on my way.

Unlike for travel between the "New York" and "Quebec" portions of the territory, Canada enforces an obligation to report for residents entering the territory at Cornwall Island, Ontario. There, travellers can proceed overland from the island to the nearest port of entry in the city of Cornwall. Consequently, the CBSA requires travellers transiting to or through Cornwall Island from New York State to "report in."

Up until 2009, when the POE was still on Cornwall Island, all traffic crossing the border from New York State funnelled through the port. This is no longer the case, however, since the port of entry was moved north of Cornwall Island and into the city of Cornwall in 2009 (see figure 2.1). Traffic currently filters from the northern span of the Three Nations Bridge, first to the Seaway International Bridge Corporation's toll booth, and then to the primary inspection lanes of the new Cornwall port of entry. Consequently, all of Cornwall Island and its several thousand residents are sandwiched between the Massena port of entry to the south, and the Cornwall port of entry to the north.

At present, all residents of Cornwall Island must first report to Canadian customs when entering Canada's mainland, even if their point of origin was the island itself. Consequently, the Cornwall port is Canada's only POE handling a mixed traffic of international travellers who began travel in the United States and domestic travellers whose travel originated in Cornwall Island, Ontario.

If the CBSA finds that a traveller has stopped on Cornwall Island without proceeding directly to the port of entry, that traveller is charged with "failure to report." Failures to report result in vehicle seizure, a $1,000 fine for release of vehicle in the first offence, $2,000 on a second, and $3,000 on a third and subsequent charges. The MCA offered to pay for a vehicle's release for Akwesasne members' first seizure and has, to date, paid well over a quarter of a million dollars to the CBSA. The policy has since been terminated. A few residents expressed concern that the MCA's willingness to reimburse first offences encouraged community members to be lax in reporting, at least until their first seizure.

Residents are physically capable of turning their car to the left, or the right, at the site of the former port of entry. Doing so enables them to freely move about the island without having first attended the port of entry in the city of Cornwall. From the perspective of the Canadian government, this would mean entering Canada without being processed at a port of entry, and would constitute a violation of the Customs Act.

It is a "poorly kept secret" that some residents employ two vehicles, one to cross Canadian customs and the other to move freely between the territory and Cornwall Island. I feel somewhat comfortable writing this, as I know CBSA officers are aware of this practice, and they probably have a better sense than I do as to how prevalent it is. This enables island residents to go home without reporting. In a couple of instances, I heard residents jokingly refer to this vehicle as the "getaway car," but others simply call it the "island car." Residents who do not own, or cannot afford, a second car do not have this option.

Considering there is no CBSA or RCMP presence on Cornwall Island, how does the CBSA determine which cars have failed to report? Licence plates are tagged at the port in Cornwall and compared with video footage of cars entering Cornwall Island from the south. If a car is seen entering the island, but not reporting to customs, or reporting out of order from the other vehicles that arrived, the driver is charged with a failure to report.

Some residents have also been charged criminally in relation to the obligation to report, either for lying about their point of origin or for dropping people off on the island before reporting. One resident typically dropped her son off at his father's home on the island before proceeding to report herself to the port of entry and go to work in Cornwall. During one of these drop-offs, the car behind her as she turned at the crossroads to drop her son off happened to be a CBSA officer driving to work (the officer must have resided in either New York State or a nearby part of Quebec). When she arrived at the port, she was charged criminally for "aiding and abetting" her son's non-compliance with the Customs Act.

Residents who falsely claim to be coming in from the island rather than New York State have also been charged for "Interference" and "Making a False Claim." Problematically, many island residents, especially adolescents arriving at the port via the United States, began answering "the island" when asked, "Where are you coming from?," as they realized it would expedite processing. They argued that this was technically true, as their vehicles traversed the island before heading into the port. In response, the first question officers are supposed to ask was officially changed in 2014 to, "Are you, your vehicle, or any goods in your possession arriving from the United States?" ("CBSA Changes Preliminary Port of Entry" 2014). In my dozens of trips across the port since this revision, I have not encountered a single instance of the new question being asked. Indeed, it could potentially open up a larger can of worms among Akwesasronon who do not view the territory as either Canada or the United States. The "flexible geography" of Akwesasne, discussed in chapter 1, renders standardizing any sort of question problematic, particularly one that relies upon a single normative understanding of national boundaries.

Consequences of Canada's Reporting-in System

The act of "reporting in" ranges from a minor to a major inconvenience. Until very recently, travellers and residents going to the island from other parts of the territory had to first drive across several kilometres of rocky, narrow, and derelict bridge in order to report. After crossing the bridge, island residents and visitors had to then turn around and drive again across those same several kilometres of rocky, narrow, and derelict bridge in order to return to the island. Though the bridge has been replaced by a smoother, slightly wider two-lane bridge, the policy remains intact.

Average wait times on the bridge are low, but during peak hours and holidays, they can grow substantially. Many of my days were organized around bridge wait times, scheduling interviews in the island in the morning so I would not have to spend the time and money required to report in from my office in St. Regis Village. It was not unusual to see cars and small trucks tired of waiting on line, turn around along the narrow two-lane bridge, their motors' roar mimicking the frustration they (and I) surely felt.

Akwesasronon often criticize the border wait times in terms of their risks to bodily health. In the aftermath of the port relocation and creation of the reporting-in system, the Mohawk Council of Akwesasne filed a human-rights complaint attacking the changes. This complaint cited one resident with bladder problems who, unable to go home to use the toilet or change, had no choice but to relieve themselves in their car while waiting in line. When I mentioned on Facebook that I was going to mention the relationship between border control and bladder control in my book, a resident replied, "OMG, my biggest fear, always. Don't eat don't drink fluids on the way over, getting out of the car and having to try and find a bush might get you shot hahahaha."

Island residents with medical conditions who are returning from the Akwesasne health clinic in St. Regis ("Quebec") must first wait in line and report to Canadian customs before returning home to Cornwall Island ("Ontario") to rest. "What if" conversations are frequent when talking about the hazards of the bridge line-ups – What if my car stalls? What if someone has an emergency and can't leave the line-up? What if someone needs to get a medication? What if children need to use the toilet? What if elders become overheated/frozen sitting in their car? This line of thinking suggests that the reporting-in system represents not simply an inconvenience but a threat to communal health.

This policy has also had a negative impact on non-resident travel and business on the island. Although Akwesasronon travellers and MCA employees are exempt from the $3.25 bridge fee charged at the northern span of the Three Nations Bridge, others must pay each time they cross the bridge. As a consequence, it costs non-Akwesasronon travellers $6.50 CAD any time they visit the island, regardless of whether they are coming from the United States or Canada (when the port was on the island, visiting was free from the United States). When driving to the island via the United States, non-residents must pay the bridge fee first when they check in, and then again immediately afterward when they turn around onto the island. Toll collectors expressed sympathy for the situation but collected the fees nonetheless. Businesses in the city of Cornwall no longer deliver to island residents, taxi drivers prefer not to take their charges onto the island, and many shops that once catered to cross-island traffic have closed down since 2009.

I asked an officer to walk me through the procedure for a vehicle seizure. I was told that drivers are asked to surrender their car keys, and the vehicle is brought to secondary inspection. They are told that their vehicle failed to report, and if they so request, they will be read a list of the date or dates for that failure. Should they wish, the Community Advocate to the CBSA can take on their case and, if it is a first offence, pay for vehicle release.[2] If someone is unable or unwilling to pay for their vehicle on the spot, it is taken to an offsite lot.

Travellers are not allowed to see the documentation on which officers base their seizure of a vehicle, although the officer may state the dates at which they refused to report, and the traveller may write down that information. If the seizure is contested, it is given a case number, and the traveller (or their advocate) is asked to send as much evidence as possible to prove that they reported. Because travellers must first pass the bridge's toll booth before reaching the port of entry, they can consult the Seaway International Bridge Corporation's records of their transit. One resident with whom I spoke received a formal apology and her car was returned by the CBSA after she brought receipts proving she had paid a bridge toll at the time she had allegedly failed to report. Another Akwesasronon was able to demonstrate that she had paid the toll on the day in question but was then accused of not reporting on additional days. The "black box" of enforcement remains a common source of frustration, reinforcing the "facelessness" of local border enforcement.

---

2 The community advocate position was created by the Mohawk government to compile complaints and concerns Akwesasne residents were having with border officers. Advocates could be authorized to follow-up on complaints on the part of residents dissatisfied with their interactions. Following the vehicle seizure policy, the advocate also took on the role of helping people get their vehicles back, authorized to pay out 1,000 CAD to release a car on a first offense. With the creation of the CBSA's Aboriginal Liaison Officer position, the advocate came to work closely with the liaison. As of 2020, neither position exists, although both the advocate and liaison were very active at the time of fieldwork alongside the rise in vehicle seizures.

That frustration is voiced in the introduction to chapter 4 in which an officer refuses to provide BT with the report concerning her confiscated tobacco.

Though the new low-level bridge and redesigned port of entry at its foot have mitigated many of the most substantial concerns about reporting in – namely long wait times and the bridge's poor construction – it has opened the door for others. The permanence of the new port of entry, which sandwiches Cornwall Island between US and Canadian ports, gives the lie to assertions like those made in 2009 that the port would be temporary. Archival information shows that the expansion of port facilities in order to accommodate community concerns for circulation has consistently been the rationale for the CBSA to build more permanent structures in the port. Akwesasne remains Canada's only "mixed-traffic" corridor, and thousands of island residents are still obligated to report in every day.

Now that traffic has become manageable, the CBSA has been able to justify demanding that Akwesasronon declare goods eligible for the remission order. Though Akwesasronon still do not pay duties on these products, they are now expected to account for everything they bring across, whereas they were previously not expected to do so. This time-consuming process would not have been possible in the old facility, where wait times could balloon to well over an hour, and officers were pressured to maintain the flow of traffic. By relieving the symptoms of the reporting-in policy, the CBSA has strengthened its underlying pathology.

Haudenosaunee Protocols

In this section, I discuss "the Edge of the Woods" as an alternative conception of borders and their regulation. I am interested in the Edge of the Woods as a Haudenosaunee tradition, in full recognition that "tradition" is a loaded word in the social sciences. I ask the reader to consider this treatment within the contemporary context of legal pluralism, in which tradition can and (often) should remain a relevant index of legal praxis.

Audra Simpson has criticized much of "Iroquois studies" scholarship for trying to force a particular notion of tradition upon Haudenosaunee peoples, and in doing so legitimating some communities and claims to authority while ignoring others – all the while furthering the ongoing colonization of North America. In recognition of this critique, I synthesize both contemporary and classical treatments of the edge of the woods with my own conversations with elders and other knowledgeable Akwesasron. I use lower case for "the edge of the woods" when referring to the physical location, and upper case, "the Edge of the Woods" when referring to protocols of exchange and condolence. As I discuss below, the edge of the woods has remained an important concept in Haudenosaunee contemporary politics well into the present. Furthermore, it can help us think through some of the tensions inherent in settler colonial states' imagining of what a border should be, and how it should be regulated.

Cornell historian Jon Parmenter recently published a spatial history of the Haudenosaunee Confederacy under the title *The Edge of the Woods* (2010). The term "the edge of the woods" (or, "the woods' edge") is rich with meaning in a Haudenosaunee context. It can be used to describe (1) the brush demarcating pertinent borders/boundaries in a territory, (2) the means by which visitors to villages presented themselves, and (3) a preliminary stage in the condolence ritual by which past chiefs' deaths were mourned and new chiefs were installed. After contact with Europeans, the term also came to refer to a preliminary stage of treaty making between Haudenosaunee and Dutch, British, French, and later American diplomats.

In the first published ethnological account of the term, Horatio Hale (1999) refers to "the edge of the woods" as *Deyughnyonkwarakda*. Concerning its etymology, William Fenton writes, "the word applies to the line of bushes usually found on the border between forest and clearing" (1998, 137). Former ARRO researcher and current chief Tobi Mitchell was kind enough to provide me with the word in Akwesasne Mohawk – *Tsieiot'te tsi kahrhahere* – and has informed me that combining the words, as Hale did, negates their meaning.

I should note that *Tsieiot'te tsi kahrhahere* is *not* the Mohawk word used to describe the Canada-US border. The word for that is *T'Karistaron*, which refers to the metal equipment dragged by government surveyors to delineate the border. In the context of this discussion, I consider the edge of the woods as, among other things, one sort of border.

The wood's edge demarcated the border between forest and clearing, a border that is both conceptual and physical. In the past, Haudenosaunee settlements were centred in a palisaded town of longhouses, frequently on hills overlooking waterways. Home life, politics, and agricultural production (all historically managed by women) were centred in the clearing while hunting, warfare, and commerce (all historically managed by men) were centred in the forest. Deborah Doxtator (1997) argues that this forest–clearing distinction persists as an integral conceptual category in contemporary Haudenosaunee practices, particularly those of gender. Audra Simpson extends Doxtator's argument to reflect upon logics of gendered space, home, and movement (Simpson 2003; but see also Venables 2010).

Historically, such a division was cyclical rather than permanent. Clearings would be left when new settlements were built in the forest, and abandoned clearings would, over time, become forest. It is uncanny, if not coincidental, that the port of entry in Massena is a clearing surrounded by woodlands at the edge of a river's shore. This is visible in the image I presented at the chapter's beginning (figure 5.4), much as the image of the border at Akwesasne shows it as, if not yet a forest, well on its way to becoming one.

The image in figure 5.6, taken from the New York State Museum website ("Mohawk Iroquois Village circa 1600" n.d.), depicts the construction of a Haudenosaunee village. It gives a sense of the spatial organization of both forest and clearing. I am indebted to Phillip White-Cree (personal communication in 2014) for pointing out that there are several "border" regions in this orientation – notably, (1) the boundary between the village's clearing and the forest, and (2) the boundary between the river coast and the forest. Visitors by waterways would first arrive at the woods' edge along the shore, and then be taken to the woods' edge at the village clearing. In both instances, the edge serves as a site of exchange between insider-outsider, villager-foreigner, and more abstractly, male and female spheres.

Parmenter's *The Edge of the Woods* examines the geographic boundaries of the confederacy, and the ways in which contact and exchange were established between the Haudenosaunee and other nations (especially European ones). He argues that freedom of movement across land rather than ownership of a particular territory was the dominant factor in Haudenosaunee policymaking, diplomacy, and warfare in the post-contact era. In other words, the confederacy was more concerned with the lines of movement on a map than the lines of demarcation. This makes sense, as wide swaths of territory were regularly traversed by traders, hunters, warriors, and diplomats. Settlements, however, were semi-permanent and relocated approximately every twenty years (Snow 1996). European settlements in a given territory would not interfere with the activities of the clearing, so long as the lines – the trailways – of movement (of goods and people) along forests and rivers were unambiguously of Haudenosaunee provenance.

As I note in chapter 3, the confederacy's vast territorial expansion during the Beaver Wars enabled it to monopolize the north-south trade in pelts acquired from Cree trappers in the north and sold at trading posts in and around Albany. In this way, the confederacy made itself into a selectively permeable boundary between Cree and Ojibway fur

Figure 5.6. "Edge of the Woods." Photo courtesy of New York State Museum.

trappers to the north and European fur consumers in the south. Haudenosaunee sovereignty involved, to paraphrase Torpey (2000), monopo-
lizing the legitimate means of movement within a given territory.

The term "the Edge of the Woods" has taken on a renewed relevance
in recent years, with the opening address, "Welcome to the Woods'
Edge," of the Conference on Iroquois Research, the longest-running
conference of its type. Although the concept has become central in
studies of Haudenosaunee history and spatiality, most recent scholarship invoking "the Edge of the Woods" focuses on it in abstract rather
than concrete terms (Jennings 1995; Shannon 2008; Parmenter 2010).
Emphasis is given to the variety of forms of exchange and diplomacy
between Haudenosaunee and Europeans. Less attention is paid to
these forms' antecedents in protocols followed when entering a foreign village – in other words, "the Edge of the Woods" as a procedure
for "reporting in," and none, excepting Fenton (1998), draws a connection between spatial protocols and the physical space that is the
woods' edge.

In "The Clearings and the Woods: The Haudenosaunee (Iroquois)
Landscape – Gendered *and* Balanced" (2010), Robert Venables describes
"the Edge of the Woods" as the term used to describe a protocol for
arrival in a Haudenosaunee village between 1535 and 1794:

Approaching humans fell into two categories: those who came in peace
and those who were enemies. Of course it was unlikely that enemies

would announce themselves, but an announcement of peaceful intentions was ritualized. [...] At the Edge of the Woods, a person was expected to light a fire or to shout loudly. Whether the people were alerted by a messenger, by smoke, or by shouts, a male or female messenger, or even a group of women and men, customarily went out to ascertain the identity of the visitor or visitors into the Clearings and into the Town. This concept was based on what the founder of the Confederacy, the Peacemaker had done to announce his presence outside of a town. (Venables 2010, 37–8, citing Wallace 1994, 54–5)

The Edge of the Woods protocol was not only a means to regulate and legitimize travel into Haudenosaunee territory; it also served as a process for delineating different types of travellers. Both of these tasks are currently functions reserved for BSOs in North America. Smoke was the primary means by which one's presence was announced, and following European contact, the smoke from muskets shot into the air served this purpose frequently (Venables 2010, 38).

When I asked the Mohawk Nation's Wampum Keeper to explain the Edge of the Woods, I was told of both the Peacemaker's self-announcement with fire at the edge of the woods and the practice's central position in the Great Law. It was unclear whether the Peacemaker was the first to announce his presence at the wood's edge, although it is certainly the first (orally) recorded instance. I was told that at the time, smoke was already an established form of communication and, in my mind, it is not unreasonable to suspect that the Peacemaker was observing an already existent practice of propriety.

Nineteenth- and early-twentieth-century anthropologists, largely concerned with Haudenosaunee political organization, focused heavily on the details of political protocol rather than its abstractions (Morgan 1851; Hale 1999; but see Voget 1984). However, their treatment of "the Edge of the Woods" emphasized the term's third meaning, as one "stage" in the condolence ritual by which new chiefs were installed, and not as a way of legitimating entry into a village. The first such account of the Edge of the Woods in condolence was presented by Canadian ethnologist Horatio Hale in 1883. He writes:

Here took place the "preliminary ceremony," styled in the Book of Rites, "*Deyughnyonkwarakda*," a word which means simply "at the edge of the woods." At this point a fire was kindled, a pipe was lighted and passed around with much formality, and an address of welcome was made by the principal chief of the inviting nation. The topics of this address comprised a singular mixture of congratulation and condolence, and seem to have

been prescribed forms, which had come down from immemorial antiq-
uity, as appropriate to the occasion. The guests were then formally conducted – "led by the hand," as the Book recites – to the Council House of
the town. (H. Hale 1999, ch. IV)

More than a century later, William Fenton clarified and expanded upon
the Edge of the Woods' role in condolence in his magnum opus, *The
Great Law and the Longhouse* (1998). He remarked that it was the second
stage of condolence by which the mourners within the longhouse come
out to meet and invite the "clear-minded," who have built fires outside.
After the clear-minded are brought into the longhouse, other rituals
of condolence can begin, leading up to the installation of new chiefs
within the mourners' clan.

Nineteenth- and early-twentieth-century scholars emphasized the
Edge of the Woods as protocol, but only focused on the narrow context
of condolence. This has changed in recent decades. For the most part,
contemporary scholars have de-emphasized the Edge of the Woods as a
clearly administrated stage of condolence (but see Pomedli 1995, 321–2)
while instead focusing on the Edge of the Woods in terms of broader
cultural notions of boundary and exchange. While there is today substantial interest in the edge of the woods as an abstract cultural concept
regarding boundaries, there remains less attention to the Edge of the
Woods as a concrete set of legal protocols regulating movement across
those boundaries.

The Edge of the Woods protocol, a preliminary stage in the induction
of new chiefs, can be seen as a similar transposition of village practice
into political structure. Strangers and visitors had, since "time immemorial," lit a fire at the woods' edge in order to be met outside the
village and brought within. This was the means by which travellers,
visitors, and strangers transitioned from outside the community to the
inside, both conceptually and physically. It was also the means by which
travellers' intent was determined, and their presence legitimated. These
same logics are employed in condolence rituals, as the clear-minded
clans light smaller fires in order to be met outside the council house and
brought inside. It demarcates the end of mourning and the practices by
which new chiefs were legitimated. Both spatial and political protocols
marked transitions from outside to inside and served as formal ground
rules preliminary to any sort of exchange.

As a spatial/political metaphor/practice, "The Edge of the Woods"
was well suited for providing context to European diplomacy. Douglas
George-Kanentiio has gone so far as to suggest that "the Edge of the
Woods Ceremony was the basis for the Two Row Wampum" (2013).

What does this have to do with border crossing in Akwesasne? There are parallels to the underlying logic of the American and Canadian reporting-in systems. Different types of entrants to a territory must be recognized and distinguished. In order for this to be done, travellers must make the polity aware of their presence. This occurs at the site of a border, the wood's edge, and involves exchange with villagers. Whereas the borderlines of Canada and the United States are invisible, wholly conceptual, and bound to a contract between states (a treaty), the Edge of the Woods is both a conceptual site of exchange and a physical one demarcated by brush and brambles.

There is, additionally, a doubling of border locations. Canada and the United States have both the port of entry and the borderline as the two dominant sites of the border. Among Haudenosaunee, there were two edges to the woods, one where travellers would arrive – the river/forest edge, and another where travellers would enter the village – the edge of the clearing/forest edge. "Border crossing," in both cases, involves traversal of not one, but two locations.

Haudenosaunee engaged in customary practices regulating movement into and out of their territory. Though different from the discrete, hard-shelled, aggressively protective, "crustacean" (Polanyi 2001) European borders, the Edge of the Woods served as another sort of border, one with its own rules, regulations, and enforcement. Before thinking of Canadian and American notions of bordering as either universal or inevitable, we would benefit from realizing that neither is the case. Haudenosaunee peoples did not have no borders but rather different borders, and ones that continue to offer a useful and viable model for regulating movement within the Akwesasne Mohawk Territory.

Conclusion

Whereas Mohawks living in Akwesasne today are required by the Canadian government to report themselves to the nearest port of entry upon entering a territory, their ancestors doubtless would have come out to the woods' edge to meet foreign travellers. Unlike Canadian and American "reporting-in" policies, the Edge of the Woods places the onus on the polity to meet the traveller, and not the other way around. Alternative methods of reporting, such as video booths at the old Cornwall port of entry on the island, similar to ones Canada already uses in remote regions, which the Mohawk Council of Akwesasne has proposed since 2009, not only exist, but are also both practical and culturally viable in a local context.

While some contemporary activists (see, e.g., Miner 2015) may argue that Indigenous peoples had no borders, such a simplification is a dangerous one. It risks reducing those peoples' territorial claims to sovereignty, and denies long-standing manifestations of that sovereignty. I offer here one example of examining an Indigenous polity's borders on their own terms. I agree with Ingold that "colonialism, then, is not the imposition of linearity upon a non-linear world, but the imposition of one kind of line on another" (2007, 2). Though some Akwesasronon certainly do resist the concept of boundaries in general, many do not reject borders on the whole. Rather, they dispute foreign borders' manifestation within Mohawk territory. Even if European styles of nationalized borderlines did not exist until a certain historical moment, there were undoubtedly both demarcation of space and formal protocols regulating movement across and within Indigenous territories.

As Wittgenstein remarked, "if I draw a boundary line that is not to say what I am drawing it for" (cited in Rael 2012, 72). A border can be a line, a port, or some combination of the two; a line can become a bridge, a wall, or a funnel. The disparity of borderline and port in the Akwesasne Mohawk Territory has created more of a fence than a bridge. Policymakers and scholars would be well advised to attend to the ways in which conventional notions of how borders work are built upon a conceptual bundling of interrelated but distinct objects. By disambiguating borderlines and ports, we can gain an insight into the interactions that make up border crossing, and the policies that force people to cross borders in certain ways.

But this is just the beginning of exploring those interactions. Having examined the policies and some of the logics that have shaped the ideals and efforts of border enforcement at the Cornwall port of entry – having looked at how, and why, Akwesasronon come to "the border" – in the next chapter I look at the strategies and ideologies employed by both border services officers and Akwesasronon in their interactions with one another. How do travellers and BSOs decide what to do and what to say when two or more sometimes mutually incompatible notions of "the border" and – more poignantly – law are manifested in a face-to-face interaction? How do they negotiate the border and each other? How do these sorts of frame disputes get resolved? To look at those interactions, the next chapter draws upon personal experiences, interviews with border officers, and interviews with frequent travellers.

Chapter Six

Processing

Every time we cross that bridge, we have to answer the troll's questions. And we never know what they'll ask.
Akwesasne resident talking about crossing at the Cornwall port of entry

Introduction

The previous chapter examined a few of the policies that regulate the movement of Akwesasronon across the Canada-US borderline. Many of these policies are unique to the area, trying to force an "ideal type" of border into a territory whose geopolitical reality defies convention. Cornwall Island, Canada's only regulated "mixed-traffic corridor," stands out among all Canadian border crossings.

This chapter asks how BSOs and Akwesasronon view their interactions with one another. My present focus is on "processing," here defined as the face-to-face interaction that takes place between a border services officer and an overland traveller at the port of entry. Processing initially takes place at a "primary inspection lane" (PIL) booth, though some travellers may be sent to secondary inspection in the port facility for further scrutiny, or payment of duties. If so many of us experience border crossing in terms of the interactions between a border officer and a traveller, it is necessary to examine them to provide a fuller understanding of the border.

What takes place in these interactions? This chapter addresses the question in two ways.

Firstly, I try to get a sense of the "flow" of processing. I demonstrate "streaming" as a "conceptual metaphor" (Lakoff and Johnson 1980) underlying the work of border officers. In thinking of borders in terms of streams and their flows, many officers implicitly adhere to an underlying sense of a natural ordering of their work in processing travellers.

Yet the naturalness of this order, the naturalness of a stream's flow, is the consequence of particular cosmologies. If I say a border is like a stream, I implicitly invoke my own understanding of what streams are, how they work, and where they come from. Streaming is one way for information, and people, to move across the border – it is a metaphorical concept operationalized for the purposes of border regulation.

Secondly, I look at what officers do at the border. I examine how officers determine when, how, and whether to employ the limits of their authority in interactions with travellers – how they navigate those streams. This involves paying attention to the use of discretion and the categories both officers and travellers navigate during processing. Both border officers and Akwesasne residents negotiate between "principle" and "practicality." Officers are required to uphold the law but often exercise leeway in the form of discretion. Akwesasronon share a dogmatic opposition to the border's imposition but also have access to a wider variety of state-recognized identifications that can expedite border crossing. Much as officers exercise leeway regarding discretion, so too do Akwesasronon often determine how they will act toward officers on a case-by-case basis.

Border officers are charged with sorting travellers into streams and ensuring that the flow of traffic does not get clogged along the way. This is, even at face value, a challenging task that demands rapid decision making and evaluation. It is complicated immeasurably at the Cornwall port of entry, where unique laws must be applied and where travellers have access to a far wider variety of framings for themselves and the border than at other crossing points.

By framings, I mean ways of articulating "what is going on," and this includes who is crossing. A traveller may cross as an American or a Canadian; as a Canadian living south of the border; as a Mohawk, Haudenosaunee, or Native American; as a Native North American or a Native Canadian, and so on. Beyond legal categories, they may frame themselves as friendly, belligerent, indifferent, and so on. They may deny the authority of the border, or of the officer. They may respond to the officer in Mohawk, only say "Fuck you," or refuse to talk at all.

Many of these framings go beyond the training officers have received. New officers are taught how to deal with belligerent travellers or ones who speak a language they do not understand. They are not, however, taught (at least at headquarters) how to deal with Indigenous travellers who deny the border's legitimacy. Part of the challenge of non-recognition is the difficulty of engaging in dialogue with it. As a result, front-line border officers often find themselves obligated to fit a Mohawk-shaped peg into a Canadian-shaped hole, and all while being pressured to maintain the cross-border flows of the travelling public.

Similarly, Akwesasronon, may be regularly subjected to framings of themselves and their territory that they do not accept or like. They may be labelled against their will as American or Canadian, or told that they crossed a border they do not recognize.

Streaming

Akwesasne is the site at which the Canada-US borderline transitions from the St. Lawrence River to the forty-fifth parallel. It is literally the place where streams (more specifically, "the river") become the border. It is also, more abstractly, a place where borders become streams. In this section, I look at the ways in which streams constitute a "conceptual metaphor" for border processing.

As Lakoff and Johnson argue,

> Metaphor is not just a matter of language, that is, of mere words. We shall argue on the contrary, human *thought processes* are largely metaphorical. This is what we mean when we say that the human conceptual system is metaphorically structured and defined. Metaphors as linguistic expressions are possible precisely because there are metaphors in a person's conceptual system. (1980, 6)

Much of border enforcement is organized in terms of the metaphor "processing is streaming." This is not my invention, but rather the way BSOs I interviewed spoke of their activities. As one officer put it,

> It's what we know, it's the literature, and it's what we're trained to deal with. I use the word "stream" and I know you visualize it as something else, but to me it's just how I'm dealing with you and what you're doing and how to best serve you. How to process you and your goods.

Here, I wish to unpack this assertion that processing is streaming and – to pursue Lakoff and Johnson's line of reasoning – some of the consequences of this metaphor.

Borders as Streams

Streams have particular characteristics that, when employed as a metaphor for processing, enable distinct ways of considering processing. Here, I emphasize three of them: (1) streams can be mapped; (2) streams flow; and (3) streams can be navigated.

Streams can be mapped. Their pathways can branch in particular directions, expanding and collapsing. I asked an officer to explain

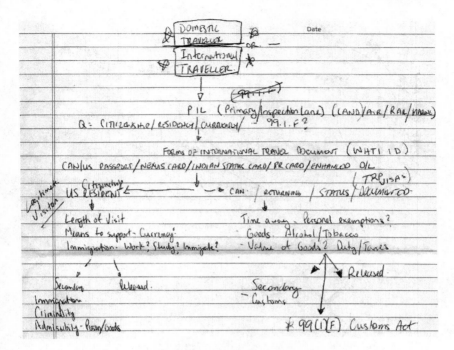

Figure 6.1. Hand-drawn "map." Image courtesy of the author.

"streaming," and he offered to draw me a "map" (see figure 6.1). In the next section, "processing," I offer a better sense of what some of the particular junctures on this map, such as "International Traveller" or "99(1) F Customs Act," mean. Here, I suggest the reader focus more on the shape of processing than the content.

As a "map" of border processing, this image suggests that the processing officer connects a variety of concerns within a singular ecosystem. But unlike a geographical map, this map – like a waterway – "flows." Questions and concerns are tied together by a very particular sort of line, a vector, or a line with an arrow at the end – suggesting an entropic force to processing, in which one question leads to another, or one answer leads to another. The stream's flow pushes travellers in particular directions. When I asked an interviewee to elaborate what he meant by "stream," he began listing questions.

What was your intent in coming to Canada? What was the purpose of your trip to Canada? You were coming to go to school. So you would likely have to have made application on your side of the border, because you're American, correct? So you would've started the process for your student visa online. And when you arrived, either flown in or driven, you would have made your declaration to the border officer. And the border officer said, "Hello/ Bonjour. Where do you live?" "I live in this part." "Where are you off to today?" "I'm heading to school, I have my student visa" (or, "I need this validated at some point"). So then the officer is then taking the information that you're giving them and deciding how you're going to be processed. So it's likely that you went to immigration, spoke to an immigration officer who validated your documents, and would then tell you what the parameters are, explain the parameters, in essence counsel you, tell you what you need to do, what you can and cannot do with that particular document. How long you have to be in Canada. So these things are, we would consider streams. So you came in that way, that is the way you are dealt with.

There is a directionality to processing streams that ultimately empties at one of two mouths – admission to Canada, or rejection. Someone can either end up in Canada, or not.

Finally, streams can be navigated. Moving through complex networks of waterways requires knowledge and skill. BSOs processing travellers into different streams are responsible for manoeuvring through complicated pathways to determine admissibility. It is officers, not travellers, who have to be familiar with the legal statutes and statuses that determine processing. Officers I interviewed spoke frequently, and with pride, of their capacity to quickly determine admissibility and any duty exemptions while maintaining "the flow of traffic." Travellers are quickly brought through a web of exhaustive customs regulations with a few questions and a document scan on the part of a knowledgeable BSO.

There are likely more ways in which the phrases "processing is streaming" and "borders are streams" represent a conceptual metaphor for the work activities of BSOs at primary inspection lanes. Even if officers themselves do not actively consider the extent to which this metaphor trickles into border work, it provides a useful tool for non-officers to get a handle on the shape of the waterways. But the metaphorical value of streams for thinking about border crossing extends to the other side of the PIL booth as well.

Streams in Haudenosaunee Worldview

Joyce Tekahnawiiaks King argues that "water is at the core of Haudenosaunee Weltanschauung [worldview]" (King 2006, 453). As in most cosmology narratives, water serves an important role within creation.

Yet the creation of rivers and streams holds a special significance in the Haudenosaunee cosmology. Their flows are not taken for granted but are understood as the product of a conflict between the Creator, Sapling, and his brother, Tawiskaron. Hewitt's *Iroquoian Cosmology* offers one version of the narrative, as told by a Mohawk elder:

> Taw 'skaron' spoiled and undid some of the things that Sapling had prepared. The rivers today in their different courses have been changed, for, in forming the rivers, Sapling provided them with two currents, each running in a contrary course, currents made for floating objects in opposite directions; or it may be that it is a better explanation to say that in the middle of the river there was a division, each side going in a direction contrary to that of the opposite side, because Sapling had intended that mankind should not have, as a usual thing, any difficult labor while they should be traveling. If, for any reason, a person would wish to descend the current, it would indeed not be a difficult matter simply to place himself in a canoe, and then, of course, to descend the current of the river; and then, if it should be necessary for him to return, he would, of course, paddle his canoe over to the other side of the river, and just as soon as he passed the division of the stream then, of course, his canoe would turn back, and he would then again be descending the current. So that is what Sapling had intended; that mankind should be thus fortunate while they were traveling about on rivers, but Taw 'skaron' undid this. (Hewitt 2009, 326–7)

The cosmology suggests that even if streams' unidirectional flow is now seen as natural, this was not originally, or perhaps inevitably, the case.

At present, however, the unidirectional flow of streams is as expected as the rain coming downwards. The motion is as solid a part of the landscape as the streams themselves. It is for this reason that "as long as the rivers flow" was a popular addendum to treaties intended for perpetuity.

Yet, as much as streams flow, those flows can also be resisted. One can push against the entropic pull of the waterways, even if doing so can be dangerous. As I discuss in the next chapter, one can refuse to cross "as American" or "as Canadian" in a variety of ways. One can employ a form of identification not officially recognized by Canada, or no identification at all, or one can simply say "Fuck you" to an officer, without explanation.

Haudenosaunee peoples have a long-standing political history of rejecting the flows of processing – refusing to move down the streams employed by Canadian or US border services officers. In Akwesasne, "going with the flow" can potentially be condemned as a tacit

acknowledgment of US or Canadian sovereignty. Much as the unidirectional flow of streams was a corruption of the landscape's natural order
on the part of the Creator's brother, the unidirectional flow of border
processing can be seen as a corruption of the continent's natural political order imposed by non-Indigenous settlers.

I feel it worthwhile to note that the metaphor of moving upstream
also has a long-standing history, not simply in Haudenosaunee cosmology and treaty making but in Iroquois studies. William Fenton (but
see Voget 1984) used the term "upstreaming" to refer to his method of
ethnohistory. Fenton described upstreaming as based on three prem-
ises: (1) basic cultural patterns tend to be stable over long periods; (2)
analysis should begin with points of greatest familiarity (generally
texts written in the recent past) and work their way backwards; and
(3) those patterns that are observable in both present and past can be
analysed and valued confidently (Voget 1984, 347; Fenton 1949, 236).
Essentially, upstreaming is built on the premise of patterning. If we
can establish a pattern in the present that matches up with the observable past, we can infer that the same pattern probably extends into the
unobservable past. There was an implicit effort in upstreaming to trace
the waters of history to their sources, where the waters (and data) are
purer.

Audra Simpson critiqued Fenton and his ilk by calling this method
"backstreaming" (2014, 109), suggesting that rather than resist the
flows of historical change, Iroquois researchers have imposed "a tradition of tradition" upon Haudenosaunee peoples. In doing so, she
suggests that, rather than resisting the currents of history, Iroquois
historians judged past practices by their own contemporary standards
of relevance. While I quote Hewitt above, I do not include anything
that departs from oral versions of the cosmology I heard in Kahnawake or Akwesasne.

The interactions between BSOs and Akwesasronon as both try to navigate the customs streams speak to a long-standing articulation of their
relationship, the Two-Row Wampum Treaty, or *Kaswentha*. The wampum belt depicts two river-faring vessels travelling side by side along
the same river. The Haudenosaunee in their canoe and the Europeans in
their ship represent a shared ethos of non-interference between Indigenous and non-Indigenous people (Muller 2009). Though recent debates
have questioned just how old the belt is, and the extent to which it can
be considered a legally binding treaty (Otto 2013; Hermkens, Noordegraaf, and Sijs 2013; Meuwese 2013; Jacobs 2013; Parmenter 2013; Otto
and Jacobs 2013; Bonaparte 2013), today the wampum belt nevertheless represents the way in which many Haudenosaunee political actors

articulate and pursue their relationship with the Canadian and US states in both court cases and discussions of the border.

To think briefly in terms of the Two-Row Wampum Treaty, many BSOs at a port of entry envision themselves in the same boat as Akwesasronon. They are captaining this vessel, and trying to navigate the often confusing and at times treacherous waters of processing as efficiently as possible. In their perspective, when Akwesasronon compete to navigate the customs stream in their own direction, they are trying to take the tiller – usurping the officers' authority and making the vessel much more likely to ground or capsize. Yet adherents of the Two-Row Wampum ethic would likely push against such a reading of the situation. The problem is not who captains the boat but how many boats are in the water. The obligations placed upon Akwesasronon at the border force them into the same vessel as officers when they should instead be in their own ship making their own way. Thus, what can be perceived (rightly or not) as hostility toward officers may be an attempt not to pilot the routes but rather to get off the boat entirely.

There is an inevitability and unidirectionality to streams that seems natural in the West. Border officers take care of the navigation for us, determining which channel or back-eddy we are in, and whether we end our journey in Canada, in the United States, or, in some rare instances, in a holding cell. But officers are, in their eyes, directing the vessel, rather than pushing it. In this sense, their position involves sorting travellers into streams rather than producing those streams.

Yet the flow of these streams can also be seen in Akwesasne as a corruption of the way things should be, and residents' resistance to those flows as simultaneously challenging and affirming who they are. In the next section, I look more closely at the ways in which BSOs and Akwesasronon jointly, and sometimes antagonistically, navigate borders.

Processing

Thinking of processing in terms of streaming offers a helpful way to conceptualize its properties but doesn't necessarily explain why officers choose to direct travellers down particular paths. In this section, I try to offer a sense of how CBSA officers process travellers at the Cornwall port of entry. More specifically, I look at how they talk about their authority, what constitutes it, and how they determine when, and to what extent, to apply that authority. I also ask how Akwesasronon choose to present themselves to CBSA officers at the Cornwall port of entry.

Processing is what BSOs *do* at ports of entry. As one officer told me at the start of our interview, "We're trained to process people, people and goods."[1] As I argued in the previous chapter, processing is often the most salient way in which "the border" manifests – through the face-to-face interactions between BSOs and travellers. Consequently, an examination of processing gets at the heart of the ways in which both BSOs and Akwesasronon experience the border.

Here I wish to argue that "inconsistency," or perhaps more accurately "uncertainty," is a defining facet of many interactions between BSOs and Akwesasronon. Inconsistency in interactions frequently results when both BSOs and Akwesasronon organize their activities along an axis of two seemingly incommensurable approaches to the border. BSOs simultaneously invoke an absolute adherence to the law and the pragmatic employment of discretion. Akwesasronon simultaneously invoke an ideological opposition to the border (principle), and a pragmatic and strategic approach to crossing (practicality).

How to Study Processing

Of the large body of scholarly research on borders, most studies do not pay much attention to processing. Most of what has been written in North America has focused on movement across the Mexico-US border and undocumented migration (see, e.g., Heyman 1995; Kearney 2004; John 2012; Hernández 2010; but for a study of the western Canada-US border see Chang 2012). While some studies have emphasized the creation and identification of people as "illegals" (Genova 2002; Ngai 2004) or the myriad technologies employed by border security (see, e.g., Zureik and Salter 2005; Pickering and Ham 2014), less has been written on the ways in which "legal" travellers traverse ports of entry.

Rather than being simply a fundamental marker of identity, citizenship is rapidly becoming understood as an economic resource employed to gain access to different countries and markets. Aihwa Ong's influential text *Flexible Citizenship* (1999) suggests that choice (choosing to travel, work, or claim one of several citizenships) is an increasingly important factor in border crossing. Yet while travellers may present themselves in different ways to smooth interactions with BSOs, most lack the opportunity or motivation to travel "as" anything other than a citizen of a particular country.

---

1 This distinction between "people" and "goods" highlights one of many potential impasses between officer knowledge and Haudenosaunee teachings, as several sacred objects are locally seen, as one Akwesasronon succinctly put it, as "parts of the community too" (discussed in chapter 2), bearing rights, responsibilities, and personhood.

Audra Simpson's *Mohawk Interruptus* (2014) implicitly suggests a worthwhile complication of Ong's work. As I mention in the introduction, Simpson demonstrates the ways in which Mohawk residents of Kahnawake see border crossing as a site for the "activation and articulation of their rights and identities." Simpson describes instances in which travellers intentionally cross the border "as Mohawk" rather than Canadian or American, despite the fact that doing so makes travel more difficult. She suggests a sort of "inflexible citizenship" at the heart of Haudenosaunee political ideologies that becomes expressed in cross-border travel. As Simpson's chapter is the most extensive (if not the only) treatment of Mohawk border crossing, my own text must be seen, at least in part, as a response to hers.

In my research in Akwesasne, I found Simpson's discussion accounted very well for part of the story but not all of it. On the one hand, Akwesasronon frequently talked about border crossing in terms of their political principles and rights when speaking to journalists or politicians, or when asked about sovereignty or nationalism or rights. In a survey of community residents, several remarked that they prefer using Mohawk ID rather than Canadian or US passports whenever they have the opportunity. Yet in Akwesasne, where many people traverse the border several times a day, most border-crossing conversations were far more banal – short and uneventful.

Many travellers emphasized practicality rather than principle when crossing the border – with the majority crossing using a Canadian or US passport. Simpson describes an incident where she shouts at a BSO, "I am a Mohawk!" (2014, 119), when the officer told her that she was American. Yet I met many residents of Akwesasne who had little problem being called American or Canadian if it meant making their dentist's appointment on time, and still others who did not mind at all. For many, an important factor was how the officer treated them at that moment – whether they had a history with the officer, or viewed them as rude, or condescending, or polite. The minutiae of each interaction, and the context surrounding it, played as great a role in what took place as long-standing Mohawk ideologies over sovereignty.

To put it simply, a more complete interrogation of the role of border and border crossing in the articulation of Mohawk rights, identity, territory, and sovereignty must take into account the many instances in which travellers choose not to articulate or activate their identity and rights. Such a study invokes Yael Navaro-Yashin's (2002) suggestion that ethnography focus not only on acts of resistance to the state but inversely on the ways in which citizenry may "embrace" the state.

This does not mean that Akwesasronon have any desire to give Canada, or the United States, any form of hug. Rather, it suggests that, just as Simpson opened the possibility of viewing the border as a site for the "activation" and "articulation" of one's rights, we should equally look at the circumstances within which one chooses to de-activate or "inarticulate" those rights. In doing so, we can get a more poignant view of the ways in which daily regulatory practices of a state can represent a "banal nationalism" (Billig 1995), a sense of the inevitability, if not legitimacy, of the nation-state's existence, and one's identity in relation to that nation-state. Among populations defined by their resistance to state norms, it is especially productive to look at the many situations in which resistance does not manifest itself.

Discretion

Officer discretion is a popular topic of inquiry in studies of policing. However, its meaning is not uniform. The term "discretion" is often used to describe a wide variety of policing activities and can even be used in mutually incompatible ways (Ericson 2007). BSOs employed the term "discretion" in a variety of ways but most frequently in the manner Ericson describes as "ethnographic," emphasizing stories and anecdotes rather than a systematic definition of the word.

Discretion, as officers described it, is seemingly fractal and paradoxical. It involves the exercise of choice alongside the forfeiture of responsibility – the embracing of a seemingly contradictory "the law's the law" approach to policing and a relativistic "you have to use your judgment" approach.

> Discretion, to me is a tough one, because what you might deem to be something you can use your discretion on might be different than what I would, might, use my discretion on, so it's very individualistic, it's based on different scenarios, and there's no "one [size] fits all," so it's dynamic in that sense in that you have to use your judgment, and use your discretion. But, you know, you also have to do what your job is, and you have to uphold the law, then you have to uphold the law.

In this sense, discretion is simultaneously acting within and outside the law. It is acting within the broad scope of an officer's mandate even if outside the tight restrictions of statute. This was suggested to me by an anecdote about traffic stops from the same officer, who had previously worked highway patrol.

> Well, you know, any time you're in a position to enforce any type of law or regulation or act of Parliament you're going to have conflict. I use the

example coming from my policing background. What is the speed limit posted on the highway, and how many of us abide by that speed limit, which is a law […] I personally don't drive 100 kilometres per hour, I tend to go with the flow of traffic […]

… [we can use] the analogy of a white lie. We rationalize it and say okay, it's acceptable for me to not necessarily tell you the whole truth because perhaps the truth will hurt.

Discretion was often understood by officers as an essential facet of the job. My efforts at employing hypothetical situations to get a better sense of the underlying rules of officer discretion ("Would I be charged duty for leaving my tent in my car, for example?") were dismissed.

"Noninvocation of the law" (LaFave 2006) offers the most productive definition of discretion-in-action as it applies to the activities of border services officers. Officers depicted discretion as their ability not to exercise the fullest extent of their legal authority or mandate – more concretely, as the ability not to demand certain forms of identification, or not to charge duties on certain goods, and so forth. Thus understood, discretion is often the ability to choose not to act in a way prescribed by the job, rather than to choose among a variety of actions permitted by the job.

At the Cornwall port of entry, discretion often involves choosing not to ask for ID, choosing to accept a legally unacceptable form of ID, choosing not to charge duties, choosing not to ask certain questions, or choosing to accept non-answers to other questions. As border officers spoke about it, their discretionary authority stemmed from their capacity to not invoke the law. As I discussed in chapter 3, once computers started requiring officers to enforce the law, even if they felt it was a bad idea, they still exercised discretion in telling travellers why they were stopped, if they did not agree with the computer.

Time and again, officers invoked the phrase "what is reasonable" when I tried to get them to elaborate on how they choose to exercise discretion. When I asked what they would do, they told me they would do what is reasonable. But what does that mean? In the next section, I ask, "What is 'reasonable' as far as officers are concerned?"

The "Reasonable" BSO

The "reasonable man" concept has a long history in the study of law and society. Past philosophers such as Aristotle and Montesquieu imagined an "ideal type" of person who represented a paradigm of either virtue or averageness against which legal orders were judged.

The idea was that laws frequently revolve around the question "Would a reasonable person do this?" Max Gluckman (1955, 1965a, 1965b) brought this concept into the anthropology of law – showing that, even if what constituted a reasonable man (or woman, or child, or elder, etc.) varied within and among cultures, legal systems across cultures employed the "reasonable person" concept in determining what is acceptable and unacceptable. The way in which officers think about "what is reasonable" is important for two reasons: firstly, it is a factor in determining how they process travellers; secondly, it complicates a long-standing theme in the anthropology of law, the "reasonable man" concept.

In brief, the "reasonable man" principle is built around the assumption that societies operate in accordance with an assumed standard for how a reasonable person would act in a given situation. Consequently, in order to determine whether something is legal, we ask, "Is this what a reasonable person would do in the same circumstance?" Legal anthropologists complicated this metric by examining how there are different social roles that maintain their own standard for "what is reasonable." A reasonable parent is not the same as a reasonable child, and neither is the same as a reasonable doctor. Nor is a reasonable man going to behave in the same way as a reasonable woman. Simply put, different social positions engender different standards for what is reasonable.

This is an important distinction for our current considerations, as a "reasonable BSO" does not necessarily follow the same standards as a "reasonable member of the travelling public." BSOs express reasonableness as the standard by which they exercise their authority whenever possible. This standard is sometimes depicted as a legal standard – that officers require "reasonable cause" to do something – but is also often depicted as a professional standard by which they judge themselves and their colleagues, regardless of legal compulsion.

This was a matter of contention during the Fallan Davis hearing – a meeting of the Ontario Human Rights Tribunal (which I attended) in which a young Mohawk woman from Akwesasne accused the CBSA of discrimination. During the hearing, a former CBSA officer disagreed with the attorney representing the CBSA as to the necessity of reasonable cause with regard to searching vehicles. The officer said that he had no problem telling people who were electronically referred at random by a computer system that it was not he but the computer that had decided to send them to secondary inspection. The CBSA lawyer resisted the officer's assertion that "We'd have to have reasonable, probable grounds to do that stuff. You have to have reasonable grounds to do what you're doing – and I know that's changed a lot over the years, but as an old-timer, there's limits."[2]

Even in searching international travellers, Canadian border services officers are legally obligated to have "reasonable cause," though this standard is legally nebulous and far looser than that regulating police (Pratt 2010). As the court found in *R v. Simmons* (1988), while "searches made at the border ... are reasonable simply by virtue of the fact that they occur at the border," more invasive scrutiny such as strip searches or cavity searches require a higher standard of justification. In other words, there is a proportionality principle for the invasiveness of searches at the border. While some form of interrogation or inspection (opening one's trunk, for example, or rolling down the windows of one's car) is reasonable given that the person is crossing a border, more invasive searches require more justification. One cannot legally conduct a full cavity search of a cross-border traveller "on a hunch." However, officers have a wide recourse when seeking to justify their hunches after the fact (Pratt 2010). An officer may decide to search a traveller on a hunch at that moment, but when called upon to justify their search in court, they can point to any one of a number of indicators to justify that search after the fact – even if they did not consciously consider those indicators at the time.

In processing international travellers, border services officers adhere to their professional notion of reasonability, even if they do not feel constrained by a legally delimited standard. Here is an example, from one of my interviews with an officer stationed in Cornwall:

> OFFICER: Police have the power for search and seizure and they have to have reasonable grounds. We [border officers] have the power of search and seizure based on the virtue of you travelling through the customs process.
> ME: So reasonable grounds aren't necessary? Anyone who crosses the border is subject to search and seizure?
> OFFICER: They can expect that they may be subject to that. As part of travelling through the border.

While an officer who searches too many vehicles without explanation may be reprimanded for causing complaints, or taking too long to expedite the flow of traffic, they typically do not have to worry about the

---

2 All quotations from the human rights tribunal were typed *in situ* as the person spoke, though I did not record them.

same legal reprisals as a police officer who stops random cars on the street and demands that the drivers open their trunks. Nor do they have to worry about the results of their search being thrown out of a court of law. While a legally delineated standard of reasonable search exists for border policing, many officers are ignorant of or undertrained in that standard (Pratt 2010).

Officers I spoke with do, however, abide by their own sense of what is reasonable. In fact, this sense was central to the ways in which officers articulated their own discretion. The term "reasonable" was referred to again and again when I asked how officers decide which questions to ask and what to expect of travellers bringing personal goods across the border. I feel it is this standard of reason the officer on the stand referenced when saying, "We'd have to be reasonable."

I asked the officer quoted previously to clarify what he meant by "reasonable."

ME: How would you define reasonable?
OFFICER: I can't go there. What's reasonable for me, and what's reasonable for you are two different things. Every scenario is so unique it's hard for me to say generically, this is what's reasonable.
ME: Okay, and there's nothing written in the Customs Act that says "reasonable is defined as ..."?
OFFICER: Reasonable is up to the officer's articulation. So I interview you, I'm asking you questions in a primary lane, there's a multiplicity of indicators that are going to be coming into play as to whether or not I believe your statements. Or whatever I see also in terms of indicators, visually, and also when we're having that exchange of dialogue and you're responding to my questions. But that's, again, there's no generic "here's the rulebook on how this works" because to me what is reasonable and to you what is reasonable will depend on a number of things, on what you're seeing, and it's very difficult to say because I'll have a viewpoint of it, because I have a lengthy law experience background and what I'm seeing and hearing, and you're going to have a totally different perspective because you don't. So it's very difficult for me to say here's what's reasonable, and here's what's not reasonable.

There are two standards for reasonability that officers employ in processing. Whether something is reasonable is at the same time (1) the standard by which they judge themselves and their coworkers ("Is it reasonable for *me* to stop this person?"), and (2) the standard by which they judge the activities of travellers and act in accordance with that judgment ("Is it reasonable for *this person* to be carrying forty pounds of fertilizer and a map to the prime minister's house in their car?").

The former, reflexive, exercise of reasonability ("Is it reasonable for me to stop this person?") does not seek a mean or median. In other words, it does not ask whether "the average officer" would consider this reasonable but rather whether "a good officer" would consider this reasonable for a traveller to be doing. Indeed, the idea is that as an officer's experience and training increase, their ability to judge "what is reasonable" also increases. The latter standard, however ("Is this traveller behaving reasonably?"), relates to "a reasonable member of the travelling public," and fits more closely with the traditional notion of the reasonable man as a typical rather than an exceptional individual. Ultimately, the two standards combine in the way border officers make their decisions, asking, in effect, "Would a good officer see this traveller as behaving reasonably?"

Canadian courts differentiate between the legal requirements and definitions of "reasonable" for border policing and inland policing. BSOs have a much wider range of powers in determining whom to stop and search than police officers. Yet the Cornwall port of entry is the one location along the Canada-US border where this distinction becomes extremely problematic.

Because thousands of Cornwall Island residents live on ostensibly Canadian soil between the Cornwall port of entry and New York State, border officers have no way of immediately determining whether or not a traveller is "international" – having started their journey in New York State – or "domestic" – having started their journey on Cornwall Island. Many people crossing at the port of entry have not crossed "the border," and therefore should not "reasonably" expect a search. Unlike at any other port of entry, the first thing BSOs in Cornwall have to do when processing travellers is determine the extent of their powers. The traveller's status determines whether they should behave like border officers or inland police. But that status is not known until after they talk to the traveller. In the next section, I examine one of several unique facets of processing at the Cornwall port of entry, the differentiation of a "mixed traffic" of international and domestic travellers.

Domestic versus International Travel: Policing by Consent

The CBSA's requirement that travellers to Cornwall Island first "report in" is simple in principle but complicated in practice. Anyone driving across the borderline into Cornwall Island must first report directly to the Cornwall port of entry. Afterward, anyone continuing onto the mainland may proceed within Canada, and anyone going to Cornwall Island may double back onto the island. One of many problems with this system in practice is that the Cornwall port of entry currently handles a "mixed traffic." Because the bridge from Cornwall Island filters directly into the port of entry in the city of Cornwall, some of the travellers crossing the bridge are "international" travellers who began their journey south of the borderline. Others are "domestic" travellers who began their journey on Cornwall Island.

A traveller's status has a substantial impact on the powers and responsibilities of BSOs in their dealings with that traveller. While border services officers have had the authority of Canadian police since the 1990s (see chapter 3), mainland policing and border policing remain different. As noted above, the legal statute delimiting "reasonable search" is much looser for cross-border travellers than it is for those who have not left Canada. A BSO may stop an eighty-year-old grandmother, search her trunk, and demand that she provide identification if she is crossing the border. If that officer finds contraband in her car, and can assert that she "looked nervous" or offer a simple explanation for the search, then that grandmother is going to jail. A police officer, on the other hand, cannot make the same demands of a citizen walking or driving within Canada. The fruits of such a search would doubtless be considered inadmissible in court.

In the above examples, the suspect's point of origin is assumed. Anyone at a port of entry is understood to be an international traveller and therefore subject to greater discretionary authority by a BSO, and anyone from inland is understood to be "domestic" (even if they are not a Canadian national) and subject to more rigorous standards of "reasonable search." Yet the status of a traveller is, initially at least, unknown to BSOs. Although offsite analysis of videos can eventually determine after the fact whether vehicles crossed the bridge from the United States, at the moment of contact a BSO has no way of knowing this. Thus, the first responsibility of BSOs is to determine what their responsibilities and powers are vis-à-vis the traveller.

In the previous chapter, I mention the prosecution of Akwesasronon travellers for stating that they were coming from Cornwall Island when, in fact, their point of origin was New York State. While the CBSA has officially changed their primary question from "Where are you coming from?" to "Are you, your vehicle, or any goods in your possession arriving from the United States?," as I write this, "Where are you coming from?" is still the question asked by BSOs. It became not uncommon for some residents, particularly youths, to state that they were coming from the island after realizing that officers did not typically ask any additional questions and simply let them proceed. Other travellers would answer "the island" without employing subterfuge, simply because the island actually was their location prior to their arrival at the port of entry. Thus, oral declarations are not entirely reliable for BSOs. Travellers may claim "domestic" status in order to expedite travel.

This poses a problem for officers. A traveller in a car is simultaneously both and neither international and domestic until their status can accurately be determined. How, then, do officers determine whether a traveller is domestic or international? The way a traveller answers can say a bit about where they are from. If a known Cornwall Island resident says "the island," they are more likely to be believed than a stranger saying "Cornwall Island." Yet this is often not enough, and risks profiling non-Mohawk travellers coming from the island – such as anthropologists, for example. Indeed, I found that I was often treated with greater scrutiny when coming from an interview on the island and declaring myself to be a domestic traveller, even if officers are legally supposed to treat domestic travellers with less invasiveness. While this did not personally bother me (I found it gave good data), it stymies social relationships between island residents and non-residents, especially non-Indigenous residents. Cornwall residents I spoke to who had friends and classmates on the island were reluctant to pay a toll and deal with border officers in order to visit their friends' homes in what is, ostesnsibly, another part of Canada.

One technique employed by BSOs with people they suspect are lying about coming from the island is to demand identification and ask additional questions. Even if identification won't determine whether or not a traveller began their journey in Canada, it could assuage any concerns as to whether they have the legal right to be in Canada. It is a way for officers to determine that "even if this person is lying, they can still legally enter the country." But do officers have the legal authority to ask for these things? This remains uncertain. A Canadian police officer cannot legally demand a passport from someone driving down the street. Yet there is no established training for "mixed-traffic corridors," and the only regulated one is Akwesasne. There are also, to date, no court cases challenging officers' powers vis-à-vis domestic travellers at the port, stating what they can or cannot do.

So, how can officers determine the limits and responsibilities of their authority without exercising that authority in the first place? One way officers in Cornwall challenge the legal nebulousness of their authority is through what Ericson calls "policing by consent." By getting travellers to give information voluntarily, or accept search voluntarily, officers do not have to compel them to do so:

> Policing by consent is the usual way in which police work gets done. Having the subject of police investigations consent to routine information checks, searches, and interrogations avoids statutory requirements. For example, a consenting suspect can be searched without reasonable grounds for suspicion. Policing by consent also reduces the visibility of police discretion. (Ericson 2007, 373)

But how do officers obtain this consent? Ericson argues that "people consent because of some combination of deference to police authority, assumed legal powers of the police, ignorance of the law, and a belief that guilt will be implied if they resist and more intrusive investigation will result" (ibid.). As John A. Hall (1994) suggests, coercion and consent, though seen as opposites are, in the sphere of government, more often complementary.

This meshes with my own experiences and those of interviewees from Akwesasne. More harshly, officers can employ legalese or accusations to coerce "consent." On one of the few occasions when I was interrogated on coming from the island, I felt compelled to provide ID to the officer after he accused me of contravening the Customs Act. I recorded my description of the incident as I drove away seconds later:

> BSO: Where do you live?
> ME: I'm coming from the island.
> BSO: That's not what I asked you. I asked you where you live.
> ME: [Surprised] I live in Montreal (this was during a post-fieldwork return visit to Akwesasne).
> BSO: Can I see your ID?
> ME: Why are you asking me for that? I came from the island.
> BSO: I'm asking you because you are in contravention of the Customs Act.
> ME: Why do you think I'm in contravention of the Customs Act?
> BSO: You have a New York-plated car and you reside in Canada.
> ME: I'm not a resident of Canada, I'm living here on a student visa, and I'm allowed to have my car. Look, here's my passport and visa. [I hand over the documents.]
> BSO: Why, if you don't mind my asking, were you on the island?
> ME: I was conducting an interview with Mike Mitchell.
> BSO: What about?
> ME: I'm doing a doctoral research project on the border. That's why I asked you those questions.

BSO: Canadian residents aren't allowed to have US-plated vehicles, there's an exception to that because you're a student and here temporarily. That's why I was asking you what I was asking. [Officer returns documents and opens lane for me to exit.]

In the above exchange, I felt intimidated by the officer's assertion that I was "in contravention of the Customs Act." My familiarity with CBSA operations left me (1) aware of what the word "contravention" meant, and (2) aware that my vehicle's status in Canada was legal; even so, I felt that the best way to mollify the BSO was through handing over ID and answering his questions.

To a considerable extent, the way in which consent is garnered stems not merely from the public's perceptions of police authority but from a toolkit employed by border officers to gain consent. The most visible tool is the use of language. By framing an utterance as a personal request rather than a legal demand, officers can often gain information without invoking their legal authority. In the preceding exchange, for example, the officer asked, "Why, *if you don't mind my asking*, were you on the island?" Many travellers do not recognize that a personalized request is not legally mandated.

Even though I knew that I was not legally obligated to answer the officer's question, if I had decided not to do so it could have increased his suspicion. He could have then come up with a reason to justify a more invasive search after the fact, saying I seemed either too nervous or too confident, for example.

Another incident earlier in my field research exemplified both the use of personalization and modal language (*can, could, may, might, should, would*), by an officer to secure consent. Again, this exchange was recorded and transcribed after the fact:

BSO: Where are you coming from?
ME: The island.
BSO: What were you doing there?
ME: I was interviewing someone.
BSO: Do you ... uh ... can I see your passport?
ME: Are you allowed to ask me for that?
BSO: I'm asking you for that.
ME: Okay [handing over passport].
BSO: Okay, thank you [returns passport]. Have a nice day.

In the above exchange, the officer did not threaten me, but asked if she could see my passport, making it clear that it was her asking for the document. Regardless of whether this sort of phrasing is taught at officers' training at Rigaud, it remains one of the means by which they secure consent for exercising their powers, particularly when unsure about what those powers are. The distinction between "Could you open your trunk?" and "Open your trunk" is a subtle one, but legally significant. I invite the reader to recall, in the previous chapter, that the American port supervisor insisted I "should" report in to the US port of entry, when I asked him about the legality of the policy.

I juxtapose these two encounters to illustrate the ways in which officers deal with uncertainty that is unique to Cornwall, but also to highlight the ways in which good "face work" translates to a smoother interaction at the border. Whereas I drove away from the first officer fuming and contemplating filing a complaint, I found little frustration with the second officer, who framed their request as personal rather than threatening, I felt more comfortable complying with their request.

Several residents of Akwesasne complained about the intentional opacity of BSOs' language in dealing with travellers. An officer could say a traveller "has broken" a law, or that they are "in contravention" of a law. They can talk about a "vehicle" or a "conveyance." They can also cite statutes with which the traveller may be unfamiliar. Akwesasronon recognized these efforts as intimidating, seeking to push them into compliance rather than elucidate the officer's motivations.

The primary statute delimiting officers' authority with regard to the mixed traffic coming off Cornwall Island is section 99(1) F of the Customs Act. It was frequently invoked by officers to justify their authority. The section reads as follows:

> (f) where the officer suspects on reasonable grounds that this Act or the regulations or any other Act of Parliament administered or enforced by him or any regulations thereunder have been or might be contravened in respect of any conveyance or any goods thereon, stop, board and search the conveyance, examine any goods thereon and open or cause to be opened any package or container thereof and direct that the conveyance be moved to a customs office or other suitable place for any such search, examination or opening.

One officer I interviewed told me that initially, section 99(1)(F) was applied widely by officers to exercise authority over travellers they were suspicious of, though this had been curtailed by supervisors as of 2013. They said that today officers are not supposed to accuse travellers claiming to be domestic of lying unless they are nearly 100 per cent certain that such is the case.

While reference to the act is typically used (intentionally or not) as a sword by officers, intimidating travellers into complying more readily than they might otherwise be inclined to do, the text of the act reads more as a shield. It requires "reasonable grounds" for officers to exercise powers on domestic travellers.

Having looked at the tools employed by BSOs to secure, or coerce, consent in local enforcement strategies, I look, in the next section, at a countermeasure: "knowing your rights."

Knowing Your Rights

Knowing one's rights offers a response of sorts to policing by consent. If "what is reasonable" was the mantra of officers, "know your rights" was that of travellers. Many Facebook posts begin or end with "Know your rights," often in capital letters. Many of my interviewees sagely stated, "I know my rights," as the preamble or postscript to discussions of their interactions with border officers. Consequently, it is worth investigating what it means when someone says, "I know my rights."

Whereas policing by consent relies upon a suspect's acquiescing to the officer's efforts at search and interrogation, the idea of knowing one's rights is organized around knowledge of which powers are legally compulsory and which require consent. In Akwesasne, knowing your rights often means knowing when not to give consent.

People in Akwesasne often talk about knowing their rights, and this can mean a variety of things. It can refer to knowing one's rights to mobility under the Jay Treaty, even though Canada, unlike the United States, does not recognize those rights. In this context, knowing one's rights involves a self-assurance regardless of whether it meshes with Canadian law. Alternatively, knowing one's rights can, and often does, refer to knowing one's rights within the law – in this context, knowing what border officers can and cannot do in their interactions with travellers.

During my fieldwork, a YouTube video of United States border-patrol stops began to circulate over Facebook among my friends in Akwesasne. The video, one of many online, shows drivers and passengers refusing to say anything to border-patrol officers other than "Am I being detained?" and "Am I free to go?" The officers asking, in a manner described in the above section, "Could I see your ID?" or "Could you tell me your citizenship?" are confounded by the traveller's refusal to consent to their requests. One popular posting was titled "Know your rights!" with a respondent writing, "That's how they'll win (police state) by intimidating everyone!"

Many Akwesasronon I interviewed offered stories of triumph, or frustration, in refusing to acquiesce to an officer's requests or demands. These are popular topics of conversation, and stories – especially those of triumph – arise unsolicited in the workplace or at the dinner table (the next chapter directly considers "border stories"). Recently, a friend told me of his experience driving through the Cornwall port of entry. As he described it, there were two people in the booth, a senior officer and one in training. My friend pulled his car into the port of entry and rolled down the windows to speak with the trainee. He answered the standard questions – "Where are you coming from?" and "Where do you live?" – but did not hand over his passport. The officer held out his hand insistently while my friend sat in the car smiling at him, knowing that he was under no obligation to produce the passport unless verbally asked to do so. The officer became increasingly exasperated as he continued to hold out his hand. Finally, after a minute or so of tension, the officer asked for the passport, which my friend produced without complaint. The officer then asked my friend why he hadn't handed over the passport from the start. My friend replied that he was under no legal obligation to do so unless asked explicitly by an officer. He then described how the senior officer told the trainee, "He's right," as the trainee grudgingly handed back the passport and wished my friend on his way. My friend smiled as he told the story about how he knew and exercised his rights.

Despite the fact that many BSOs I spoke with suggested that one of their duties is to inform people of their rights, such a model can be at odds with a consent model for policing. Officers' ability to gain consent is often contingent upon a traveller's not knowing their rights.

Doing What's Right versus Doing What's Easy: Principle versus Practicality

In the preceding sections, I offered a brief window into the sometimes ambivalent, always complex, relationship between BSOs and "the law." I argued that at the Cornwall port of entry, border work often sits at various points along a spectrum ranging from an inflexible adherence to the rules, in which "the law's the law," and a flexible and pragmatic interpretation in which "you have to use discretion." While these two orientations to law may seem contradictory, they are, in fact, mutually constitutive facets of border policing. In this section, I suggest that Akwesasronon are involved in a similarly contradictory yet constitutive relationship with legal norms in their own relationships with the border.

Akwesasronon traversing the Cornwall port of entry navigate between a principled, idealized notion of what the border and its enforcement *should* be and a practical, pragmatic desire to traverse the border and conduct their business expeditiously. The ways in which Akwesasronon interact with BSOs, and the public more generally, reflect both facets of decision making simultaneously.

I offer this anecdote as an example. On 12 March, several community members affiliated with Akwesasne's local "Idle No More" movement began circulating a petition to "end apartheid" in Akwesasne. The petition argued that the CBSA's reporting-in policies were discrimination tantamount to apartheid. It demanded that the port of entry return to Cornwall Island, effectively ending the reporting-in system, arguing that the CBSA had a moral and legal obligation to ensure equal treatment of travellers. The first person to sign the petition was Chief Brian David, who stated for local news cameras:

It gives me pleasure to be the first to sign this petition. Since talks with CBSA there have always been three or four options on the table. One was to build a permanent port in Cornwall, and the other was to build the port in the United States, the third option was to reopen this port here [on *Kawehnoke*], and of course the fourth option was to move the port entirely. In examining those options, the CBSA has never really known for sure how thick the ice was in terms of whether or not they'd be welcome back, and indeed, I think this is a good time that we re-examine, take the pulse of the community strategically at this time to make that determination as to how the community feels about whether the post should be reopened, customs port here, and hopefully it will generate the kind of dialogue and discussion that's needed in order to bring this message back to CBSA. So it's with that in mind that I sign the petition. (Seaway Today 2013)

As Akwesasronon affiliated with the petition hosted a demonstration at the People's Fire, across from the former site of the port of entry on Cornwall Island, another community member began circulating a counter-petition. The organizer of the counter-petition, a lifelong Cornwall Island resident, told me, "We fought to get the CBSA off the island, and I don't want them back here." The counter-petition read, "We, the undersigned do not want CBSA to come back to *Kawehnoke* [Cornwall Island]."

As we discussed the position of the counter-petition, the organizer, a former chief, told me, "It comes down to doing what's right versus doing what's easy." She continued by noting that history has shown that people who do what's right will ultimately win out. In this instance, "doing what's right" meant keeping Canadian Border Services off Mohawk land, even if this necessitated the difficulty of reporting in regularly.

In the end, too few Akwesasronon signed either petition to offer a good gauge of the community's interest in the CBSA's return to the island.

Chief David ultimately signed both petitions – the one in favour of the port's return, and the one against it. He remarked, "If one of the functions of leadership is to promote and provoke dialogue on critical political issues, than [sic] we haven't strayed from that" (Oakes 2013).

How to interpret the chief's signing of both petitions? Rather than performing a simple act of shrewd politicking, Chief David was acting in recognition of an ambivalence, not an indifference, that defines the ways in which Akwesasronon often make choices in relation to the border.

In Akwesasne, people want, at the same time, to do "what is right" and "what is easy." Journalists have represented Akwesasne as a community divided into two camps: idealists (or ideologues) and pragmatists (or opportunists) (for a recent example, see Smith 2014; for earlier examples, see Hornung 1991; Johansen 1993). However, one can also think of Akwesasne as a community in which each individual is divided, to varying degrees, between idealism and pragmatism. Such a conception, in my mind, better recognizes Akwesasne as a singular community – more united over shared uncertainties than divided by them.

Another chief echoed the former chief's distinction between "what's right" and "what's easy." As we sat in the kitchen of the Mohawk Council of Akwesasne's administration building, he told me that, "at the end of the day," people's decisions come down to choosing between "principle" and "convenience." However, unlike the former chief, he held the view that history has shown that convenience will always win out. People have to get to work or to school, get home, do their grocery shopping, and so on, he said. When crossing the border, he makes sure to answer officers' questions as clearly as possible and provide whatever ID makes processing easiest. Rather than see himself as abandoning principle, he saw Washington, D.C., and Ottawa as more fruitful venues for enacting change.

One visible way in which Akwesasronon navigate between practicality and principle in everyday life is in their interactions with border services officers. While officers exercise choice as to what streams to place travellers in, and what sorts of questions to ask, Akwesasronon exercise choice as to how they present themselves, and how they respond to those questions. Contestations and articulations of "status" represent one of the main points of contention between Akwesasronon and BSOs. It is also a nexus of the shared uncertainties of officers and travellers. In the next section, I examine what "status" means in the context of anthropology's broader literature and the processing of cross-border travellers.

Status (and, to a Lesser Extent, Contract) Documents

A person's ability to enter and travel within a nation-state is first and foremost determined by citizenship status – the number the person drew in what Ayelet Shachar (2009) calls, "the birthright citizenship lottery." We cannot choose what citizenship we are born with, even if that citizenship often determines, more than anything else, the qualities and possibilities of our life. As one BSO succinctly put it,

> A lot of people had the impression [... that] you are getting a passport because, well, not only are you, your government is saying that you are a US citizen, but that you are a good person [but it has nothing] to do with that. You could be a really bad person and you are still getting a passport. [...] You can be denied entrance, but not a passport.

The most significant economic and social opportunities many will encounter in life will be determined at birth by their nationality. Further, one's experience of rights or discrimination as a member of a minority group is tied to birth rather than choice. This is especially true among Indigenous populations, whose legal status is intimately and inexorably tied to what Circe Sturm calls "blood politics" (2002). In Akwesasne, a person's ancestry ("blood") can determine what sorts of taxes they pay, what sort of hiring preferences they may or may not receive, where they can reside, what sorts of support they are eligible for, and so on.

Status is conventionally presented in the form of identification documents. Many travellers do not have a choice of documents, using only a passport for international travel. For overland travel between Canada and the United States, other WHTI-compliant documents include an enhanced driver's licence or a Nexus card.[3]

Akwesasronon have access to several unique options in border crossing. Many Akwesasronon hold US citizenship, Canadian citizenship, and/or citizenship in the Haudenosaunee Confederacy, which produces its own passport – though that passport is seen by Canada as a

---

3 The ports of entry surrounding Akwesasne do not have Nexus lanes, however.

"fantasy document." Many also hold status as a Native American from the United States, and status as a member of a First Nation from Canada. Some documents are also produced locally by contingents within Akwesasne that do not accept the authority of Canadian, American, or Longhouse governments. During the Fallan Davis hearing, Davis stated that she travelled using one of eight "purple cards" produced by a group of residents who see themselves as subject only to "natural law." At trial, she stated that in the early 2000s, she could present any photo ID, including a health card or a BJ's Wholesale Club Card, to a border officer. Additionally, in years past, many Akwesasronon would present ID to American officers but not to Canadian officers – simply looking at the officers until let go. Because of the diversity of statuses and related documents held by Akwesasronon, choice of status documentation, or non-documentation, represents an easily observable way in which different border-crossing strategies are brought to bear.

The United States accepts "status documents" showing that a traveller has Native American or First Nation status in either Canada or the United States as valid for cross-border travel, while Canada only accepts Canadian "status cards." American officers at the Massena port of entry have also tacitly accepted a wider variety of documents at the border than their Canadian colleagues, though they always demand some sort of photo ID.

The choice of documentation reveals different facets of a person's legal status to the officer. ID that is legally acceptable for admission may not be sufficient for other requirements of border crossing. A Canadian passport may guarantee admission into Canada, but it does not demonstrate membership in Akwesasne, therefore, eligibility for duty exemption under the remission order. Officers may ask a traveller who has provided a passport as ID to also provide a status card, not to determine admissibility but to determine duty exemption. Similarly, older documents cannot be scanned by officers, necessitating the manual entry of information, which may hold up traffic. Officers sometimes ask for licences and other documentation to facilitate processing.

Yet these sorts of requests are rarely framed with clarity to Akwesasronon, who are not told why they are asked for such diverse identification documents. As one Facebook post stated, "CBSA is asking for licences along with Status cards b/c it'll speed up the process – invasion of privacy anyone?" Another resident responded, "It goes a lot faster, all they have to do is swipe it ... I'm not sticking up for CBSA but I give it to them to avoid the hassle and limit the time it takes to get through ... that's just me though." The original poster replied, "I probably would've attempted to speed up the process but her [the officer's] language made it seem mandatory, which I don't agree with. I'm down with speeding up the process as long as they don't step outside their boundaries/powers." The final word on the posting, from another community member, "Weh, I used my licence once and they asked if I had any other ID to prove I was Canadian. The girl working said anyone can get an Ontario licence, and if I didn't prove I was Canadian, they could refuse to let me in." The final traveller, having been previously asked for their licence, came to assume that the licence itself was acceptable documentation for cross-border travel. The conversation thread highlights a simultaneous empathy with the difficulty of CBSA officers' efforts to do their jobs as efficiently as possible and frustration at the inconsistencies in enforcement. It also suggests that the wide variety of identification documents available to Akwesasronon travellers can be as much a liability as a boon.

Akwesasronon travellers express a simultaneous desire to be processed both in the same manner as non-Indigenous travellers and distinctly as rights-bearing Indigenous people. Ultimately, in their efforts to recognize the distinct rights and status of Indigenous North Americans, border officers may end up asking them for more rather than less documentation. BSOs may ask an Akwesasronon traveller for a passport to determine admissibility, a status card to determine duty exemption, and a licence to scan. In the broader context of Indigenous minority rights, this demonstrates the ways in which state efforts to recognize minority rights may prove an inconvenience if not a negation of those rights in practice. Efforts at targeting a specific population as rights-bearing necessitates a burden of proof-of-membership within that group. In the context of Akwesasne, this means that in order to prove that they are eligible for more relaxed border regulations, Akwesasronon are, at times, subjected to stricter border regulations.

Akwesasronon employ a variety of strategies for organizing and presenting ID. One MCA official told me that he recommends people stick their status card inside their passports much as I put my Canadian visa inside my US passport. Another told me that he used his passport unless travelling with alcohol, at which point he would provide his status card. Another resident who used different vehicles for cross-border travel (see my discussion of the "island car" in the previous chapter) told me that he placed a different piece of ID in each vehicle, so he would not forget. With a smaller profile than passports, cards are also easier to travel with. Others told me that they simply used their US passports whenever possible, and only handed over a status card when asked.

For many others, choice of a status card was not simply about "convenience" and duty exemption but was rather a means to cross "as" a Mohawk from Akwesasne. Though accepted by the Canadian government, many of these cards are decades old – one elder resident proudly showed me a card that looked like it was produced nearly half a century earlier.

The above examples, far from being exceptional, stand in contrast to Audra Simpson's ethnographic vignettes of border refusal (Simpson 2014, ch. 5). They are less dramatic but more representative than those she cites. In Akwesasne, choosing to cross with an identity document produced by Canada or the United States represents the norm rather than the exception. That choice frequently reflects a desire to move throughout the territory without hassle. In a community survey, less than 4 per cent of respondents listed a Haudenosaunee passport among the top three documents they use (though several stated they would prefer to use one if they were more likely to be recognized). Numerically, residents tend to prefer ease of travel over conflict and contestation and choose documents accordingly. Nevertheless, many residents complain of irregularity in terms of which documents are accepted by which officers, and on which side of the border. Officers are not always clear about which documents are accepted, and are often inconsistent. Akwesasronon Facebook status updates regularly lament a run-in in which an officer refused to accept a form of identification that the person had used successfully in previous crossings.

The uncertainty about documentation is shared on both sides of the PIL booth. While Akwesasronon have difficulty determining which identification officers would prefer to see, BSOs experience similar uncertainty about what to expect in their encounters. In the case of questionable ID, officers experience a variety of pressures to accept the ID and "de-escalate" any potential conflicts, or to scrutinize the ID in accordance with their training. A video file circulating on the internet highlighted this dilemma. It features a covertly filmed exchange between a Mohawk traveller from Akwesasne and a Canadian BSO with a poor reputation in the community.

BSO: Where are you travelling from?
MOHAWK TRAVELLER: Hogansburg.
BSO: Where do you live?
MT: The island.
BSO: May I see your ID please? Where are you going today?
MT: Home.

BSO: What brings you to Hogansburg?

MT: Visiting.

BSO: Visiting?

MT: Yeah.

BSO: Who?

MT: Does it matter?

BSO: Yeah.

MT: For what reason?

BSO: The nature of your trip to the US and who you're visiting could depend on who you have with you, what you're bringing back ...

MT: Co-workers.

BSO: Do you have any goods to declare?

MT: Nope.

[At this point, several dozen seconds elapse as the officer looks at the traveller's ID. As the phone capturing the exchange is repositioned to capture the officer, one can see the traveller drumming his thumbs at the side of his car. The officer continues looking at the document and at his computer screen.]

BSO: Your vehicle?

MT: Yeah.

[Another very long pause]

BSO: Have you ever thought about getting a new one? [Holds up the ID]

MT: It seems to work.

BSO: Because the face is ... I can't really see you there.

MT: You see me here, right?

BSO: See what I'm saying though? How do I know that that's you? [Hands back the ID] I believe what you're saying right now, that's you, but ... have a good day.

[The traveller drives off.]

Though the video was taken as evidence of BSO aggression toward Akwesasronon, the exchange, in transcription, may invite more sympathy with the officer. In this instance, the traveller was likely able to successfully cross the border with an invalid ID card and a tense exchange with a BSO because of his status as a Mohawk resident of Akwesasne. Yet the terms of the exchange, and the ID most readily available to the traveller, were engendered by that status as well.

One officer I interviewed confided in me his frustrations over longstanding customary enforcement practices of providing differential treatment for Akwesasronon. He said that it was problematic to determine based on phenotype who is and is not Mohawk, saying, "Some of these Mohawks are fucking redheads." Another officer, very well-liked in Akwesasne, jokingly suggested I turn off the recorder when I asked her how she differentiated Mohawk travellers. She said,

> This is ... maybe you should turn your machine off ... but no. I am being very stereotypical but of course it's by looks, and their talking. When they speak they have a degree, again, I hope that this is not ... I'm not trying to sound bad ... but you are the one who asked me the question. A bit of a grunt to their speak, and they don't even look at you some of them. Again, when you are talking of working on a border crossing [...] it's a funnel, you are alone in your vehicle and my job is to put you, and everything that's around you, your vehicle, in a funnel. And my end is to get you out at the bottom [...] and this is all in a few seconds.

I doubt anyone who knows this officer would ever call her racist (many Akwesasronon cited her as "one of the good ones," though the above remarks could be interpreted as racist). Rather, as I see it, the officer took pains to identify Akwesasronon as distinct and positively recognize that distinction in her interactions with them. Ironically, officer efforts to accommodate Indigenous difference by not subjecting travellers to certain forms of scrutiny may rely upon reinforcement of what would otherwise be considered racialized suppositions. In other words, officers recognize the responsibility to accommodate Indigenous cross-border travellers in different ways, and the manner in which they determine who has access to that accommodation is linked to assumptions about what Indigenous people look like – for example, darker skin, and long (but certainly not red) hair.

Akwesasronon choices of ID, or choices not to provide ID, often reflect their own efforts at articulating and activating their rights as Indigenous Mohawk people. Yet these choices also often reflect a pragmatism and practicality among a people who have to cross the border several times daily. Choice of ID is both informed by and formative of the ways in which BSOs process travellers. At the Cornwall port of entry, where officers are mandated by custom and law to treat Akwesasronon equally and exceptionally, the choice of what ID to accept, and what questions to ask, is rarely a simple one. Status is simultaneously at the heart of Indigenous rights and a central problem in those rights' activation.

Inconsistency

A BSO in Cornwall summarized his job as "long periods of boredom interspersed with sudden periods of terror." The same could be said of many Akwesasronon's experiences with border enforcement and processing.

Many unwritten, quasi-unofficial policies have been created (and contested) at the port of entry over the years. These policies have frequently involved the "non-invocation" of the Customs Act in an effort to foster good relations with the Akwesasne community – creating new law, such as the Akwesasne Residents Remission Order, to formally sanction what would otherwise be considered non-invocation of a law. In other words, creating new formal regulations that state the law does not apply in such and such a case is a possible solution to relieving officer anxieties over the legality of their practices. With the remission order, rather than breaking the law when an officer does not charge customs on some goods held by an Akwesasne resident, that officer is instead following an order-in-council specific to the area. But the creation of new law risks opening new and different anxieties for officers, and the creation of more rules that can be misunderstood or misapplied. Often, travellers don't know what to expect from officers, and officers don't know what to expect from travellers.

A former chief stated that much of the current tension between BSOs and Akwesasronon stems from inconsistency.

> What's hard is the inconsistency of being stopped. If the person knows they'll be stopped for five minutes each time, that's okay. But he comes back a few hours later, and the officer waves him through in ten seconds. When that thing goes back and forth – that's the inconsistency. The difficulty is, if you ask me once, and ask me again, then you should ask me a third time, ask me a fourth time. But when you go through and don't get asked again, you aren't asked, and then the time after that, you're asked questions, "Open your trunk" […] inconsistencies, that's what we find there.

This anecdote parallels one I presented in chapter 1, in which a Mohawk resident of Akwesasne expressed annoyance at being asked "cultural" questions by border officers, saying, "You ask ten of us a question, you get ten different answers." Inconsistency is something experienced by both Akwesasronon and Canadian border officers. It is something they consistently expect when they meet.

We can compare the Canadian model for enforcement, which has emphasized codifying new legislative sanctions for non-invocation of the law, with the American model employed at the port of entry in Massena. The US border service is generally viewed as more consistent and preferable to the Canadian service. As far back as anyone I spoke with remembers, US officers have been armed and demanded ID. Yet US officers accept a wider range of identification documents than their Canadian counterparts, and are legally bound, at least in part, by American recognition of the Jay Treaty. The United States' position that Native American governments have sovereignty and that Indigenous North Americans have the right to cross into the United States also aligns with the position of Mohawk nationalists.

Some Notes on Small Talk

Not all that is spoken in processing constitutes processing. Nevertheless, seemingly inconsequential dialogue may be viewed by BSOs as intelligence gathering, as they try to get a sense of the completeness and veracity of a traveller's declarations. Asking, "How did you like the film you saw?" may be a way for the officer to try to verify whether someone is telling the truth about going to the movies, but it may also be a way to show they genuinely care, or a way to pass the time when they are bored. In practice, it often accomplishes all these things. When I told an American officer I was going to spend the day looking for snow tires, she told me, with a grin, "I'm not supposed to give people directions, but if you want a good cheap place for tires, I think you should go here." I was genuinely grateful for her advice, and it rendered me friendlier to her in the future and more willing to answer questions or accept a search if she chose to perform one.

As with many sorts of engagement with the border, I encountered ambivalence about "friendly" interactions between officers and crossers. Some residents found it pleasant getting to know officers. Others felt that these exchanges slowed lines and made the drive across the port even longer. Some travellers, myself included, had difficulty knowing when it was appropriate to end an exchange. Usually it's the officer who says "Goodbye," or "Have a nice day," and not the other way around.

But when a border-crossing interview seems to turn into genuine small talk, unrelated to processing, this distinction is less clear. The disruption of that order, in which the onus is on the traveller, rather than the officer, to end a conversation can be unsettling. I found myself looking backwards at the line of cars stacking up behind me, as I spoke with officers about my research project, my snow tires, and my little sister in Washington, D.C., wondering what the drivers of those cars must be thinking, and whether I was annoying them.

Akwesasronon I spoke to expressed ambivalence about socializing with officers at the booth. Some found it nice that officers attempted to be friendly, especially when they made small efforts toward learning a few words of Mohawk. Others were annoyed, or frustrated. It is sometimes difficult to tell when processing ends and socializing begins: are questions asked for intelligence purposes, or out of genuine interest? Is there even a difference? Historically, the best intelligence gathering among officers has been accomplished through friendships with community members.

Some residents I spoke to were frustrated by the time added to their journey by socializing. One woman told me she had been frustrated after waiting behind her cousin's car for several minutes. She said, with an eye roll, that she called her cousin later that day to ask what the problem was. The cousin replied, "Oh, I was just visiting" with the officer at the booth.

Such ambivalence concerning the friendliness of officers complicates efforts by both the CBSA and their connections within the Mohawk government to "put a friendlier face" on local officers and contributes to the uncertainties of a given interaction. Some residents prefer faceless officers, and merely desire robotic efficiency whenever they are obliged to report at a port of entry. Others value efforts made by BSOs to personalize interaction. Even if nearly all residents with whom I spoke appreciated the fact that one CBSA officer began saying *She:kon* (Greetings) to travellers from Akwesasne, a vocal minority complained, with one resident telling me, "They've taken everything from us, and now they're taking our language."

Community ambivalence toward efforts at personalizing interactions during processing can result in frustration on the part of officers and administrators, leading many efforts at improving relations to feel like a "no-win situation," or not worth the trouble. This can contribute to fatalistic attitudes on the part of many officers, who feel that their actions do not matter in the eyes of Akwesasronon. It can also further contribute to the inconsistency of border services that many in Akwesasne lament.

Conclusion

Of the interactions that take place between officers and Akwesasronon, the pre-eminent one is processing. For many travellers, processing and the border are effectively synonymous. Yet, the waters of processing can be muddy, and in Akwesasne, even the vectors of their flow can be unclear.

As with rivers or streams, one could argue that it is impossible to step across the same border twice, and this is often a source of frustration for both Akwesasne residents and border services officers. I began this chapter with a quotation from a Mohawk resident of Akwesasne:

"Every time we cross that bridge, we have to answer the troll's questions. And we never know what they'll ask." The resident was expressing her frustration at the inconsistency of Canada border services in and around the territory.

Officers, too, are also often frustrated by the inconsistency of their interactions with Akwesasronon travellers. This shared inconsistency may have a historical basis, though it is most immediately rooted in the complexities and flows of processing. Processing involves an interplay of discretion, adherence to the law, reasonableness, coercion, consent, ambiguity, and uncertainty. At the same time, processing, like cross-border traffic, has a flow that must be accounted for, even if resisted. Uncertainty offers a problematic that Akwesasronon and Canadian BSOs share. It becomes the platform for a form of intimacy – not indifference, but its opposite. In recognition of shared participation in the choppy waters of local and national norms and laws relating to the border, Akwesasronon and BSOs may have more in common than is immediately apparent. Cultural sensitivity-training materials, operating on a principle of one-mindedness, may benefit from emphasizing these shared uncertainties as a platform for greater one-mindedness between BSOs and Akwesasronon.

Counter-intuitively, one source of the inconsistency that frustrates both officers and Akwesasne residents is the formal and informal enforcement practices that seek to accommodate Akwesasronon as a distinct rights-bearing group. This is not to say that some officers do not also view Mohawk travellers with suspicion as potential "smugglers." Yet at the same time, efforts to recognize specific rights for Mohawks have engendered either (1) reliance upon racialized understandings of the community in which travellers are expected to look or sound a certain way in order to be recognized as Mohawk; or (2) a greater and often confusing documentary burden of proof for Mohawk travellers than for non-Mohawk travellers. Efforts at targeting Mohawk people for non-invocation of the law as well as requirements to produce documents to identify status-member travellers have added complexity to an already unique border-crossing environment.

Groucho Marx once famously said (while playing a political leader in the film *Duck Soup*), "These are my principles, and if you do not like them ... well, I have others." This quotation says something about how principle operates in political practice. Though doing so through the voice of satire, Marx recognizes that principles are not monolithic and do not exist in a vacuum. They are simultaneously fundamental and flexible. Border officers have principles and rules and, when necessary, they have the option of employing others. Akwesasronon have principles and statuses and, when necessary, they have the option of employing others.

This chapter offers a sense of some of the interactions that take place when Akwesasronon and Canadian border services officers meet in the contentious space of border crossing. But what happens afterwards – after a traveller from Akwesasne has had a tense exchange with a border services officer? Or a funny exchange? Or an uneventful one? These interactions do not disappear when the car drives off into mainland Canada, or when the booth closes. These interactions linger; their stories are told on the radio, on the internet, and in person. In the telling, they may change; harsh words may seem harsher or softer; embellishments may be added, and details may change. Much as ethnography frequently relies upon anecdotes to describe a much bigger picture, anecdotes about exchanges at the border in Akwesasne often come to represent the border itself.

In the next chapter, "Talking Borders," I examine what Akwesasronon take away from their interactions. I look at the stories people tell of their interactions with BSOs, the ways in which those stories "make" the border, and how people incorporate the knowledge from these stories into future interactions. In doing so, I suggest ways in which the tales of "what happened" come to determine "what happens next."

Chapter Seven

Talking Borders

Does a story have to have *really happened* in order to be true? No, I haven't said that right. In order to communicate a truth about relationships, or in order to exemplify an idea. Most of the really important stories aren't about things that really happened – they are true in the present, not in the past.
 Gregory Bateson and Mary Catherine Bateson, *Angels Fear* (2005, ch. 3)

Introduction

Let us talk about borders. Or rather, let us talk about talking about borders. How do the conversations people have about borders – and border enforcement – define borders and border enforcement? How do they define the storyteller and the world they live in? This concern is at the same time theoretical and epistemological.

Border stories are of theoretical concern because anthropologists have long theorized the role of stories in constructing the spaces we live in and the people we interact with. Stories, especially myths, hold a long-standing prominence in anthropological inquiry. Whether it was collecting or categorizing myths around the world (Frazer 1951) or salvaging the myths and other stories told by purportedly "vanishing" populations (see, e.g., Parker 1968; Hewitt 2009; H. Hale 1999), stories of one sort or another have long been seen as a window into the way a population sees the world. Stories have also been examined in terms of their function, as a true or false science (Tylor 1958; Lévi-Strauss 1966; but see Segal 2004), or perhaps most intensively by Claude Lévi-Strauss as a means of reconciling the underlying paradoxes of human thought. In short, stories matter for a lot of reasons.

While border stories may not seek to resolve paradoxes like Lévi-Strauss's myths, they often hinge upon moments of irony or confusion.

They are also a way of making sense of, and in the process making, the complicated borders in and around Akwesasne.

Border stories are, firstly, an epistemological concern. Much of the information I gathered, as with any ethnography of law enforcement, comes from second-hand and third-hand accounts of interactions. They are the stories people tell of their own and others' encounters at or with the border. What can one "do" with these stories? Initially, I attempted to verify stories, particularly second-hand accounts, seeking first-hand corroboration to find out whether they "actually happened," but such a project proved difficult if not impossible. I later came to examine these stories not so much for what they said about what happened in the past as for the truths they reveal about the tellers and the futures they create among believers.

By looking at which sorts of border stories emerge, circulate, and become popular, we can get a sense of the themes that are relevant and believable in the present. These stories people tell are worthy of study in themselves, and not simply as an indicator of "what happened." These stories are what people talk about over dinner or in the break room or what they post online. They are the way people bring the border home with them. And both travellers and officers bring the borders described in their stories back with them to the port of entry. They are, to paraphrase Geertz, the stories we tell ourselves about ourselves (1977, 452). They are as much the border's reality as its reflection.

This chapter discusses what both Akwesasronon and BSOs take away from their interactions at the border. As much as border crossing "takes place" in the interactions between officers and crossers, the border comes into being again and again in the stories that circulate about those interactions. Regardless of whether these stories are rooted entirely in fact, they are used, as Bateson and Bateson suggest, "in order to communicate a truth about relationships, or in order to exemplify an idea. Most of the really important stories aren't about things that really happened – they are true in the present, not in the past" (2005, ch. 3).

Beyond focusing on the content of border stories, we can look at what sorts of stories circulate most frequently, and how people listen and respond to those stories. I identify the themes that recur in border stories and consider why some themes prevail over others. We can also look to the media through which they circulate – not just in informal conversations but also by phone, radio, television, and the internet. I show that the border is simultaneously undermined and reinforced by media and communications technology.

Does a Story Have to Have Really Happened to Be True?

When I first wrote this section, I chose the word "rumour" to describe border stories. The Google definition of "rumour" as "a currently circulating story or report of uncertain or doubtful truth" (Google n.d.; accessed 2015) meshed with my own understanding. The phrase "of uncertain or doubtful truth" suggests a certain dubiousness. "Rumour" is a messy term as an analytic, defined differently across populations. Like rumours themselves, the term is hard to grasp.

As a researcher, I approached these stories with doubt, looking to confirm or refute their veracity. This was an overwhelming task, given the sheer volume of stories, and also one that distanced me from the role these stories played in the imagination of the tellers and audiences and the ways in which that imagination came to define people's own conceptions of the border.

I have elsewhere (Kalman 2015b) privileged the term "story" over alternatives such as "myth" or "legend" when discussing oral history (Vecsey 1986). I do the same here. Stories typically lack the same degree of ingrained scepticism. Border stories are another sort of cosmology, a story about the ongoing creation of the world. As Bateson and Bateson (2005) have suggested, thinking in stories is something fundamentally, though not solely, human. This is no doubt the case in Akwesasne, where learning and exchanging through stories hold special significance in both "traditional" and "contemporary" contexts.

Ultimately, the distinction between a rumour and a story lies with the listeners and not the content of the stories, or their veracity (one could say the framing). This distinction is rarely made explicit, though there were certainly stories that people told with a grain of salt and others that were taken to be true.

Earlier in this chapter, I offered a quotation from Gregory Bateson's and Mary Catherine Bateson's *Angels Fear: Towards an Epistemology of the Sacred* (2005) in which they considered how humans think with stories. Much has been written about this theme before and since, but the Batesons' brief anecdote, told in the form of a dialogue between a father and daughter that is no more "true" than an unverifiable story someone tells to illustrate a point, offers a powerful perspective. If we think of these stories in terms not of whether they happened in the past but of what they say about the present, then they represent ways in which the border is made, and remade, at ports of entry and along borderlines and also wherever and whenever these stories are told.

In a community like Akwesasne, where stories of officer misconduct spread like wildfire (smoke rising to be seen by all) and are, indeed, a popular topic of conversation, these accounts form, in part, the "reality" of the border and its enforcement. The same could be said of border services officers' stories about their own interactions. Border services officers in Cornwall, in particular, are known as a tight-knit group because of the unique stresses of that posting. In the terms introduced at the beginning of this chapter, these stories frame border enforcement in Akwesasne. Regardless of whether they "really happened" in the past, they provide context for interactions in the present.

Below, I offer a few examples of stories from either side of the booth, and trends they suggest in terms of what sorts of stories are most popular and believable.

The *Fallan Davis v. CBSA* human rights tribunal that I followed centred on charges of discrimination by a Mohawk woman who chose to end her pregnancy after her car was singled out to be scanned by X-rays from a mobile VACIS machine, a scanner generally used only for much larger commercial vehicles. This occurred in 2007. Nearly everyone who mentioned the trial to me told me that she had been in the car at the time of the scan. I was surprised to learn from Fallan Davis's testimony that she had been standing outside the car alongside other officers. Nevertheless, she has charged that radiation concerns were the reason she chose to end her pregnancy.

Thematically, this story bolstered ongoing indignation in Akwesasne toward officers. Officers were vilified as the sort of people who would force a pregnant woman to stay in her car while it was scanned by radioactive materials. It also included certain tropes that seem to make up the most popular stories concerning mistreatment by border officers. Most of the stories that widely circulate involve the mistreatment of a youth or elders, women, or someone with a physical condition that is seen as making them more vulnerable. Stories of incidents with male travellers are told, though they are less common. In the Mohawk Council of Akwesasne's preliminary presentation to the Canadian Human Rights Commission concerning complaints, ten examples were presented; seven involved women, and of the three male travellers, two were explicitly described as youths. Roughly half of the incidents described involved a traveller with an illness.

These incidents are the ones most commonly and effectively used to introduce the border situation in Akwesasne to unfamiliar audiences, especially in the context of human-rights violations. Curiously, though the most commonly told stories of abuse involved women, youths, elders, and/or the disabled, of my interviewees who filed complaints, nearly all were adult males. This could account for a discrepancy between the capacities for qualitative and quantitative inquests into officer complaints. While numerically most complaints come from middle-aged men, community perceptions of tensions focus on the abuse of women, children, and the elderly.

If stories told by Akwesasronon about officers focused on the mistreatment of women, youths, and elders, stories told by officers about Akwesasronon emphasized lawlessness and violence. One officer told me how he learned from colleagues who had been stationed in the customs house during the 2009 protests that Mohawk protesters had lit a car on fire in the parking lot. This story was offered to provide evidence of the tense working environment that existed when he arrived, and the state of community-CBSA relations at their nadir in 2009. Yet when I asked a port supervisor who was there at the time about it, he told me unequivocally that there had been no car set on fire. Nevertheless, protesters who were camped beside the customs house lit several "peace fires" within the vicinity for their own purposes.

Most of the stories of violent exchanges reported to me by officers involved a male Akwesasronon traveller, typically one suspected of smuggling, who employed violence, or the threat of violence, against an officer. Stories that stood out involved shots fired at the customs house, and smugglers driving away as an officer inspected their trunk, dragging the officer, whose clothing had gotten caught on the car.

This poses a methodological and analytical consideration for thinking about the border in Akwesasne. Of course, it is useful to distinguish between stories that are easily verified or falsified. However, this is often not possible. Still, the stories that circulate reflect and produce both officers' and Akwesasronon attitudes about border interactions. The storytelling itself is one of the ways that the border manifests in casual conversation, at the dinner table, in the bar, and even in the customs lane.

Self-Fulfilling Public Enemies

In her ethnography of Turkish nationalism, *Faces of the State*, Yael Navaro-Yashin demonstrates the ways in which Turkish ideas of the state can result in a self-fulfilling prophecy, with the state taking on those very characteristics attributed to it (2002, 31, 40). The argument can extend beyond Turkey into notions about states more generally; expectations built around an "othering" of the state (especially perhaps the surveillance state) distanced from the citizenry can result in the creation of that very state. In Akwesasne, the othering of the Canadian and American governments is a built-in facet of Mohawk nationalism and not, as in other contexts, conceivable as a failure of the state to effectively "embrace its people." For many in Akwesasne, the Canadian and American states work best when they are illegitimate and impotent.

Within my interviews, I found many stories, but only one explicit mention of rumour. The interviewee was himself a former police officer who had also worked as a liaison with the CBSA. He was driving home to the island after a game of golf in the United States. The CBSA officer said to him, "I heard a rumour that you have a DUI" (DUI stands for "Driving Under the Influence" [of alcohol]) and demanded to see his licence. My interviewee told the officer, "Fuck you," and asked where he had received the information. This was the first and only time I heard this cool and even-tempered man use profanity. Eventually, he showed the officer his licence but refused to hand it over; after driving home he filed a complaint against the officer. He ended the story with the question, "Is that how they operate, rumour and innuendo?"

The officer who asked my interviewee for his licence was himself known as a blight upon the community. This officer, I later learned, was responsible for more complaints than any other officer since the MCA had opened a file for collecting complaints. Though he had since left (or been driven out of) Akwesasne, mention of his name provoked stories of his racism and abuses of authority. As to what happened to him, I heard stories that his career ended when he, an alcoholic, fell down drunk and hit his head in the shower. I also heard stories that he simply transferred to another port of entry. The first variant was more popular, the second more likely. Both define the ways in which BSOs are seen by the community.

At present, another officer has become the focus of community ire, with stories of his misconduct proliferating in chats and online. Whenever he was in a PIL lane, Akwesasronon would post the lane online so people could avoid him. There was even a video posted of him online. The officer is known and nicknamed for his distinctive hairstyle and was featured in the video discussed in the previous chapter.

I encountered this officer when heading home one evening from dinner and board games at a friend's place in Akwesasne. When I saw the hair, my heart started beating slightly faster – a mix of excitement and nervousness. "This is the guy, the one everyone complains about," I thought. "Maybe I'll get some great data. Maybe he'll send me to secondary inspection." I resolved to treat him like any other officer and simply let the exchange play out. After asking a few of the primary questions, he asked me to open the trunk of my car. After poking into my backpack, he returned my passport and said to me, "Have a nice day." My heartbeat slowed down to normal as I continued home. This was the first (and ultimately the only) time that any Canadian officer searched my car in my year of daily commuting to and from Akwesasne.

Did I seem nervous or petulant because of the rumours I had heard? Did that play a role in his decision to search my car? I would not be surprised either way. In a year of fieldwork, my tensest exchanges with officers often came after I had been interviewing residents with particularly unpleasant stories to tell about their own encounters – even when I attempted a friendly demeanour. It may well be that I brought empathy with the reimagined scenarios of these stories in my car with me when I drove into the port of entry.

We can take Navarro-Yashin's argument one step further in suggesting that not only the state but also the citizenry can produce a self-fulfilling prophecy under similar conditions. This is one way to consider how expectations of officer aggression have the potential to become the reality in Akwesasne. Expecting an abusive officer may yield one; expecting a non-compliant traveller (especially one from Akwesasne) may produce that very traveller. Repeating the rumour that he has been a drunk driver can stir a sober citizen to bellicosity. A citizen's expectation that a BSO will be a hard-ass can lead that officer to wonder why the passenger in front of them seems "off."

Jokes

Not all stories about exchanges at the border are indignant accounts of injustice or tension. There are many other sorts of interaction that take place, but perhaps the sort of communication most salient in people's memories is joking. Joking between officers and travellers is undoubtedly what Radcliffe Brown calls asymmetrical. "A jokes at the expense of B, and B in return teases A only a little" (1940, 195). Border officers can tease travellers indiscriminately, but travellers tease border officers at their own risk.

Below I offer two examples of "joking" exchanges between BSOs and Akwesasronon. The first example is a Facebook posting from Akwesasne's "How's the Bridge" group (which I discuss below). The second was posted in Akwesasne's newspaper, *Indian Time*, as part of the "Life at the Border" section. The mere presence of a newspaper section that chronicles exchanges (and in particular humorous ones) suggests the significance of border interactions in everyday life for many Akwesasronon.

Facebook Anecdote

So, I go across the Cdn bridge last night and wait in line at customs. Finally made [it?] to the booth, and the customs officer asked, "Where are you coming from?" I say, "Hogan." He looks down at his papers, "OK, I have a question for you ... which part of the human body is the largest organ that can regenerate itself?" ... "What?"... He looks down again and repeats himself. I yelled out, "The skin!" (The officer in back of him shouts, "That's true!"). He looks at me and says, "Noooo, it's the Liver ... Have a good nite ..." Bahahaha! That's a first for me ... ☺

Life on the Border: *Indian Time* – **Vol. 22, Issue No. 40 – 7 October 2004**

Stories and Opinions on the US and Canadian Customs

Going through the U.S. Customs one day, my aunt was [in another car] directly ahead of me. As she went through I watched the agent look in the back of [the] vehicle and then she passed him a briefcase from the front seat. He looked inside and then handed it back to her and away she went.

When we pulled up to the same agent he asked the usual questions, which included the notorious, "Do you have $10,000 or more in cash?"

"Nope," I said.

"C'mon!" he joked. "I know you do!"

"No, I thought it was in that briefcase up there," I joked back. A sneaky, evil look came across his face and he said,

"So did I!"

Just a little customs story ...

Signed, Niece of an innocent woman

Both stories involve a shared joke between officers and crossers, yet suggest deeper power imbalances at work. In a comment on the Facebook posting, one resident wrote, "I so would have been pulled in for answering that question!" I am unsure what answer would have merited getting pulled in. The "Niece of an innocent woman" described the officer's look as "sneaky" and "evil" without suggesting that the officer was play-acting. One wonders what the consequence would have been if the crosser had told the officer that they refused to answer biology trivia or to go along with an officer's gentle teasing about carrying $10,000 across the border.

Humorous exchanges between officers and travellers are in some sense the most irrelevant sort of interaction one can observe. They do not determine the admissibility of travellers or their goods. At the same time, the unspoken rules of who can joke, and in what way, tend, in my experience, to reinforce rather than undermine the distinctness of officers' position and authority. In this regard, joking is a serious business.

This is not to say that such interactions between officers and citizens/travellers do not help put a personal face on the state. Joking can bring them together, just as Radcliffe Brown suggests.

At the same time, when the limits of these encounters are reached, the power dynamics between officers and travellers manifest most strongly. This is undoubtedly an asymmetrical joking relationship, one in which the rules for propriety are set and enforced by officers. They may be allowed to ask silly questions or poke fun at the project of a naive young anthropologist, but reciprocal teasing is not possible, particularly with regard to issues of smuggling or terrorism. Any joke about terrorism told to a border officer will surely bomb.

As we drove off to lunch one day, a friend told me of a non-Indigenous co-worker who had commuted to work in Akwesasne for more than a year. After hundreds of trips across, he told me, his co-workers became friendly with officers, sharing chit-chat, and joking around while crossing. Toward the end of his employment, an American officer he had gotten to know had asked him, "Are you bringing anything across?" The man replied, sarcastically, "I'm smuggling diamonds." "I wish you hadn't said that," was the officer's response. At this point in the story, my co-worker looked directly at me. "They took his car apart. It took hours, and I think they helped him put it back together." This story was more a warning about joking than a joke itself.

How's the Bridge? Border Stories in Digital Space

Even if most crossings are uneventful, the sheer volume of crossing by residents ensures an interesting story every week or so, at a minimum. Stories about "the border" and "border crossing" are a popular conversation topic in Akwesasne. But where and how do these stories circulate?

Stories are recounted both in person and in other media. For over a decade, residents experiencing trouble at the port of entry have texted one another on their phones. When the port of entry was on Cornwall Island, it was not unusual for residents living near the port to come by and keep an eye on proceedings, even, at times, to intervene. This is less common now, though text messages have been used to document the frequency of stops and searches. One resident filed a complaint after showing, via text messages to his family, that he had been stopped daily at the port of entry over several weeks.

A popular Facebook group entitled "How's the Bridge" emerged following the relocation of the port of entry off the island. The group, initially designated to share wait times so that residents could avoid tedious line-ups, also became a forum to discuss all manner of border issues, provide legal advice, describe problems with border officers, and even offer recommendations about which lanes to avoid. At present, the group has more than 1,200 members, though a few dozen contribute more often than anyone else.

I used the "How's the Bridge" page frequently in order to plan my return trips to Cornwall after a day in the office in St. Regis Village. If the lines were long, I'd make plans with friends south of the borderline, or head over to Massena to do some grocery shopping. The site was shown to me by several colleagues, who also contribute infrequently. I attempted to join the group on two occasions, but was not added by the administrators on either. It is, however, a public group, which anyone can access, and residents semi-regularly remind one another that it is probably monitored by Canadian border-enforcement officers. I suspect that that is why a covertly recorded exchange between a resident and a BSO was eventually taken off the group site. There has been, to my knowledge, no reference to or advice about illegal activities on the forum. The participants, like most other people in Akwesasne, simply want to move about their territory without impediment.

Later in this section, I reproduce a couple of exchanges that received high levels of attention from group members. Though the site remains open-access, I use pseudonyms for the residents involved in these exchanges to add a layer of anonymity should they someday choose to delete or remove their posts.

The website is an open forum for border stories, with those that are particularly interesting, compelling, personal, or troubling receiving the widest reception, and therefore remaining at the top of the page for longer. Many of the most active threads involve residents' collective attempts to make sense of uncertainties, drawing upon personal and second-hand histories to guide themselves – to determine "what was going on" at the border.

This was markedly the case in a post from January 2015, in which a resident, Tom, asked "Anyone get pulled in for 'ABOR' and not told what it means?" I present the conversation below, using pseudonyms for those involved. In the ensuing comments, fellow community members tried to make sense of a referral classification, drawing upon their own knowledge and expectations of the port and officers.

27 January 2014

TOM: Anyone get pulled in for "Abor" and not told what it means?
LISA: We got pulled in for "Nat."

LISA: [Posts picture of referral slip]

LISA: I'd assume the ABOR could be assumed to stand for ABORiginal and that the NAT stands for NATive.

TOM: That's what I thought, Lisa, but I wanted to see what it means ... lol but Thx I'll look into that one too.

GINA: Ask your community advocate Wesley Benedict lol.

TOM: Pffff lol.

GINA: Lmao! Lemme see what I can do I may know someone who can find out there.

LEANNE: Pull sum strings there, Gina. Lol.

TOM: Right lol CBSA don't like me cus I question everything they do.

TOM: That would be awesome, Gina, because I'm helping a person file a complaint with Ottawa against cbsa for being ABORiginal.

MARTIN: Their gonna hate me!! LOL I've been pulled over 3 times and every time I demanded "the hell for?" They don't answer then I tell them I'm not pulling over until I'm informed wy ... Then the eye rolling starts lol.

TOM: Lol. Yep once they give that smart-ass attitude I fawking give it right back. Honestly, the more people to question their "motives" and reporting their behaviour the better and maybe this abuse of authority will subside.

CALVIN: Nat is when you answer no to alcohol or tobacco, never heard of abor, maybe questioning your native status in canada?? ... probably one of the new ones council warned about.

LISA: But as you can clearly see in the picture they didn't cross off the boxes for Goods Declared or Duty Free Purchase, so No Alcohol and Tobacco does sound good for NAT, but so would the little boxes clearly created for that type of declaration. Also, shouldn't the reason still be 99(1)(f) which is the generic detain and search notation under Canadian Customs Act??

GINA: Apparently issue with guards not using proper codes, could be that ... sounds like a bullshit party line to me.

TOM: Yep, smells like bullshit to me too ... because you know they're superhuman and never make mistakes.

TOM: I say this because the guards in question have been at this port for years ... so it's not the new guards. So tell your source to try again lol jk.

The participants in this discussion are collectively trying to make sense of opaque classifications by the CBSA. Some explanations emerge as more plausible than others, but most hinge on the assumption that Indigenous people are being singled out for additional controls by customs. It is worth noting that "Calvin," the resident who explained that NAT stands for "No Alcohol or Tobacco," is a retired CBSA officer from the community. The former officer's speculation that "Abor" refers to Aboriginal status is reasonable considering a status card is an accepted form of identification for entering Canada. At the same time, Akwesasronon are sensitive to being singled out as Indigenous, and many assume that they are profiled and given harsher treatment for that reason.

Ultimately, the message board's conclusion is not so much a clearcut understanding of what these CBSA codes mean so much as a pronouncement of the foetidness of the "bullshit" in their explanations. This story resonates, because for many residents, to borrow from Geertz (1977), CBSA activities are "bullshit all the way down," and that is what is expected of the organization. It resonates with expectations of border services' opacity, uncertainty, abuse of power, and possible use of profiling. Much like the (false) radio interview at this chapter's start, it is already meaningful in those terms. Just like the storied "turtles all the way down" anecdote Geertz employs to discuss the point at which cultural analysis reaches infinite regression, the moment of infinite regression in analysing an encounter with a border officer is often not so much what exactly happened and why, but the fact that something smells. This in turn sets up a situation in which hostility toward officers is a reasonable, if not always necessary, approach.

Another series of exchanges, starting in 2014 and continuing to the present, chronicled a resident's difficulties after finding his vehicle flagged, first on his way to a show at the "SVTC" (which I believe stands for Seaway Valley Theatre Company in Cornwall). Through his posts, "the flagged man" sought to demonstrate his problems, get a sense of why he had been flagged by the CBSA, and seek advice from fellow Akwesasronon. I reproduce the exchange below. I have included only those messages directly posted by "the flagged man," though there were dozens more related posts in between. One worth particular mention that I have not included is an image showing a copy of the text of Section 99(1) (F) of the Customs Act with the headline, "What is reasonable?"

17 July 2014

JAMES: CBSA got all "99(1)f" on me this evening. Just crossing from the Island and pulled in for a secondary search. Not fun when you're on your way to a show at the SVTC. Good thing they had three officers doing the search. Only took about 10 minutes. They couldn't figure out why I carry a hard case full of calibrated testing instruments.

JAMES: [Posts a picture of referral form]

JACKIE: What's a 99(1)(f)? No freedom rights of travelling within the country like everybody else ...

TOM: I can't google it for some reason, but what I remember is they use this section as an excuse to search your vehicle when you're coming from the island ... basically claiming you failed to report from the US. However, they still need a reason justifying their search. File a complaint at the Ottawa head office. Anyone finding themselves in this situation should file a complaint. This is wrong. The more you know your rights, the less they can do this to us.

LUCINDA: Here's a link to the customs Enforcement Manuals. 99(1)(f) is referenced in manual 2 of 3, on page 2.

LUCINDA: http://vancouverlaw.ca/immigration-lawyer-resources/.

JACKIE: Who pulled you over, James, and thank you, Lucinda, I now know what is a 99(1)(f).

JAMES: Pulled in by Primeau. Then searched by Spencer, Roy and ??? (Roy and the other guy didn't have ID tags. I asked for names right off the start).

KAILEY: Oh for real. We had an engineer working for MCA years back who got followed then surrounded and stopped in Ottawa due to all of his trips to Akwesasne. Heck, nobody here can actually be involved in science or engineering y'know. That's an automatic red flag.

JACKIE: Lol.

21 July 2014

JAMES: BOOM! 2 searches in 4 days. On a roll baby. I have TWO 99(1)(f)s now, sukkas. How many do you have? [Posts a picture of referral sheet]

DANI: Basturds.

MITCH: Did u ask what the f is? Now they added 10–15? Im still trying to get an answer on this.

DANI: Now that you went into secondary search you're on the list expect it to happen more until they pull you in more times with nothing happen to me.

JAMES: Bring it on. I'm ready.

JACKIE: Sometimes RCMP sent them info often wrong info about a person and CBSA has to pull the person over. It happened to me. I asked why and the supervisor looked on his computer. I told him it was false info and they removed my red flag from the computer after talking to RCMP.

TOM: File complaint ... it's harassment.

JAMES: I filed two complaints. One for each offense on the CBSA website. Plus I sent all my info to MCA Wes Benedict.

1 September 2014

JAMES: Use this link to file complaints. It works! Goes right to district manager in Ottawa. Had a response (phone call then meeting in person) within a couple weeks. Http://www.cbsa-asfc.gc.ca/co.../feedback -retroaction-eng.html. Easy to file a complaint from your phone while sitting in loooooong lineup while only two lanes are open.

GREY: Awesome. You're today's digitip on the radio.

SKYLA: Bump. PowWow Day on the Island – heavy traffic. Cbsa only has two lanes open during heavy traffic, so backed up to the bridge. Feedback: one of the busiest local traffic days annually (Akwesasne PowWow) and the cbsa only has two lanes open???

Of course traffic is backed up to the bridge as of 9:30 am on the first day of the Akwesasne PowWow. The CBSA officer asked us where we were coming from twice – of course we answered the same both times she asked us (we were coming from our home on Cornwall Island).

It's very interesting that the CBSA in Cornwall Ontario seems to never have more than one or two lanes open for traffic any time Akwesasne has an event that creates very high local traffic.

8 September 2014

JAMES: Got myself another 99(1)(f) baby!! Get'em like Pokemon cards (just the picture though). That's three now. At least the officers were polite and friendly. All three were "the good ones." [Posts a picture of the referral sheet]

JACKIE: Very strange … ask them why? Ask to see what's on your file?

JAMES: I did last time. They said it was my trailer. This time I was carrying HVAC units on my trailer for a client to deliver them. I made a trip to the POE to sort this out last time around. Guess the flag is back on my file.

TOM: Whats a 99 1f anyways? lol.

JAMES: The right to stop and search domestic travellers in a mixed traffic corridor. It was added to the CBSA Customs Act in 2011 (I think) no doubt as a result of 2009.

MEHGAN: You're flagged.

26 May 2015

JAMES: Got a letter from the regional office. They track all my complaints and respond every time. It works. [Posts image of reply to complaint]

The year-long odyssey of James, the "flagged man," met an unsatisfying conclusion, as the CBSA's response to his complaint, which included his concerns regarding overall wait times, remarked that "complete reviews of each of your complaints submitted regarding border wait times at the Port of Cornwall have been conducted and have determined that, on each of those occasions, we have been operating within the established service standards." Nevertheless, he maintained good humour throughout the ordeal and was pleased to have, at the very least, received a response.

The "How's the Bridge" group offered a forum for the resident to share his grievances, receive affirmation from fellow community members, seek advice, and speculate on the sources of his problems. It is worth noting one resident's intimation that the CBSA reduces service when Akwesasne has events, and that James makes sure to refer to some CBSA officers in positive terms as "the good ones" (presumably, as opposed to "the bad ones," or, more pessimistically, everyone else).

Border Media

Here I wish to turn the reader's attention to the media through which border stories circulate, paying particular attention to the technological facets of storytelling. In the above case of James, he communicated his problems with Canada Border Services through several media. After being stopped in person, he posted his concerns online, and received links to legal advice and statutes from friends. In a subsequent thread, one resident remarked that his case became the topic of a local radio show. Finally, he received a reply to his complaints from Canadian customs in the mail, after suggesting to his fellow residents that they take advantage of the long wait times to fill out complaints on their smart phones. Face-to-face communication, internet, telephone, and radio were all involved.

This use of technology to transcend the geopolitical divides imposed by the Canada-US border meshes well with a common thread in the anthropology of media and globalization – namely, the argument that new media technologies help bring people (virtually) closer together, and therefore subvert the restrictions on mobility imposed by borderlines (see Appadurai 1995; 2001; 2008). It can go even further; in providing advice about border crossing, these sites facilitate physical as well as virtual mobility. Media technologies, in this respect, both transcend and undermine borders.

Yet in Akwesasne, the situation is more complicated than this. As much as media technologies may subvert borders, they also reinforce them. As suggested by Collyer (2003), the regulations, service regimes, and available technologies within a particular nation can reinforce rather than undermine national borders in cyberspace. While Facebook does not care from which side of the border a resident logs in, in Akwesasne, people's geophysical location vis-à-vis the border affects their internet access. Even without any sort of customs regulation in many parts of the territory, their place of residence determines whether they have dial-up or high-speed internet. It influences how much money they pay (or do not pay) for electricity, and what radio and television stations they have access to. In this regard, media technologies reinforce "the border" in Akwesasne as much as they may undermine it. I illustrate this point and expand upon my discussion of mobile service with the anecdote below.

Welcome to Akwesasne

Early in my fieldwork, I invested in an old, US-based, mobile phone to use when calling my family in New York and/or while I was in the southern (US) portion of Akwesasne. I decided that since I would be spending so much time across the borderline, it would be good to avoid roaming fees. After all, sometimes my only sense of "the border" within the Akwesasne Mohawk Territory happened when my phone buzzed and notified me that I had left my country of service.

At one point, I found, much to my frustration, that both my US and my Canadian phones were on roaming. The US phone wrote, "Welcome to Canada," and the Canadian one wrote "Welcome to the US." I took a photograph of the two phones next to each other and posted it on Facebook (I've included the image in figure 7.1). One friend replied in the comments, "Welcome to Akwesasne."

Mobile phones are an avenue in which the border is both contested and created. While phones make it possible to send messages about border officers or simply to call a friend or family member wherever they reside, they also determine the fees for a call. Even if phone signals do not rely strictly speaking upon where someone is standing relative to the borderline, phone service is often contingent upon the border's location.

Calling from St. Regis Village to the city of Cornwall is cheaper than calling from St. Regis Village across the street to what is ostensibly New York State. As I mention in the prologue, a roaming signal is often the only tangible marker of "the border" in many parts of Akwesasne, as one's phone chimes crossing a border that the carrier would otherwise ignore. I found myself driving up and down the street in order to call a

Figure 7.1. Mobile phone welcome messages. Photo courtesy of the author.

friend simply to avoid international roaming fees (my cheapness knows no borders). A few times, I was wary of doing so, driving close enough to "the border" that I could receive a proper signal but not so close that I would be obligated to "report in" afterwards. When I called the phone company to adjust false roaming charges, I was surprised when the respondent was familiar with Akwesasne and simply wiped the charges without further question.

Mobile phones are not the only communication forum in my anecdote. The punchline "Welcome to Akwesasne" came from an Akwesasronon friend on Facebook. I had no way of knowing from "which side" of Akwesasne she sent her message – in that capacity the website rendered the border irrelevant, yet the fact that she had home internet revealed something about her location. High-speed internet only came to St. Regis Road south of the borderline a year and a half after I concluded my primary fieldwork. One friend planned his weekends around visiting a family home on Cornwall Island so he could take care of his downloads for weekly media consumption.

The internet, widely heralded as breaking down national borders, relies upon infrastructures and fees that are highly nationalized. This case is even more severe beyond North America, where censorship laws and firewalls determine what sorts of activities take place on which side of the bordered internet. Ultimately it was through Facebook, a website that seemingly undermines national boundaries but is nevertheless bound to nationalized access, that we could share our sense of humour about Akwesasne as a place where a person can be simultaneously in both (neither) Canada and (nor) the US, and must pay the price accordingly.

What does one *do* with this shifting landscape of stories, space, and communication? Much like crossing the border for a slice of pizza, one cannot easily imagine a court case, speech, academic article, or political movement focused on the hassle of navigating an invisible borderline to access an invisible communication network. This is not the colonialism of residential schools or of armed standoffs, nor is it the resistance or refusal inherent in rights cases, protests, and angry altercations. Yet it is the product of that same set of stories. It is part of the possibilities and limitations of everyday life there. At this juncture, it is worth reiterating a point that I made in chapter 3: these incursions of settler colonialism may not easily map onto common conceptual frameworks. Yet they show just how far into everyday life settler colonialism penetrates. Their seeming insignificance may make them a drop in the bucket, but in a place like Akwesasne, there are enough drops to fill that bucket to overflowing.

Conclusion

Most border crossing in Akwesasne is banal, not an occasion for shouting matches or funny anecdotes but a simple exchange of a few words. My record for crossing was three words:

BSO: From?
ME: Hogansburg.
BSO: Citizenship?
ME: US.
BSO: Status?
ME: Student.
BSO: [Looks for student visa and returns passport] Have a nice day.

Brief "non-events" like this represent the majority of encounters as Akwesasronon cross the border. Yet even a single traumatic encounter is one too many for either a BSO or a resident. A funny encounter may be retold again and again, with embellishments where necessary. Akwesasronon and border officers select these stories when telling and retelling accounts of "what is going on" at the border, and bring these stories with them when they meet officers at a primary inspection lane.

Earlier in this chapter, citing Yael Navarro-Yashin, I looked at the ways in which interactions between "the state," or, more accurately, state actors and (going beyond Navarro-Yashin) the citizenry can become a sort of self-fulfilling prophecy. In other words, the imagined future can become the present. Here, I have looked at the ways in which stories people tell about the border help create the border. In other words, the imagined past can also become the present. Regardless of whether those stories are true in the past, they are part of "the border's" cosmology – its ongoing creation. They are mythic in the Lévi-Straussian fashion, stories about the creation of "the border," something that is logically paradoxical yet nevertheless exists. Though situated within a wider range of history and past relationships, these stories, their themes, and their repetition can become "self-fulfilling prophecies" in their content, their framing, and the media through which they circulate.

One's capacity to send and receive those stories, regardless of their content, is determined by practical considerations linked to the means of communication. Posting a story on Facebook or a web forum is one matter; calling or texting is another; and driving over to a cousin's place to tell that story at the dinner table is another still. The ability to access a communication forum is often contingent upon where the person and the intended audience are located relative to the borderline. In this regard, communications technologies simultaneously undermine and reinforce the border in Akwesasne.

Akwesasronon and BSOs sometimes drive away from an interaction with a story. They take that story with them when they leave the port and circulate it among friends, family, and colleagues. The story may undergo revisions with retellings, but in order to remain believable, it has to fit an already existing framework delimiting how Akwesasronon and BSOs are expected to act. That story, repackaged, retold, and retransmitted, comes back to the port of entry, setting the context for future interactions that in turn produce new stories and set the standards for their believability. They reproduce the already existing framework delimiting how Akwesasronon and BSOs are expected to act. Though we do not declare them at the border, travellers often arrive in a car loaded with stories. Regardless of whether these stories were true in the past, if they are true in the present, they will likely remain so in the future.

Conclusion

A Lesson in Mohawk

20 June 2013

I arrived at the health centre enthusiastic for my first day with the ambulance service. Walking into the lobby, I told the receptionist my name, and she asked me to have a seat while they contacted someone from the service. A few minutes went by, and I looked up from my book, glancing around to see if anyone I recognized had arrived.

A woman came by and spoke to me, perhaps seeing confusion on my face. "Shekon," she said to me, with a slight smile on her lips. I spent a moment trying to determine whether we had met, or if she was my contact in the ambulance service. Neither seemed to be the case. She repeated, "She ... kon," slowly enunciating each syllable. She continued, "It means hello ... you say it ..." continuing to smile like an elementary school teacher.

I replied, trying to sound friendly, "Shekon. I knew what that meant actually. I've been working out here for about a year now ..." I assumed she would follow up with a question about what I had been doing working out of Akwesasne, and that would start a conversation about the border and her experiences. But this was not the case. At least, not directly.

Her face briefly flashed into one of dissatisfaction, and she began speaking in Mohawk; this time, far more rapidly than I'd heard other Mohawk speakers communicate. After she finished speaking, she said, "You didn't understand that, did you?," with her face returning to the bemused smile I had seen earlier. I replied, confounded, "No, I'm sorry, I didn't ..." And she walked away before I had the chance to say anything else.

Introduction (to the Conclusion)

The above anecdote is taken from the same day's field notes as the prologue to this book. That prologue involved overt depictions of cross-border traversal, pointing out borderlines and ports of entry and interactions with border services officers. It emphasized the ways in which a single day in Akwesasne can involve multiple trips across the borderline. Yet the border is not just a line on a map or a port of entry. It is also a particular type of conversation. I have begun this conclusion with a conversation that, though not taking place at the border, is very much *of* the border.

I have chosen to analyse the conversation here to consider, in microcosm, several of this book's assertions. These assertions are (1) that "the border" does not always take place "at the border"; (2) that border crossings are, among other things, a particular type of conversation; (3) that these conversations not only describe but also create their terms of reference; and (4) that neither ideological dogma nor pure pragmatism are sufficient to account for what takes place in these conversations. After this analysis, I justify and unpack my efforts at offering a "balanced" approach to studying border and elaborate upon three core themes in this approach: framing, flexibility, and one-mindedness.

The woman was acting as a gatekeeper (or border officer) of sorts in determining, through a variety of conversational techniques, how to place me. Our exchange was about her, in part, figuring out "what are the terms of recognition" (Simpson 2014, 40) between us. But it was not simply about figuring out who she was to me; it was also about *making* me something to her (and vice versa).

What was going on? How to make sense of a conversation in which my interlocutor's approach to me seemed to alter substantially, from wanting to teach me a word in her language to trying to befuddle me with that language? One way to consider this conversation is through the lens of "frame shifting," which I discussed in the previous chapter. Frame shifting is the act of employing linguistic techniques to change what a conversation is about. This is something everyone does, but it is also a core facet of the way border officers shift the flow of an interview with a traveller for their own purposes. In the above conversation, the woman did something very similar to what border officers do in her efforts to shift the frame of our conversation. Initially, she seemed to be trying to teach me her language, but by the end, this was no longer her goal. Ostensibly, she was finding out who I was, but in the process of doing so, she not only defined "what is going on" but also "who gets to say what is going on."

We shifted between three framings of the situation, two offered by her, and one by me. When she began the exchange by trying to get me to repeat "She:kon" after her, she framed the conversation as one of benevolent education. The roles were clear: I was an unfamiliar outsider, and she was a familiar insider. I could have accepted this framing and repeated the word after her, but this did not sit with the way I had come to see myself relative to Akwesasne. Without giving it conscious thought, I replied that I understood what she was saying and offered a secondary framing, a readjustment of our roles. I was a familiar outsider, and she was a familiar insider. She could have accepted this framing and asked me about my work, but this did not sit with the way she saw herself relative to me. She offered a third frame. By speaking rapidly to me in Mohawk and not waiting for a response, she contested my suggestion that I had familiarity, this time without the beneficence of her first frame. The desire was not to share but to affirm a relationship in which she knew something and I knew nothing. She was more interested in teaching me that I was ignorant than in teaching me Mohawk. And having succeeded in doing that, she left.

Frame shifting is one of several analytical frameworks offered in this text, and one of several ways to interpret our interaction. This sort of analysis is useful in drawing attention to the ways in which our exchange was simultaneously reflective and productive of my position in Akwesasne as an outsider. It helps make sense of our interaction without relying upon her Indigenous identity, or narratives of resistance or colonialism. One could imagine a similar scenario elsewhere, in which an outsider gets "put in their place" by an insider through that insider's fluency with a vernacular language and familiarity with "the local." This happens every day at American and Canadian ports of entry, local sports bars, and academic conferences, to name a few places. There is little culturally or regionally specific about wanting to put someone in their place and using the tools available at the time to do so. By many measures, this conversation could have taken place anywhere – there is something universal to it.

But this conversation did not take place just anywhere. It took place in the Akwesasne Mohawk Territory. While frame shifting can account for seeming inconsistencies in an interaction's content (was she "really" being friendly?), it does little to offer context. It does not explain why I was at the health centre to begin with, why she was able to speak Mohawk and expect I could not, nor why she felt impelled to approach me. Nor does it account for the affect underlying our exchange. Frame shifting is a way for me, as an anthropologist, to make sense of our interaction after the fact, but it does little to tell me how she would make sense of it if someone were to ask her, "What happened?"

Even if "putting someone in their place" is a widespread phenomenon, the manner in which each instantiation is understood is not.

Border officers at a port of entry may attribute it to "doing their jobs," a sports bar patron may attribute it to "home team pride," and a snooty academic may attribute it to something Bourdieusian. Along those same lines, the woman I met in the waiting room may have understood her actions as an act of resistance *as* a Mohawk, or an affirmation of her identity as an Indigenous person. This is something most border officers, sports bar patrons, or academics could not do. By many measures, this conversation could only have taken place in Akwesasne – there is something unique to it.

Such an interpretation is privileged in the literature of settler colonialism focused on "the grounded everyday life of *feeling citizenship*" (Simpson 2014, 191; her emphasis). Even if a similar sort of exchange takes place in a wide variety of contexts, there are certain interpretations (and feelings) that can only be claimed by Mohawk people. This is a powerful analytic lens because it helps point to the very real role the state has played in diminishing the livelihoods of Indigenous populations, and the agency, ingenuity, and resilience with which these populations have maintained their identities. It is good at accounting for the "big picture" of settler colonialism.

Yet it is less successful at accounting for the "small picture" – those facets that render each interaction distinct. To ground this argument, it risks suggesting that while non-Mohawks may argue with border officers because they are angry, upset, frustrated, hiding something, exhausted, or simply having a bad day, any time a Mohawk traveller argues with border officers it is in order to exercise their rights and resist the state – at least at some level. This is not the way many of my interlocutors voiced narratives about their interactions with officers unless, perhaps, I prompted them to do so. Resistance, or refusal, is one way in which Indigenous actors may ground or understand their actions, but it is by no means the only one.

I have taken an alternative approach in looking at how resistance, refusal, Mohawk citizenship, and colonialism are several of many possible frames employed by Akwesasronon as they try to live their lives in a difficult situation. Akwesasronon are not slavishly beholden to Mohawk political ideology; nor, on the other hand, are border officers slavishly beholden to legal statute. Neither Akwesasronon nor border officers are, in the words of Garfinkel (1967), "cultural dopes." It is thus necessary to give equal credence to the ways in which settler colonialism has set the stage for a very particular border and the universality of the efforts undertaken by human beings who are trying to live their lives there.

Walking the Line: An Overview of This Text

My goal in this text has been to strike a balance between analytical frameworks that emphasize the universality and those that emphasize the uniqueness of the border in Akwesasne. In doing so, I have sought to synthesize two approaches to the study of human action. Though I brought forward these frameworks in the introduction, it may be useful to reiterate them here more concisely.

The first could be called, in the words of Baudouin Dupret, "praxe-ological" (2011; Dupret, Lynch, and Berard 2015; but see also Garfinkel 1967). It looks at the ways practice is primary and ideology is the means by which sense is made of practice. The second could be called "ideo-logical." It looks at the ways ideology is primary, and practice is the means by which ideology is enacted. In Akwesasne, both permutations proliferate. Ideology often informs practice, and practice often informs one's interpretation of ideology. The border is an especially pertinent space for such a study, as we observe a parallel in the actions of bor-der officers. For them, law often informs practice, and practice often informs their interpretation of law.

By some interpretations, arguing that practice is grounded in ideol-ogy *and* ideology is grounded in practice is contradictory. I risk either saying nothing by saying everything with a truism or simply making a logically inconsistent statement. Neither is my intention. Rather, I point to the ways in which the border is a place where seeming contradictions flourish and become necessary. This is especially true in the "impossible border" of Akwesasne, a space literally and figuratively at the boundar-ies of settler states. Below I highlight some of these contradictions, their historical origins, and their manifestations.

Akwesasne is Canada, the United States, *and* Mohawk territory. Alter-natively, it is all, some, or none of those things. Akwesasne came to the border, *and* the border came to Akwesasne. The community and port of entry personnel have been both united *and* divided by the border. The border is an invisible line across the landscape *and* a highly visible site of fences, cameras, and law-enforcement personnel. Officers follow the letter of the law *and* exercise discretion. Similarly, Akwesasronon cross the border "as Mohawks" in rejection of state authority *and* cross in whatever manner is convenient for a given situation. The "reality" of the border is grounded in first-hand experiences *and* stories that, techni-cally speaking, may or may not be "true."

How did this come to be? How did so many contradictions come to proliferate in a single site? They are the product of complex and them-selves often self-contradictory laws, histories, and policies that have

imposed "the border" on an Indigenous population and charged officers with maintaining that border. Haudenosaunee peoples and especially Mohawks have not been mute witnesses to these histories. They
have a long history of inhabiting border regions and recognizing their
advantage. Yet the evolution of the "modern nation state" imposed a
border regime on Akwesasne that had analogues in their traditional
regulation of space but no precedent in its rigidity. The attempt of
Canada and the United States to impose an ideal type of border in an
irregular space like Akwesasne was problematic prior to the relocation
of the Canadian port in 2009 but has become impossible since. In consequence, both states have instituted policies requiring travellers in the
territory to "report in" as a means to control the movement of bodies
across borderlines.

I began this study with a "simple supposition" that border crossings
are, among other things, a particular type of conversation. This is evi-
dent in face-to-face conversations between Akwesasronon and border
officers at ports of entry. These conversations "frame" border crossing
for many travellers who experience the border not as an invisible line
but as a brief interaction between themselves and a border officer. The
border also appears in stories filtered through courtrooms, public discourse, and social media. These stories "make" the border as much as
they are "made by" it.

In trying to unravel "what is going on" at the border, and more poignantly, what happens when different people have different ways of
understanding "what is going on," I have repeatedly employed three
analytic themes: flexibility, framing, and one-mindedness. Flexibility
refers to my emphasis on the ways in which seeming self-contradiction
does not challenge definitions of Akwesasne and border work but rather
is part of their definition. Framing refers to my dual exploration of the
ways in which the border is framed through face-to-face interaction,
and the ways in which those interactions frame normative assumptions
about law, identity, geography, and sovereignty. Finally, one-mindedness
refers to drawing parallels between two seemingly disparate parties, in
this case border officers and Akwesasronon. The organizational structure of this volume has sought to emphasize these parallels whenever
possible.

Akwesasne – a Flexible Inflexibility

I refer to Akwesasne as a "flexible geography." I choose this phrasing
to suggest that Akwesasne is not simply a hybrid composite of many
markers but a matrix of possibility. Akwesasne and its residents can be

"both," "either," or "neither" any combination of features. These possibilities play out in the choices travellers make when they cross a border. A resident may try to explain to a border officer that they've never left Canada, while arguing with another officer over whether Akwesasne is a part of Canada.

Yet Akwesasronon are not, as some officers have suggested, simply Machiavellian strategic actors always choosing whatever identification gets them across easily. Many choose not to do things "the easy way." Sometimes Akwesasronon choose not to be flexible, or do not see this as a choice to begin with. I am arguing against a model by which *some* Akwesasronon are always flexible and *some* are never flexible. Rather, while recognizing that individuals make choices in alignment with their own proclivities and histories, I am arguing that the context of an interaction matters as well. To requote one Mohawk chief, some people don't have problems answering questions but this depends on how the questions are framed. The framing, the context, of an interaction matters.

Similarly, border officers define their own activities along a spectrum ranging from pragmatic discretion to a positivist adherence to the law. They are not, as some Akwesasronon have suggested, robots. Sometimes over the course of a single conversation, officers will argue that the law is black and white while subsequently pointing out shades of grey. Like Akwesasronon, some officers have a greater proclivity for being either easy-going or "hard asses," but the way they treat travellers is also rooted in the context of each situation. Both officers and Akwesasronon are flexible as to when they can be inflexible.

Uncertainty at the border has become a sort of evil twin to the possibilities enabled by flexibility. Border officers find themselves uncertain about what sort of traveller they'll encounter, and travellers often find themselves uncertain about what sort of demands will be placed upon them. In this space of uncertainty, the border can become a self-fulfilling prophecy, with travellers demonstrating the animosity officers expect, and officers fostering the conflicts they seek to avoid.

Framing Borders

Of the social theories employed in this monograph, Erving Goffman's frame analysis (1974) has held special prominence. My exploration of the framing of borders in face-to-face interaction is more akin to Goffman's own approach than its subsequent iterations in media studies and political science. Goffman suggested that face-to-face interaction is a process by which experiences come to be seen as "real." It is through face-to-face interactions between officers and travellers that the "realness" of the border, and other categories of the state, is challenged and affirmed.

Frame analysis is especially fruitful in the study of borders. As I have suggested, border crossing often frames the experience of cross-border travel. It is in interacting with officers rather than crossing an invisible line that the border becomes "real" for much of the travelling public.

Yet frame analysis also engages with borders and bordering in another way. Frame analysis argues that experiences are themselves bounded and defined. Context defines content, and context-making occurs at the borders of an experience. If we think about bordering as a universal facet of human cognition, then we can see the ways in which "the border" is not solely a modern social or historical construct. Rather, the experience of borders is intimately entwined with the ways in which experience is itself bordered.

Though *Frame Analysis* is Goffman's magnum opus, it is weakest where it should be strongest – in looking at "frame disputes," when several actors disagree as to what is going on. Goffman sees these disputes as "exceptional," but it is in the creation and resolution of such disputes that the role of power in framing is most visible. Much as my waiting-room interlocutor claimed and exercised the power to frame our exchange (and I, in this conclusion, have exercised a similar power to reframe it), border officers and Akwesasronon employ a wide variety of tools in order to claim the advantage in determining "what is going on" at the border. Power brings people to the border, and determines the success with which they may transcend it.

One-Mindedness

While this book has been *about* the diverse experiences of the border in and around the Akwesasne Mohawk Territory, its skeleton has been structured by my understanding of the Haudenosaunee concept of one-mindedness. One-mindedness – recognizing what seemingly disparate parties share – is a first step toward peacemaking. Such an interpretation fits well with the terms of frame analysis, suggesting that frame disputes can be resolved, in part, by first paying attention to shared framings. My inspiration here is the Thanksgiving Address, which calls people into one-mindedness through a recognition of what is shared. What is shared by border officers and Akwesasronon travellers is not all positive, but it is, perhaps, more than either party initially assumes.

Whenever possible, I have sought to offer balance to the voices of border services officers and Akwesasronon. Both parties have been implicated in histories outside their control that continue to set the terms for their interactions. While they may have different understandings of what a border is, both officers and Akwesasronon understand their roles and responsibilities along a spectrum between dogmatism and pragmatism, in spite of uncertainty. "Rumour and innuendo" are part of the ways in which both parties make sense of the border, as the stories they tell have the potential to bring that border into being.

My efforts at emphasizing parallels have brought more than a few overly long sentences and paragraphs into being. Yet my goal has been to proceed beyond the basest terms of a multi-sited ethnography in order to render parallels and commonalities as starkly as possible. I have done so both to make a broader statement about the border as a shared space and to bring these comparisons to the forefront.

Peace building is a stated goal of both border services personnel and Akwesasne's Mohawk governments. Over the past several years in Akwesasne, I have watched tempers cool after the 2009 protests, flare over vehicle seizures, and flare and cool again over several other issues. New facilities and a new bridge have facilitated the ease of cross-border travel, helping to soothe relationships by addressing the symptoms – but not the cause – of many travellers' dissatisfaction with the border. Undoubtedly, the imposition of the Canada-US border on Akwesasne will remain an impediment, perhaps an insurmountable one. Further, the strongest onus for change must be placed on border services officers, who, unlike Akwesasronon, are trained and paid to deal with the border. Unlike Akwesasronon, they arrive at the border every day by choice, and can leave it behind when they go home in the evening. Very few Akwesasronon or border officers come to the port of entry looking for a fight. It is my hope that in recognizing how much they have in common, both can help the border look more like a bridge and less like a barrier.

Conclusion (to the Conclusion)

To conclude, I would like to return to my "Mohawk Lesson." My lesson ultimately was not about speaking Mohawk but about my ignorance in such a complex territory. As I see it, part of the lesson was not simply the fact that I was ignorant but the importance of my seeing myself as ignorant. Yet recognizing one's condition of not knowing "what is going on" is not an end in itself but the start of something else.

In this book, I have eschewed predictive models for what border officers and Akwesasronon *do*. Rather, I have looked at the ways in which both make sense of "what is going on" when "what is going on" involves the border – a space as multifaceted as Akwesasne itself. The book has been about "framing borders" – the ways in which borders are framed, and the ways in which borders frame so much of experience in and around Akwesasne.

Much as national borders are perhaps most interesting not in their rigidity but in their permeability, so too are the borders of mind and memory in which the idea of "the border" is permeable rather than rigid. "What is going on" is not simply out there for the world to grasp; it is something we make through our shared efforts at grasping it.

Conclusions have something in common with borders. They serve as a sort of gateway, the last step between "reading" and "having read" something. This chapter has not offered new content to the book, with the exception of my "Mohawk Lesson" anecdote. Yet it has served as a sort of wrapper. And in repackaging the ideas, it makes something new of them. In saying "this is what was going on for the last several hundred pages," I can alter those pages' meaning without changing their text.

In the same vein, the phrase "Have a nice day" not only marks the end of one's border-crossing experience but makes something of Canada, the United States, and everything in between. So, too, do conclusions make something of that which they encapsulate. And conclusions, like borders, in order to claim that special ability to frame must, at some point, conclude. Have a nice day.

References

Abel, Timothy J. 2002. "Recent Research on the Saint Lawrence Iroquoians of Northern New York." *Archeastnortham Archaeology of Eastern North America* 30: 137–54.

Adelman, Jeremy, and Stephen Aron. 1999. "From Borderlands to Borders: Empires, Nation-States, and the Peoples in between in North American History." *The American Historical Review* 104 (3): 814–41. https://doi.org/10.2307/2650990.

Alcantara, Christopher, and Ian Kalman. 2019. "Diversifying Methodologies: A Haudenosaunee/Settler Approach for Measuring Indigenous-Local Intergovernmental Success." *Canadian Journal of Political Science / Revue Canadienne de Science Politique* 52 (1): 21–38. https://doi.org/10.1017/S0008423918000409.

Alfred, Gerald R. 1995. *Heeding the Voices of Our Ancestors: Kahnawake Mohawk Politics and the Rise of Native Nationalism.* Toronto; New York: Oxford University Press.

Alfred, Taiaiake. 2005. *Wasáse: Indigenous Pathways of Action and Freedom.* Peterborough, ON; Orchard Park, NY: University of Toronto Press, Higher Education Division.

– 2009. *Peace, Power, Righteousness: An Indigenous Manifesto.* 2nd ed. Don Mills, ON; New York: Oxford University Press.

Alfred, Taiaiake, and Lana Lowe. 2005. "Warrior Societies in Contemporary Indigenous Communities." Victoria, BC: University of Victoria.

Amit, Vered. 2002. *The Trouble with Community: Anthropological Reflections on Movement, Identity and Collectivity.* London; Sterling, VA: Pluto Press.

Anderson, Benedict R.O'G. 2006. *Imagined Communities: Reflections on the Origin and Spread of Nationalism.* Rev. ed. London: Verso.

Anzaldúa, Gloria. 1999. *Borderlands = La Frontera.* 2nd ed. San Francisco: Aunt Lute Books.

Appadurai, Arjun. 1995. "The Production of Locality." In *Counterworks: Managing the Diversity of Knowledge*, edited by Richard Fardon, 204–25. London; New York: Routledge.
– 2001. *Globalization*. Durham, N.C.: Duke University Press.
– 2008. "Chapter 2: Disjuncture and Difference in the Global Cultural Economy." In *Modernity at Large: Cultural Dimensions of Globalization*, 27–47. Minneapolis: University of Minnesota Press.
Bateson, Gregory. 1972. *Steps to an Ecology of Mind*. New York: Ballantine Books.
Bateson, Gregory, and Mary Catherine Bateson. 2005. *Angels Fear: Towards an Epistemology of the Sacred*. Cresskill, NJ: Hampton Press.
Billig, Michael. 1995. *Banal Nationalism*. London; Thousand Oaks, CA: Sage.
Biolsi, Thomas. 2005. "Imagined Geographies: Sovereignty, Indigenous Space, and American Indian Struggle." *American Ethnologist* 32 (2): 239–59. https://doi.org/10.1525/ae.2005.32.2.239.
Blackburn, Mark. 2011. "Haudenosaunee Passport Confiscated." APTN National News. 19 July. http://aptnnews.ca/2011/07/19/haudenosaunee-passport-confiscated/.
Bonaparte, Darren. 2007. "Too Many Chiefs, Not Enough Indians." Hogansburg, NY: The Saint Regis Mohawk Tribal Council.
– 2008. *Creation and Confederation: The Living History of the Iroquois*. 1st ed. Akwesasne, QC; Akwesasne, NY: Wampum Chronicles.
– 2009. *A Lily among Thorns: The Mohawk Repatriation of Káteri Tekahkwí:Tha*. 1st ed. Akwesasne, QC; Akwesasne, NY: BookSurge Publishing.
– 2012. "October 23, 1812: The Skirmish at St. Regis." Text. Indian Country Today Media Network.com. 11 November 2012. Reprinted at: http://wampumchronicles.com/skirmishatstregis.html.
– 2013. "The Disputed Myth, Metaphor and Reality of Two Row Wampum." Indian Country Today Media Network.com. 8 September 2013. https://indiancountrytoday.com/archive/the-disputed-myth-metaphor-and-reality-of-two-row-wampum-HZdxpRUzukqu5YtkiRW5dg.
– 2017. "Akwesasne: A Border Runs through It." Indian Country Today Media Network. 25 February 2017. https://indiancountrytoday.com/archive/akwesasne-a-border-runs-through-it-pkQx1eIPO0i2OsN2wNONtw.
– n.d. "The History of Akwesasne from Pre-Contact to Modern Times." Accessed 5 June 2013. http://www.wampumchronicles.com/history.html.
Bowling, Ben, and James Sheptycki. 2012. *Global Policing*. Los Angeles: Sage Publications.
Branch, Legislative Services. 2012. "Consolidated Federal Laws of Canada, Customs Act." 1 October 2012. http://laws-lois.justice.gc.ca/eng/acts/C-52.6/FullText.html.

Busatta, Sandra. 2009. "Sovereignty, History and Memory: Mohawk Smuggling as an Act of Sovereignty within the Making of Mohawk Identity." MA thesis, University of Wales, Lampeter.

"Canada's Best Places to Live 2014: Full Ranking." 2014. *MoneySense* (blog). Accessed 25 October 2015. http://www.moneysense.ca/canadas-best -places-to-live-2014-full-ranking/.

Carey, Elaine, and Andrae M. Marak. 2011. *Smugglers, Brothels, and Twine: Historical Perspectives on Contraband and Vice in North America's Borderlands.* Tucson: University of Arizona Press.

Carlson, Kathryn Blaze. 2011. "Ottawa in 'Explosive' Situation over Rejected Iroquois Passport." *National Post.* 12 July 2011. https://nationalpost.com /news/canada/ottawa-in-explosive-situation-over-rejected-iroquois -passport.

"CBSA Changes Preliminary Port of Entry." 2014. *Indian Time.* 16 January 2014.

Chalfin, Brenda. 2006. "Global Customs Regimes and the Traffic in Sovereignty." *Current Anthropology* 47 (2): 243–76. https://doi.org/10.1086/499548.

– 2008. "Sovereigns and Citizens in Close Encounter: Airport Anthropology and Customs Regimes in Neoliberal Ghana." *American Ethnologist* 35 (4). https://doi.org/10.1111/j.1548-1425.2008.00096.x.

Chang, Kornel S. 2012. *Pacific Connections: The Making of the U.S.-Canadian Borderlands.* Berkeley: University of California Press. http://site.ebrary .com/id/10558454.

Clifford, James. 1988. *The Predicament of Culture: Twentieth-Century Ethnography, Literature, and Art.* Cambridge, MA: Harvard University Press.

Cockburn, Neco. 2008. "Smuggling's Price." *Ottawa Citizen,* 21 November 2008. http://www2.canada.com/ottawacitizen/news/story.html?id=ecc66684 -6dde-4924-bea7-9e54ff7b6063.

Collyer, Michael. 2003. "Are There National Borders in Cyberspace? Evidence from the Algerian Transnational Community." *Geography* 88 (4): 348–56.

Côté-Boucher, Karine. 2008. "The Diffuse Border: Intelligence-Sharing, Control and Confinement along Canada's Smart Border." *Surveillance & Society* 5 (2). https://doi.org/10.24908/ss.v5i2.3432.

– 2013. "The Micro-Politics of Border Control: Internal Struggles at Canadian Customs." PhD diss., York University, Toronto. http://yorkspace.library .yorku.ca/xmlui/handle/10315/27585.

– 2015. "The Paradox of Discretion: Customs and the Changing Occupational Identity of Canadian Border Officers." *British Journal of Criminology,* April, azv023. https://doi.org/10.1093/bjc/azv023.

– 2018. "Of 'Old' and 'New' Ways: Generations, Border Control and the Temporality of Security." *Theoretical Criminology* 22 (2): 149–68. https://doi .org/10.1177/1362480617690800.

Côté-Boucher, Karine, Federica Infantino, and Mark B. Salter. 2014. "Border Security as Practice: An Agenda for Research." *Security Dialogue* 45 (3): 195–208. https://doi.org/10.1177/0967010614533243.

Das, Veena, and Deborah Poole, eds. 2004. *Anthropology in the Margins of the State*. School of American Research Advanced Seminar Series. Santa Fe, NM: School of American Research Press.

Deer, Tracey, Linda Ludwick, Christina Fon, Adam Symansky, Catherine Bainbridge, Ernest Webb, et al. 2008. *Club Native*. [Montréal]; New York: Rezolution Pictures; National Film Board of Canada. Distributed by Women Make Movies.

Diamond, Jared M. 2005. *Guns, Germs, and Steel: The Fates of Human Societies*. New York: W.W. Norton.

Dickson-Gilmore, E.J., and Chris Whitehead. 2002. "Aboriginal Organized Crime in Canada: Developing a Typology for Understanding and Strategizing Responses." *Trends in Organized Crime* 7 (4): 3–28. https://doi.org/10.1007/s12117-002-1002-5.

Donnan, Hastings, and Thomas M. Wilson. 1999. *Borders: Frontiers of Identity, Nation and State*. Oxford: Berg.

Doxtator, Deborah Jean. 1997. "What Happened to the Iroquois Clans? A Study of Clans in Three Nineteenth Century Rotinonhsyonni Communities." London, ON: The University of Western Ontario.

Dupret, Baudouin. 2011. *Practices of Truth: An Ethnomethodological Inquiry into Arab Contexts*. Amsterdam; Philadelphia: John Benjamins Pub. Co. http://public.eblib.com/choice/publicfullrecord.aspx?p=794523.

Dupret, Baudouin, Maurits Berger, and Laila Al-Zwaini. 1999. *Legal Pluralism in the Arab World*. The Hague; Boston: Kluwer Law International.

Dupret, Baudouin, Michael Lynch, and Tim Berard. 2015. *Law at Work: Studies in Legal Ethnomethods*. http://search.ebscohost.com/login.aspx?direct=true&scope=site&db=nlebk&db=nlabk&AN=989248.

Elliott, Michael. 1996. "Review of Life and Death in Mohawk Country by Bruce E. Johansen." *Studies in American Indian Literatures*, Series 2. 8 (2): 93–6.

Ericson, Richard V. 2007. "Rules in Policing: Five Perspectives." *Theoretical Criminology* 11 (3): 367–401. https://doi.org/10.1177/1362480607079583.

Fenton, William N. 1949. "Collecting Materials for a Political History of the Six Nations." *Proceedings of the American Philosophical Society* 93 (3): 233–8.

– 1998. *The Great Law and the Longhouse : A Political History of the Iroquois Confederacy*. Norman: University of Oklahoma Press.

Fine-dare, Kathleen, and Steven L. Rubenstein, eds. 2009. *Border Crossings: Transnational Americanist Anthropology*. Lincoln: University of Nebraska Press.

Fogelson, Raymond D. 1974. "On the Varieties of Indian History: Sequoyah and Traveller Bird." *The Journal of Ethnic Studies* 2 (1): 106–7.

– 1989. "The Ethnohistory of Events and Nonevents." *Ethnohistory* 36 (2): 133–47. https://doi.org/10.2307/482275.

Foster, Michael K. 1974. *From the Earth to Beyond the Sky: An Ethnographic Approach to Four Longhouse Iroquois Speech Events*. Ottawa: National Museums of Canada.

Frazer, James George. 1951. *The Golden Bough: A Study in Magic and Religion*. New York: Macmillan.

Garfinkel, Harold. 1967. *Studies in Ethnomethodology*. Englewood Cliffs, NJ: Prentice-Hall.

Geertz, Clifford. 1977. *The Interpretation of Cultures*. 1st ed. New York: Basic Books.

Gellner, Ernest. 1983. *Nations and Nationalism*. Ithaca, NY: Cornell University Press.

Genova, Nicholas P.De. 2002. "Migrant 'Illegality' and Deportability in Everyday Life." *Annual Review of Anthropology* 31 (January): 419–47. https://doi.org/10.1146/annurev.anthro.31.040402.085432.

George-Kanentiio, Douglas M. 2006. *Iroquois on Fire: A Voice from the Mohawk Nation*. Westport, CT: Praeger.

– 2013. "Edge of the Woods Ceremony Was the Basis for the Two Row Wampum." *The Post-Standard – Syracuse.com* (blog). 4 August 2013. http://blog.syracuse.com/opinion/2013/08/two_row_wampum_edge_of_the _woo.html.

Gluckman, Max. 1955. *The Judicial Process among the Barotse of Northern Rhodesia*. Manchester: Manchester University Press; Rhodes-Livingstone Institute.

– 1965a. *Politics, Law and Ritual in Tribal Society*. Chicago: Aldine Pub. Co.

– 1965b. "Reasonableness and Responsibility in the Law of Segmentary Societies." In *African Law: Adaptation and Development*, edited by Hilda Kuper and Leo Kuper, 120–48. Berkeley: University of California Press.

Goffman, Erving. 1959. *The Presentation of Self in Everyday Life*. Garden City, NY Doubleday.

– 1967. *Interaction Ritual Essays on Face-to-Face Behavior*. [1st ed.]. Garden City, NY: Doubleday.

– 1974. *Frame Analysis : An Essay on the Organization of Experience*. Cambridge, MA: Harvard University Press.

– 1981. *Forms of Talk*. Philadelphia: University of Pennsylvania Press.

Google. n.d. "Define: Rumour – Google Search." Accessed 23 November 2015. https://www.google.ca/search?q=rumour&ie=utf-8&oe=utf-8&gws _rd=cr&ei=cWZTVsnMG4P--AH1lIPIAw#q=define:+rumour.

Government of Canada. 1995. Customs Act RSC 1985. Ottawa. https://laws -lois.justice.gc.ca/eng/acts/C-52.6/FullText.html. Accessed 5 September 2020.

Griest, Stephanie Elizondo. 2018. *All the Agents and Saints: Dispatches from the US Borderlands*. 1st ed. Chapel Hill: University of North Carolina Press.

Hale, Alan S. 2017. "Seven Nations of Canada Prepared to Head Straight to the Crown." *The Cornwall Standard Freeholder*, 28 June 2017.

Hale, Horatio. 1999. *The Iroquois Book of Rites*. Philadelphia: D.G. Brinton.

Hall, John A. 1994. *Coercion and Consent: Studies on the Modern State*. Cambridge, UK; Cambridge, MA: Polity Press.

Hays, Matthew. 2013. "Mohawk Girls: A Native Take on *Sex and the City*." *The Globe and Mail*, 11 July 2013. http://www.theglobeandmail.com/arts /television/mohawk-girls-a-native-take-on-sex-and-the-city/article13169828/.

Hele, Karl S., ed. 2008. *Lines Drawn upon the Water: First Nations and the Great Lakes Borders and Borderlands*. Waterloo, ON: Wilfrid Laurier University Press.

Hermkens, Harrie, Jan Noordegraaf, and Nicoline van der Sijs. 2013. "The Tawagonshi Tale: Can Linguistic Analysis Prove the Tawagonshi Treaty to Be a Forgery?" *Journal of Early American History* 3 (1): 9–42. https://doi .org/10.1163/18770703-00301006.

Hernández, Kelly Lytle. 2010. *Migra!: A History of the U.S. Border Patrol*. Berkeley and Los Angeles: University of California Press.

Hewitt, J.N.B. 2009. *Iroquoian Cosmology*. London: Forgotten Books.

Heyman, Josiah McC. 1995. "Putting Power in the Anthropology of Bureaucracy: The Immigration and Naturalization Service at the Mexico-United States Border." *Current Anthropology* 36 (2): 261–87. https://doi.org /10.1086/204354.

Holcombe, Sarah. 2018. "Book Reviews: Mohawk Interruptus: Political Life across the Borders of Settler States." *PoLAR: Political and Legal Anthropology Review*, PoLAR Online, February.

Hooper, Len. 1988. "Racist T-Shirts Anger Mohawks." *Cornwall Standard Freeholder*, 17 September 1988.

Hornung, Rick. 1991. *One Nation under the Gun*. Toronto: Stoddart.

Hrabluk, Lisa. 1996. "Mohawks Confused about Past, Court Told." *Cornwall Standard Freeholder*, 6 November 1996.

Ingold, Tim. 2007. *Lines: A Brief History*. New ed. Abingdon, Oxon; New York: Routledge.

International Boundary Commission. n.d. "International Boundary Commission Official Web Site." Accessed 23 October 2013. http://www .internationalboundarycommission.org/products.html.

Jacobs, Jaap. 2013. "Early Dutch Explorations in North America." *Journal of Early American History* 3 (1): 59–81. https://doi.org/10.1163/18770703-00301006.

Jamieson, Ruth. 1998. "'Contested Jurisdiction Border Communities' and Cross-Border Crime – the Case of Akwesasne." *Crime, Law and Social Change: An Interdisciplinary Journal* 30 (3): 259–72.

Jennings, Francis. 1995. *The History and Culture of Iroquois Diplomacy: An Interdisciplinary Guide to the Treaties of the Six Nations and Their League.* Syracuse, NY: Syracuse University Press.

Johansen, Bruce Elliott. 1993. *Life and Death in Mohawk Country.* Np: North American Press.

John, Rachel St. 2012. *Line in the Sand: A History of the Western U.S.-Mexico Border.* Princeton, NJ: Princeton University Press.

Johnson, Benjamin Heber, and Andrew R Graybill. 2010. *Bridging National Borders in North America: Transnational and Comparative Histories.* Durham, NC: Duke University Press.

Johnston, Darlene. 1986. "The Quest of the Six Nations for Self-Determination." *University of Toronto Faculty of Law Review* 1: 44.

– 2015a. "'Don't Blame Me, It's Just the Computer Telling Me to Do This': Computer Attribution and the Discretionary Authority of Canada Border Services Agency Officers." *The Max Planck Institute for Social Anthropology Working Papers,* no. 166.

– 2015b. "The Peacemaker I Presume: Journeys up the Historical Streams of Iroquois Scholarship." *Iroquoia: The Journal of Iroquois Studies* 1 (1): 81–108.

– 2018. "Proofing Exemption: Documenting Indigeneity at the Canada-US Border." *Anthropologica* 60 (1): 212–22. https://doi.org/10.3138/anth.60.1.t20.

Kaplan, Thomas. 2010. "Iroquois Lacrosse Players Lose Passport Dispute with the British." *The New York Times,* 16 July 2010, sec. Sports. http://www.nytimes.com/2010/07/17/sports/17lacrosse.html?_r=1&scp=1&sq=Iroquois%20lacrosse&st=cse.

Karon, Dan. 1988. "Mohawks Seize Customs Station." *Ottawa Citizen,* 15 October 1988.

Kearney, Michael. 2004. "Borders and Boundaries of State and Self at the End of Empire." In *Changing Fields of Anthropology: From Local to Global,* 251–73. Lanham, MD: Rowman & Littlefield.

Khosravi, Shahram. 2007. "The 'Illegal' Traveller: An Auto-Ethnography of Borders." *Social Anthropology* 15 (3): 321–34. https://doi.org/10.1111/j.0964-0282.2007.00019.x.

King, Joyce Tekahnawiiaks. 2006. "The Value of Water and the Meaning of Water Law for the Native Americans Known as the Haudenosaunee." *Cornell Journal of Law and Public Policy* 16 (4): 449. https://doi.org/10.1177/1023263x0901600404.

Konrad, Victor, and Heather N. Nicol. 2008. *Beyond Walls: Re-Inventing the Canada-United States Borderlands.* Border Regions Series. Burlington, VT: Ashgate.

LaFave, Wayne. 2006. "The Police and Nonenforcement of the Law – Part II." In *Police and Policing Law,* edited by Jeannine Bell, 200–59. The International Library of Essays in Law and Society. Aldershot, Hants: Ashgate.

Lakoff, George, and Mark Johnson. 1980. *Metaphors We Live By*. Chicago: University of Chicago Press.

Laskaris, Sam. 2011. "Border Official Salts the Wounds of Passport Seizure." *Windspeaker* 29 (5): n.p. Available at http://ammsa.com/publications/windspeaker/border-official-salts-wounds-passport-seizure.

Lévi-Strauss, Claude. 1966. *The Savage Mind: (La Pensée Sauvage)*. London: Weidenfeld and Nicolson.

Malinowski, Bronislaw. 1922. *The Argonauts of the Western Pacific: An Account of Native Enterprise and Adventure in the Archipelagos of Melanesian New Guinea*. London: G. Routledge & Sons.

Merriam-Webster. n.d. "Smuggle." https://www.merriam-webster.com/dictionary/smuggle#examples. Accessed 2015.

Meuwese, Mark. 2013. "The States General and the Stadholder: Dutch Diplomatic Practices in the Atlantic World before the West India Company." *Journal of Early American History* 3 (1): 43–58. https://doi.org/10.1163/18770703-00301006.

Miner, Dylan. 2015. "Gaagegoo Dabakaanan Miiniwaa Debenjigejig (No Borders, Indigenous Sovereignty)." *Decolonization* (blog). 2015. https://decolonization.wordpress.com/2015/10/01/gaagegoo-dabakaanan-miiniwaa-debenjigejig-no-borders-indigenous-sovereignty/.

Mitchell, Michael. 1969. *You Are on Indian Land*. National Film Board of Canada. http://www.nfb.ca/film/you_are_on_indian_land/.

Mohawk, John. 2005. *Basic Call to Consciousness*. Summertown, TN: Native Voices.

The Mohawk Council of Akwesasne. 2007. "Homeland Insecurity." Mohawk Council Government Webpage. Winter 2007. http://www.akwesasne.ca/node/252?q=node/287.

"Mohawk Iroquois Village circa 1600." n.d. Accessed 14 November 2015. https://www.nysm.nysed.gov/IroquoisVillage/slideonea.html.

Morgan, Lewis H. 1851. *League of the Ho-Dé-No-Sau-Nee, or, Iroquois*. Rochester, NY Sage.

Muller, K. 2009. "Holding Hands with Wampum: Haudenosaunee Council Fires from the Great Law of Peace to Contemporary Relationships with the Canadian State." PhD diss., Queen's University, Kingston, ON.

Navaro-Yashin, Yael. 2002. *Faces of the State: Secularism and Public Life in Turkey*. Princeton, NJ: Princeton University Press.

Ngai, Mae M. 2004. *Impossible Subjects: Illegal Aliens and the Making of Modern America*. Princeton, NJ: Princeton University Press.

Niezen, Ronald. 2003a. "Culture and the Judiciary: The Meaning of the Culture Concept as a Source of Aboriginal Rights in Canada." *Canadian Journal of Law and Society* 18 (2): 1–26. https://doi.org/10.1017/s0829320100007687.

– 2003b. *The Origins of Indigenism: Human Rights and the Politics of Identity.* Berkeley, CA: University of California Press.

– 2009. *The Rediscovered Self: Indigenous Identity and Cultural Justice.* Montreal: McGill-Queen's University Press.

Oakes, Ian. 2013. "Demonstration for CBSA Move Held at People's Fire." *Indian Time*, 28 March 2013, 31 #12 edition.

Obomsawin, Alanis, Donna Read, Don Haig, Savas Kalogeras, Claude Vendette, Francis Grandmont, and National Film Board of Canada. 1997. *Spudwrench Kahnawake Man.* Montreal: National Film Board of Canada.

Ong, Aihwa. 1999. *Flexible Citizenship: The Cultural Logics of Transnationality.* Durham, NC: Duke University Press.

Otto, Paul. 2013. "Wampum, Tawagonshi, and the Two Row Belt." *Journal of Early American History* 3 (1): 110–25. https://doi.org/10.1163/18770703-00301006.

Otto, Paul, and Jaap Jacobs. 2013. "Introduction: Historians and the Public Debate about the Past." *Journal of Early American History* 3 (1): 1–8. https://doi.org/10.1163/18770703-00301006.

Parham, Claire Puccia. 2004. *From Great Wilderness to Seaway Towns: A Comparative History of Cornwall, Ontario, and Massena, New York, 1784–2001.* Albany: State University of New York Press. http://site.ebrary.com/id/10594936.

Parker, Arthur Caswell. 1968. *Parker on the Iroquois.* Edited by William Nelson Fenton. Syracuse, NY: Syracuse University Press.

Parmenter, Jon. 2006. "After the Mourning Wars: The Iroquois as Allies in Colonial North American Campaigns, 1676–1760." *The William and Mary Quarterly* 64 (1): 39–76.

– 2010. *The Edge of the Woods: Iroquoia, 1534–1701.* East Lansing: Michigan State University Press.

– 2013. "The Meaning of Kaswentha and the Two Row Wampum Belt in Haudenosaunee (Iroquois) History: Can Indigenous Oral Tradition Be Reconciled with the Documentary Record?" *Journal of Early American History* 3 (1): 82–109. https://doi.org/10.1163/18770703-00301006.

Pendergast, James F., Claude Chapdelaine, and J.V. Wright. 1993. *Essays in St. Lawrence Iroquoian Archaeology.* Dundas, ON: Copetown Press.

Pickering, Sharon, and Julie Ham. 2014. "Hot Pants at the Border: Sorting Sex Work from Trafficking." *British Journal of Criminology* 54 (1): 2–19. https://doi.org/10.1093/bjc/azt060.

Pleasant, Jane Mt. 2010. *Traditional Iroquois Corn: Its History, Cultivation, and Use.* Ithaca, NY: Natural Resource Agriculture and Engineering.

Polanyi, Karl. 2001. *The Great Transformation.* Boston: Beacon Press.

Pomedli, Michael M. 1995. "Eighteenth-Century Treaties: Amended Iroquois Condolence Rituals." *American Indian Quarterly* 19 (3): 319–39. https://doi.org/10.2307/1185594.

Pratt, Anna. 2005. *Securing Borders: Detention and Deportation in Canada*. Law and Society. Vancouver: University of British Columbia Press.

– 2010. "Between a Hunch and a Hard Place: Making Suspicion Reasonable at the Canadian Border." *Social & Legal Studies* 19 (4): 461–80. https://doi.org/10.1177/0964663910378434.

Price, S.L. 2010. "Pride of a Nation." *Sports Illustrated*, 19 July 2010. https://www.si.com/vault/2010/07/19/105961100/pride-of-a-nation.

Radcliffe-Brown, A.R. 1940. "On Joking Relationships." *Africa: Journal of the International African Institute* 13 (3): 195–210. https://doi.org/10.2307/1156093.

Rael, Ronald. 2012. "Boundary Line Infrastructure." *Thresholds* 40: 76–82. https://doi.org/10.1162/thld_a_00134.

"Regional Schools in Decline?" 2015. *Cornwall Standard Freeholder*. Accessed 25 October 2015. http://www.standard-freeholder.com/2015/04/20/eastern-ontario-regional-schools-in-decline-fraser-institute-highlights-cornwalls-lheritage-holy-trinity-as-bright-spots.

Richter, Daniel K., and Institute of Early American History and Culture. 1992. *The Ordeal of the Longhouse: The Peoples of the Iroquois League in the Era of European Colonization*. Chapel Hill, NC: Published for the Institute of Early American History and Culture, Williamsburg, Virginia, by the University of North Carolina Press.

Rickard, Clinton. 1994. *Fighting Tuscarora: The Autobiography of Chief Clinton Rickard*. Syracuse, NY: Syracuse University Press.

Sallot, Jeff. 2002. "Smuggler's Alley Is No Easy Street." *The Globe and Mail*, 30 September 2002. http://www.theglobeandmail.com/news/national/smugglers-alley-is-no-easy-street/article1026761/.

Scheff, Thomas. 2006. *Goffman Unbound!: A New Paradigm for Social Science*. Boulder, CO: Paradigm Publishers.

Schielke, Samuli. 2010. *Second Thoughts about the Anthropology of Islam, or How to Make Sense of Grand Schemes in Everyday Life*. ZMO Working Papers 2. Berlin. http://nbn-resolving.de/urn:nbn:de:0168-ssoar-322336.

Scott, James. 1998. *Seeing like a State: How Certain Schemes to Improve the Human Condition Have Failed*. New Haven, CT: Yale University Press.

Seaway Today. 2013. "No Man's Land: Where Some Are Idle No More." Youtube Video, Akwesasne, 12 March 2013. http://youtu.be/MZfetDKUpKs.

Segal, Robert. 2004. *Myth: A Very Short Introduction*. Oxford; New York: Oxford University Press.

Shachar, Ayelet. 2009. *The Birthright Lottery: Citizenship and Global Inequality*. Cambridge, MA: Harvard University Press.

Shannon, Timothy J. 2008. *Iroquois Diplomacy on the Early American Frontier*. New York: Penguin.

Sheffer, Anne Colette. 2009. *Facework in Coercive Interactions: Evidence from Police Field Interrogations*. Buffalo: State University of New York at Buffalo.

"She:Kon/Greetings: The Mohawk Council of Akwesasne." 2015. The Mohawk Council of Akwesasne Homepage. Accessed 1 October 2015. www.akwesasne.ca.

Simpson, Audra. 2003. "To the Reserve and Back Again: Kahnawake Mohawk Narratives of Self, Home and Nation." PhD diss., McGill University.

– 2007. "On Ethnographic Refusal: Indigeneity, 'Voice' and Colonial Citizenship." *Junctures: The Journal for Thematic Dialogue* no. 9. http://junctures.org/index.php/junctures/article/viewFile/66/60.

– 2008. "Subjects of Sovereignty: Indigeneity, The Revenue Rule, and Juridics of Failed Consent." *Law and Contemporary Problems* 71 (3): 191–215.

– 2014. *Mohawk Interruptus: Political Life across the Borders of Settler States*. Durham, NC: Duke University Press.

Smith, Don. 2014. "The Pulse of the Community: Port of Entry Dividing Cornwall & Akwesasne – by Don Smith." *The Cornwall Free News*. Accessed 23 March 2014. http://cornwallfreenews.com/2013/03/the-pulse-of-the-community-port-of-entry-dividing-cornwall-akwesasne-by-don-smith/.

Snow, Dean R. 1996. *The Iroquois*. Oxford, UK; Cambridge, MA: Blackwell.

Staff. 1988. "Angry Mohawk Mob Surrounds Canadian Customs on Friday." *Massena Observer*, 20 October 1988.

Sturm, Circe. 2002. *Blood Politics: Race, Culture, and Identity in the Cherokee Nation of Oklahoma*. Berkeley: University of California Press.

– 2017. "Reflections on the Anthropology of Sovereignty and Settler Colonialism: Lessons from Native North America." *Cultural Anthropology* 32 (3): 340–8. https://doi.org/10.14506/ca32.3.03.

Tarbell, Reaghan, Paul M. Rickard, Ravida Din, Mushkeg Media Inc., and National Film Board of Canada. 2009. *Little Caughnawaga to Brooklyn and Back = Le petit Caughnawaga = Nikanatá:'a Caughnawaga Tsi niió:re ne Brooklyn Taióterahte*. Montreal: National Film Board of Canada.

Taylor, Alan. 2002. "The Divided Ground: Upper Canada, New York, and the Iroquois Six Nations, 1783–1815." *Journal of the Early Republic* 22 (1): 55–75. https://doi.org/10.2307/3124858.

Thompson, David, and David Adams. 1817. *Part of the St. Lawrence River [between Cornwall, Ont. and St. Regis, Que., Showing Eastern End of Cornwall Island, Western End of Île-Jaune]*.

Torpey, John C. 2000. *The Invention of the Passport: Surveillance, Citizenship, and the State*. Cambridge: Cambridge University Press.

Trigger, Bruce G. 1987. *Children of Aataentsic: A History of the Huron People to 1660*. Montreal: McGill-Queen's University Press.

Trigger, Bruce G., and James Pendergast. 1978. "Saint Lawrence Iroquoians." In *Northeast*, vol. 15 of *Handbook of North American Indians*, edited by Bruce G. Trigger, 357–61. Washington, DC: Smithsonian Institution Press.

Turner, Frederick Jackson. 1893. "The Significance of the Frontier in American History 1983." Presented at the American Historical Association, Chicago, 12 July 1983.

Tylor, Edward B. 1958. *Primitive Culture*. [New York]: [Harper].

US Customs and Border Protection. (n.d.) "Crossing the Border via Foot, Vehicle, or Air without Visiting an Official Port of Entry." Accessed 1 October 2014. https://help.cbp.gov/app/answers/detail/a_id/782/kw/port%20of%20entry.

Van Houtum, Henk. 2005. "The Geopolitics of Borders and Boundaries." *Geopolitics* 10 (4): 672–9. https://doi.org/10.1080/14650040500318522.

Vecsey, Christopher. 1986. "The Story and Structure of the Iroquois Confederacy." *Journal of the American Academy of Religion* 54 (1): 79–106. https://doi.org/10.1093/jaarel/liv.1.79.

Venables, Robert W. 2010. "The Clearings and the Woods: The Haudenosaunee (Iroquois) Landscape – Gendered and Balanced." In *Archaeology and Preservation of Gendered Landscapes*, edited by Sherene Baugher and Suzanne M. Spencer-Wood, 21–55. New York; London: Springer.

Voget, Fred. 1984. "Anthropological Theory and Iroquois Ethnography: 1850 to 1970." In *Extending the Rafters: Interdisciplinary Approaches to Iroquoian Studies*, 1st ed. Williams Press, Inc. Albany: State University of New York Press.

Wallace, Anthony F.C. 1970. *The Death and Rebirth of the Seneca*. 1st ed. New York: Knopf.

– 2012. *Tuscarora: A History*. Albany: State University of New York Press. muse.jhu.edu/book/19942.

Wallace, Paul A.W. 1994. *The White Roots of Peace*. Illustrations by John Kahionhes Fadden; foreword by Chief Leon Shenandoah; epilogue by John Mohawk (republication of the 1946 edition). Santa Fe, NM: Clear Light Publishers.

Weber, Max. 1958. *From Max Weber: Essays in Sociology*. New York: Oxford University Press.

White, Richard. 1991. *The Middle Ground: Indians, Empires, and Republics in the Great Lakes Region, 1650–1815*. Cambridge; New York: Cambridge University Press.

White-Cree, Phillip. 2014. "Entsiakwakaen:Ion Tsi Ni Kionkwe:Non." *Onkwetake*, August 2014.

Whitman, Walt. 1892. *Leaves of Grass*. Philadelphia: David McKay.

Wilson, Edmund, and Joseph Mitchell. 1960. *Apologies to the Iroquois*. New York: Farrar, Straus and Cudahy.

Wilson, Thomas M., and Hastings Donnan, eds. 2012. *A Companion to Border Studies*. Chichester: Wiley-Blackwell.

Winegard, Timothy. 2009. "The Forgotten Front of the Oka Crisis: Operation Feather/Akwesasne." *Journal of Military and Strategic Studies* 11 (1–2). http://jmss.synergiesprairies.ca/jmss/index.php/jmss/article/view/30.

Zureik, Elia, and Mark Salter, eds. 2005. *Global Surveillance and Policing: Borders, Security, Identity*. Cullompton, Devon; Portland, OR: Willan.

Index